Finding Harmony in
Ever-Changing Waters

One Woman's Perspective

Insights and Discoveries
Cruising the Inside Passage to Southeast Alaska

Jandira Burgess with Tom

Photos by Tom and Jandira Burgess
Cover Photo by Laurel Daniel

DEDICATION

The list is long, longer than there is room on this page, but if there was room, the list of people that have influenced my life, both "positively" and "negatively," would be quite extensive. The positive influencers are easy to explain, the negative ones...not so much, but both have played a vital role in shaping who I am today. There were the encouragers who believed in me, offered advice when asked, but in the end, trusted me to make the best decisions for my life. And then, there were the naysayers who rained on my parade, played the devil's advocate, and didn't trust that I knew my own heart. Both, in their own way, helped me to look within and find the strength, courage, and wisdom to discover and take the path that would lead me home to my True Self. I am grateful for the part each has played in my life...but...

I have chosen to dedicate this whole space to one man, my beautiful husband, Tom. He was my most ardent encourager when I embarked on the writing of this daily trip journal, and his belief in me never faltered. When I doubted myself, he simply dismissed my lack of confidence, insisting I had everything I needed right there inside me to succeed.

Tom recognized that as a writer, I needed quiet, uninterrupted time and space and made sure this happened for me. He understood my life-long passion to touch people's lives with my words, and the focus and drive it would take to accomplish this and did everything he could to help me realize my dream.

From doing the nightly dishes so I could write, to reading each day's journal entry for clarity, readability, and accuracy, he supported me every step of the way. I would often ask him to write his own thoughts and interpretations of that day's events or explain technical or navigational information that was above my head, and he would jump right in and do so. And when it came time to edit the journal for publication, once again he read each entry and offered constructive advice as I wrote and rewrote until I was satisfied it was as good as I could make it.

My gratitude for Tom runs deep. I appreciate his love and devotion to me more than I have words to adequately express, so I will simply say, "Thank you My Love, from the bottom of my heart. I love you so much."

ACKNOWLEDGMENTS

Though our family and friends might not be visible on the pages of this book, they have profoundly impacted its creation. To the 70+ folks who read and responded to my daily journal posts and then later encouraged me to turn them into a published work, I offer my sincere and heartfelt appreciation.

To my son, Rupa, who has challenged me always to face my fears...not be defined by them...to move past them to discover the exhilaration of finding my own inner courage, I am grateful beyond words. I love you and honor your free-spirited way of moving through the world on your own terms and the example you have set for me to do the same.

To my mom, Polly, for instilling in me the belief that I can do anything I set my mind to do. At 95, you are still an inspiration to all who know you.

To Kathy Briar-Lawson and Hal Lawson, I offer my deepest gratitude. Kathy read my manuscript with a keen eye for detail and offered suggestions that improved it as a whole, while Hal asked probing questions like, "What audience do you want to reach?" and "What themes are you trying to get across?" Together, they shared wisdom gleaned from their years of university teaching, research, and publishing. Thank you both for your advice to maintain my writer's voice, trust my writer's instinct and be true to myself and my vision through the writing process.

Finally, I would like to acknowledge the New York Book Publishing Company team members who were assigned to see me through the publishing process. To a person, they were skilled, helpful, and insightful as they guided me through the process of bringing my manuscript to print. From editing to formatting to book cover design and more, they were patient, kind, and respectful of my work. I owe a huge debt of gratitude for their professionalism from start to finish.

CONTENTS

PREFACE I

INTRODUCTION II

PREPARING TO CAST OFF....................................... VI

DAY 1 1
CLEARING CUSTOMS AT VAN ISLE, SYDNEY
DESTINATION: MONTAGUE BAY

DAY 2 3
DESTINATION: THROUGH DODD NARROWS TO NANAIMO AND
THE DINGHY DOCK PUB

DAY 3 6
LAYOVER DAY: NANAIMO

DAY 4 8
DESTINATION: CROSSING GEORGIA STRAIT TO BALLET BAY

DAY 5 10
DESTINATION: LUND

DAY 6 13
DESTINATION: BIG BAY AND YUCULTA RAPIDS

DAY 7 15
DESTINATION: FORWARD HARBOR
THROUGH GILLARD, DENT, GREEN POINT AND WHIRLPOOL
RAPIDS

DAY 8 18
DESTINATION: PORT MCNEILL

DAY 9 20
LAYOVER DAY: PORT MCNEILL

DAY 10 21
DESTINATION: SKULL COVE

DAY 11 24
ROUNDING CAPE CAUTION
DESTINATION: FURY COVE

DAY 12 28
LAYOVER DAY: FURY COVE

DAY 13 31
SECOND LAYOVER DAY: FURY COVE

DAY 14 34
DESTINATION: FANCY COVE, HUNTER ISLAND

DAYS 15-16 37
DESTINATION: SHEARWATER RESORT

DAY 17 39
DESTINATION: RESCUE BAY, SUSAN ISLAND

DAY 18..43
LAYOVER DAY: RESCUE BAY
DAY 19..46
DESTINATION: KYNOCH INLET, THE FIORDLANDS
DAY 20..49
LAYOVER DAY: KYNOCH INLET
DAY 21..52
SECOND LAYOVER DAY: KYNOCH INLET
DAY 22..57
DESTINATION: WINDY BAY, POOLEY ISLAND
DAY 23..61
DESTINATION: KHUTZE INLET
NEW INSIGHTS: SOMETHING TO PONDER....................63
DAY 24..65
DESTINATION: BISHOP BAY HOT SPRINGS
SOMETHING TO PONDER: 69
FUNNY DILEMMA: DRY VERSUS WET
DAY 25..72
HARTLEY BAY FOR FUEL/WATER/GARBAGE DROP OFF
DESTINATION: COGHLAND ANCHORAGE
DAY 26..75
DESTINATION: BAKER INLET
DAY 27..81
LAYOVER DAY: BAKER INLET
DAY 28..85
DESTINATION: PRINCE RUPERT
DAY 29..88
LAYOVER DAY: PRINCE RUPERT HARBOR
DAY 30..91
DESTINATION: FOGGY BAY
DAY 31..94
LAYOVER DAY: FOGGY BAY
DAY 32..98
DESTINATION: KETCHIKAN, ALASKA
DAY 33..102
LAYOVER DAY: KETCHIKAN
DAY 34..105
SECOND LAYOVER DAY: KETCHIKAN
DAY 35..108
DESTINATION: SYKES COVE
DAY 36..112
DESTINATION: PUNCHBOWL COVE, MISTY FIORDS
DAY 37..116

LAYOVER DAY: PUNCHBOWL COVE
DAY 38 122
DESTINATION: WALKER COVE, MISTY FIORDS
DAY 39 126
LAYOVER DAY: WALKER COVE
DAY 40 129
SECOND LAYOVER DAY: WALKER COVE
DAY 41 133
DESTINATION: FITZGIBBON COVE, MISTY FIORDS
DAY 42 137
DESTINATION: YES BAY
DAY 43 140
WEATHER LAYOVER DAY: HELM BAY
DAY 44 142
DESTINATION: MEYERS CHUCK
DAY 45 146
DESTINATION: BERG BAY
DAY 46 149
DESTINATION: WRANGELL
DAYS 47-48 152
THROUGH WRANGELL NARROWS
DESTINATION: PETERSBURG
DAY 49 157
DESTINATION: THOMAS BAY, RUTH ISLAND
DAY 50 161
LAYOVER DAY: THOMAS BAY
DAY 51 164
DESTINATION: CLEVELAND PASSAGE
DAY 52 166
DESTINATION: TRACY ARM COVE
DAY 53 170
DESTINATION: JUNEAU
DAY 54 172
LAYOVER: JUNEAU
DAY 55 175
DESTINATION: BACK TO TRACY ARM COVE
DAY 56 179
DESTINATION: TRACY ARM/NORTH AND SOUTH SAWYER
GLACIERS (FINALLY!!!)
DAY 57 188
LAYOVER DAY: TRACY ARM COVE
DAY 58 190
DESTINATION: BACK TO JUNEAU

DAY 59 193
LAYOVER DAY: JUNEAU
DAY 60 196
SECOND LAYOVER DAY: JUNEAU
DAY 61 197
DESTINATION: COOT COVE INLET IN FUNTER BAY
DAY 62 200
DESTINATION: PAVLOF HARBOR, FRESHWATER BAY
DAY 63 203
DESTINATION: APPLETON COVE, BARANOF ISLAND
DAY 64 205
DESTINATION: BABY BEAR BAY, BARANOF ISLAND
DAY 65 208
HEALTH LAYOVER DAY: BABY BEAR BAY
DAY 66 210
SECOND HEALTH LAYOVER DAY: BABY BEAR BAY
DAY 67 213
DESTINATION: SITKA
DAY 68 216
LAYOVER DAY: SITKA
DAY 69 218
SECOND LAYOVER DAY: SITKA
DAY 70 221
THIRD LAYOVER DAY: SITKA
DAY 71 223
DESTINATION: BACK TO BABY BEAR BAY
DAY 72 227
DESTINATION: DEAD TREE ISLAND
(TRUNCATED TO APPLETON COVE)
DAY 73 230
DESTINATION: TAKATZ BAY
(TRUNCATED TO DEAD TREE ISLAND)
DAY 74 233
DESTINATION: TAKATZ BAY
DAY 75 238
LAYOVER DAY: TAKATZ BAY
DAY 76 242
DESTINATION: WARM SPRINGS
DAY 77 247
DESTINATION: CHAPIN BAY, ADMIRALTY ISLAND
DAY 78 253
DESTINATION: PORTAGE BAY
DAY 79 255

DESTINATION: PETERSBURG
DAY 80 260
LAYOVER DAY: PETERSBURG
DAY 81 263
DESTINATION: WRANGLE NARROWS/EXCHANGE ISLAND
DAY 82 267
DESTINATION: MEYERS CHUCK
DAY 83 270
DESTINATION: KETCHIKAN
DAYS 84-85 275
LAYOVER DAYS: KETCHIKAN
DAY 86 279
THIRD LAYOVER DAY: KETCHIKAN
DAY 87 282
FOURTH LAYOVER DAY: KETCHIKAN
DAY 88 284
FIFTH LAYOVER DAY: KETCHIKAN
DAY 89 288
SIXTH (AND HOPEFULLY) FINAL LAYOVER DAY: KETCHIKAN
DAY 90 291
DESTINATION: FOGGY BAY
(TRUNCATED TO BULLHEAD COVE)
DAY 91 294
DESTINATION: PRINCE RUPERT
DAY 92 297
DESTINATION: CAPTAIN COVE
DAY 93 301
DESTINATION: MATH ISLANDS/CLEAR PASSAGE
DAY 94 305
DESTINATION: IRE INLET
DAY 95 307
DESTINATION: TUWARTZ INLET
DAY 96 312
DESTINATION: KHUTZE BAY
DAY 97 316
DESTINATION: KYNOCH INLET
DAY 98 321
FIRST LAYOVER DAY: KYNOCH INLET
DAY 99 326
SECOND LAYOVER DAY: KYNOCH INLET
DAY 100 330
DESTINATION: RESCUE BAY
DAY 101 333

DESTINATION: SHEARWATER MARINA
DAY 102 336
DESTINATION: OCEAN FALLS
DAY 103 339
DESTINATION: ROSCO INLET, QUARTCHA BAY
DAY 104 344
DESTINATION: CODVILLE LAGOON
DAY 105 347
DESTINATION: PRUTH BAY
DAY 106 350
LAYOVER DAY: PRUTH BAY, CALVERT ISLAND
DAY 107 354
SECOND LAYOVER WEATHER DAY: PRUTH BAY
DAY 108 358
AROUND CAPE CAUTION
DESTINATION: WALKER GROUP COVE
DAY 109 361
DESTINATION: PORT MCNEILL, NORTH ISLAND MARINA
DAYS 110-111 364
DESTINATION: BOOTLEG COVE
DAY 112 368
DESTINATION: VINER SOUND
DAY 113 372
DESTINATION: SIMOOM SOUND
DAY 114 376
DESTINATION: KWATSI BAY
DAY 115 380
DESTINATION: LAGOON COVE MARINA
DAY 116 382
DESTINATION: FORWARD HARBOR
DAY 117 386
DESTINATION: SHOAL BAY, PHILLIPS ARM
DAY 118 389
DESTINATION: LUND HARBOR MARINA
DAY 119 392
LAYOVER DAY: LUND HARBOR MARINA
DAY 120 396
DESTINATION: BALLET BAY
DAY 121 399
LAYOVER DAY: BALLET BAY
DAY 122 402
ACROSS GEORGIA STRAIT
DESTINATION: NANAIMO

DAY 123 405
LAYOVER DAY: NANAIMO
DAY 124 410
DESTINATION: PORT BROWNING MARINA, HAMILTON COVE
DAY 125 412
LAYOVER DAY: HAMILTON COVE
DAY 126 414
FINAL DESTINATION: PORT OF FRIDAY HARBOR
THE NEXT CHAPTER... 417

PREFACE

We all have personal dreams and aspirations that we hold in the deep recesses of our hearts. These might be adventures to experience, places to visit, skills to learn, insights to discover about ourselves and each other as we navigate the ever-changing circumstances of our daily lives. In *Finding Harmony in Ever-Changing Waters*, you will read how one such dream came to fruition.

My soon to be husband, Tom, and I had long dreamed of cruising the Inside Passage into Southeast Alaska on our motorsailor, Havis Amanda, so in the spring of 2022, we decided to embark on this journey. Our love of water and all things nature beckoned to us, calling us north to explore the incredible beauty and wildlife that we knew awaited us there.

Along with hundreds of color photos that grace the pages of this daily trip journal (and serve to tell a story all their own), this personal account of our four-month long cruise details the adventures and misadventures we experienced as we navigated the "ever-changing waters" of this wild and wonderous part of the world. More than just a typical trip log, you will find the spiritual insights and personal discoveries we gleaned along the way.

So, whether you are a beginning sailor, a seasoned sailor, or perhaps have no interest in sailing or cruising whatsoever, we invite you to take this magical, mystical journey with us with the hope that someday, you will be inspired to discover and follow your own personal dreams.

So, put on your explorer's hat, don your rain gear (it is the Pacific Northwest, after all) and come on aboard!

INTRODUCTION

Harmony, Exploration, and Adventure...three words that describe, in part at least, our philosophy of life. Our goal is to live an examined, intentional life in harmony with each other and those with whom we share our planet while fulfilling our need for adventure and exploration.

Tom and I love exploring nature's beauty, meeting interesting people, learning new skills, and pushing ourselves past our comfort zones. We are adventurers at heart. It is who we are, what we do, how we live.

We challenge ourselves to live a limitless lifestyle, to make decisions for our lives based on our desires, passions and dreams yet to be fulfilled. We choose not to be limited by our ages, health issues, the good opinions of others, or a host of other excuses that we humans use to procrastinate following our life-long dreams.

That doesn't mean, of course, that we don't consider our ages or health issues, just that we don't let them dictate our choices. We don't just sit back and talk about what we want to do...we decide and do it...we make it happen, working around any obstacles that show up along the way.

So, when we began talking about our cruising plans for the spring and summer of 2022, it was apparent we were both leaning toward exploring the Inside Passage to Southeast Alaska. Tom had long dreamed of sailing this route, and I was definitely on board to make that trip as well. As we talked about our goals for the trip, I shared with Tom my intention to chronicle each day's events in a journal format.

The following account of our trip north is primarily written from a woman's perspective...my perspective...but with Tom's wisdom, wit, and technical expertise sprinkled throughout. It began as a simple account of who, what, when, where, how, and why.

Basically, I just set out to log the day's happenings so we would have a record to refer to on our next journey north.

The goal was to document destinations, routes, weather, anchorages, marinas, and newfound friends.

But that is not entirely what happened...not by a long shot.

My basic who, what, when, where, how, and why daily trip journal took on a life of its own. Yes, it still had many of the basic log-type details that might be included in a skipper's logbook, but I also found myself intuitively adding mine and Tom's personal insights and musings, descriptions of our failures and successes, and philosophical ways of making sense of what we experienced each day.

This daily journal that was originally meant just for Tom and me turned into a way to take our friends and family along with us, connect with and keep them close, allowing them to experience, if not firsthand, at least vicariously through us, what it's like to cruise for four months straight on a boat. So, this journal that was meant for two morphed into a journal that went out to over 70 folks every day...every day, that is, that we had enough signal strength for them to carry across the "waves."

In this journal, I shared how we have chosen to live an examined, intentional life...how we lit a candle each morning and set positive intentions for our journey that day...how we asked our Heavenly Helpers from all different walks of spirituality to guide and protect us and our loved ones near and far. I included quotes from inspirational texts we read daily as part of our morning Quiet Time, our thoughts and interpretations of these readings, and how we might apply these insights to our daily lives.

I wrote about the "good" times and the so-called "bad" times and tried not to minimize or blow out of proportion each day's happenings. Some days were typical, mundane even, while others were filled with excitement and intense emotion. I wanted to share it all so that you could see what a journey of this kind looks and feels like day in and day out.

From one day to the next, our emotions ranged from joy to sadness, peace to frustration, patience to angst, pride, amazement, wonder, and everything in between:

We experienced the joy of sharing this incredible journey together,
The sadness of watching a frantic humpback whale surrounded by whale-watching boats too close for its comfort,
The peace of gliding through water blanketed by early morning mist,
The frustration of dealing with mechanical and technical breakdowns,
The patience to heal from health issues like COVID, food poisoning, bronchitis, a urinary tract infection, and falling into the engine bay,
The angst of docking and tying up the boat in high winds and the pride of successfully doing so,
And amazement and wonder at seeing whales, bears, eagles, otters, loons, ravens, and other creatures living in a harmonious, symbiotic relationship with one another.

All these emotions had to be experienced and worked through, and we did our best to meet and handle each with ease, joy, and grace...sometimes successfully and sometimes...well...

I spoke of Mother Nature and the insights we gained when we stopped, looked, and listened to the examples she set for us each day...examples that inspired us, made us laugh, and sometimes even made us cry. She offered a blueprint, a template of sorts, to guide our lives. Each time we opened our hearts to her profound teachings, we found ways to pattern our existence after them.

While documenting these insights, I rediscovered my "writer's voice." I reconnected with my inner muse. I remembered how good it felt to put pen to paper and allow my thoughts to spill onto the page. How much fun it was to work and rework a piece of writing until it was clean, crisp, concise, and flowed like a river.

And, as friends and family members responded to the daily journal entries with their own thoughts, feelings, and similar examples from their own lives, whether relating to cruising or other personal life experiences, I felt a deep satisfaction that perhaps, as I have always dreamed, my words had touched the hearts of those who read them.

I felt joy and a deep, rewarding sense of peace. I felt like I had come home to myself...followed through with one of my lifelong dreams to share myself and my experiences through the written word. I felt excited to see what the next chapter of my "writer-self" life would look like, where it would take me, and what I would learn about myself and my world that I could then pass on to my readers.

As the title of this journal suggests, Tom and I looked for and found harmony in ever-changing waters, both literally and figuratively. We did our best to not only accept but be grateful for what the Universe presented to us each day as a beautiful "gift" and for the blessings in it. In short, we learned to love "what is." As we practiced gratitude for the "isness" of every moment and embraced the importance of going with the flow of Mother Nature and applying her lessons for growth, we found harmony within ourselves, each other, and our ever-changing world.

It is my wish that as you read about our adventures, as well as our misadventures, you will be inspired to find harmony in your own ever-changing waters.

PREPARING TO CAST OFF...

I am going to share some seemingly mundane information because I want you, the reader, and possibly future cruiser, to understand just a snippet of what is involved in planning a boat trip of this length into the wilds of Canada and Alaska. It takes a good bit of planning, but if you take time to plan well and don't panic when things don't go as planned, everything will be fine...or it won't...but if it isn't...think what a great opportunity it will be to accept and be grateful for "what is" and put your problem-solving skills to the test. I mean...really....what could be better? Practice makes perfect...or so they say.

Tom and I try to live by the anacronym EWOP, which stands for Everything Works Out Perfectly. So, if things do go awry, we practice this favorite mantra and try our best to "walk our talk." And you know what? Things do tend to work out...one way or another. Even if at first we can't see the blessing in the so-called "bad" thing that has occurred, when we step back and view it from a higher, eagle-eye perspective, we can, more often than not, confidently say: "EWOP!"

But back to the task at hand: mundane but important information straight ahead.

There were a gazillion tasks that Tom and I had to do for the boat, ourselves and my mom to make sure we were prepared for all the many "what ifs" that might occur while we were away. We each made extensive to-do lists to accomplish before our cast-off day on April 29th.

On Tom's to-do list were tasks like checking all the many systems on the boat (heater, generator, batteries, engine, navigation, auto-pilot, radios, refrigeration/freezer, water, sewage, steerage, cook stove, etc.), changing fluids (oil and antifreeze), and examining all the sails (jib, main, mizzen, spinnaker) for rips and overuse. And then, there were the extra fluids, pumps, lines, fenders, filters and other vital items that he had to order and keep on board in case of emergencies. Fire extinguishers and flares had to be professionally inspected and approved, and PFDs (personal flotation devices) were also examined. And did I mention bear spray? Definitely a must if you plan to get off your boat and dinghy or kayak to shore to explore.

None of this, mind you, takes into account all the many tools that must be on board to fix anything that breaks, fails, overflows, stops up, quits, malfunctions, or simply goes belly-up and dies. If, as a sailor, you don't have at least some basic fix-it tools and skills, if you don't know your boat and all its many quirky systems inside and out, and you find yourself in a difficult situation where you have to hire the work done, be prepared because boat work is expensive! That is, if you are close enough to a marina to be towed in and can find a boat maintenance person to do the work for you once you get there. Best make sure your Boat US towing insurance is current!

And oh...your yearly boat stickers must also be up to date, another to-do on Tom's list. And do you have valid passports or picture IDs that Canada will accept to allow you to cross the border? Also, be sure to go to the Canadian Border Patrol (CBP) website to see what foods, alcohol, and other items are prohibited to bring across the border. This can change from month to month.

I had my own to-do list as well, starting with creating an inventory of what supplies we already had on board (canned goods, dry goods, paper products, spices, basic first aid products, prescriptions meds, over-the-counter drugs, bug spray, itch cream, various cleaning and toiletry supplies and on and on and on...).

Then, after taking inventory, I made long lists of what we needed to purchase to sustain us for four months on the water. Places to provision would be scattered along the way, but stores in remote areas do not always have an adequate selection of fresh fruits and vegetables, so that had to be planned for as well.

After making lists of what needed to be purchased, the amount of each item had to be calculated: like how many boxes of rice, jars of marinara sauce and peanut butter, packages of pasta, pounds of coffee and tea, can goods (tuna, black beans, black olives, chicken, tomatoes, and chicken broth were some of our favorites), rolls of toilet paper and paper towels...well...you get the picture.

And then, we had to purchase these items (Costco, here we come!), haul them on board, and find places to store them that would be easily accessible but not in the way of our day-in and day-out living. Mind you, this was no easy feat. I guess it's a good thing that I love to organize stuff cause there sure was a lot of that to do!

Another part of my to-do list centered around ensuring my 95-year-old mom and her little dog had everything they needed while we were traveling. Mom and Little Buddy live in an assisted living community here in Friday Harbor, so all her basic needs are met, but I hired three outside caregivers to step in in case something happened that required extra assistance for her. I also set up Amazon subscriptions for a few disposable items she regularly used to be shipped to her on an ongoing basis. Thankfully, she did great while we were cruising.

Even though it was a lot of work, Tom and I enjoyed all the planning and preparation. As each day went by, our anticipation built, and our excitement grew until the day finally came to cast off the lines and sail away from the harbor. We felt such a sense of exhilaration as we entered San Juan Channel and headed toward Van Isle Marina to check into Canada, then on to Montague Bay for our first night's anchorage and fish and chips at the infamous Hummingbird Pub. Yum!

Time to untie the lines and cast off...

Whoo-hoo! We are on our way!

Port of Friday Harbor

Good-Bye Friday Harbor...

See you at summers end!

DAY 1

CLEARING CUSTOMS AT VAN ISLE, SYDNEY
DESTINATION: MONTAGUE BAY

And we're off!!!

We woke up to a light drizzle that had ceased by the time we left the dock. It was the first day of our four-month journey up the Inside Passage into Southeast Alaska, and several of our dear boat neighbors came out to see us off. Thanks, Rand, Peter, Teri, Jeff, and Joan!

The further we traveled up San Juan Channel, the more consistent the rain became, accompanied by very dense fog. Needless to say, we had our radar turned on and watched diligently for other boats and floating logs. We had donned our rain gear, so we stayed dry and reasonably warm.

As we were motoring past Spieden Island, we saw what we initially thought were whales before realizing they were sea lions feeding on salmon. They were flipping the salmon up in the air…toying with them before making breakfast of them. There was a lot of blood! Man, do these guys know how to hunt and fish! It was a sea lion-feeding frenzy!

We checked into Canadian Customs at Van Isle Marina in Sidney, BC without a hitch and then continued on our way to Montague Harbor, where we were scheduled to meet my dear friend, Mooh, for dinner. We had a lovely evening at the Hummingbird Pub, with each of us getting fish and chips. It was not quite as good as Downriggers in Friday Harbor, but I would say it was close. Our server was a young friend of Mooh's who bore the same name as my maternal grandmother, Ruby. I must tell you that Grandma Ruby would have thought me daft to have embarked upon this journey at 71 years of age...or any age for that matter... but thankfully, she is not here to give me an earful on the subject.

While at the pub, we saw a man with a Sea Shepard jacket on, and we struck up a conversation with him, asking if he knew Peter Brown, our boat friend, who used to be a filmmaker and photographer for the Sea Shepard organization. He did! Small world.

Mooh graciously drove us back to the dock. We kayaked back to the boat, sat out on the stern until we got too cold, and then went inside. The sense of excitement we had both felt at finally embarking upon our journey gently turned into a contented peace. We crawled into bed and fell straight to sleep.

Jandira, Tom, and Mooh at the Hummingbird Pub

Good Night from Montague Harbor - End of Day 1

DAY 2

DESTINATION: THROUGH DODD NARROWS TO NANAIMO AND THE DINGHY DOCK PUB

The Dinghy Dock Pub in Mark Bay

Dodd Narrows is a very skinny passage where the currents can run high when flooding (flowing in) or ebbing (flowing out). It is crucial to travel through the Narrows at slack tide (in between ebbing and flooding) or the rapids may have their way with you. Slack tide on this day was 11:17 on the dot, so after crawling out of bed at 6:30 for a 7:45 leave time, and thanks to Tom's expert navigation and timing skills, we arrived precisely at 11:17. How cool is that?

But to back up a bit, before we reached the Narrows, actually not long after we left Montague Harbor, the boat exhaust temperature alarm went off, so when we arrived in Nanaimo, Tom removed the exhaust elbow and chiseled out all of the accumulated corrosion in hopes that would solve the problem. We are crossing our fingers that we will have no more issues with it, as we have a five-and-one-half hour transit across Georgia Strait tomorrow, and it can sometimes be quite dicey.

Once we dropped anchor in Mark Bay, a bustling bay located in front of the city of Nanaimo, we paddled over to eat dinner at the Dinghy Dock Pub. This floating restaurant is a favorite of locals and tourists alike. We had returned from supper and were sitting on the back deck enjoying the evening when we were entertained by our first "boat rodeo" of the trip.

Our boat, Havis Amanda, is a Nauticat (a motor sailor built in Finland back in 1984), so when we saw two Nauticats, one following the other, come into the bay, we were immediately interested. Our interest peaked even further when we noticed that one had no one at the helm. Wait, what???

After closer examination, we realized that the boat was being driven from a dinghy tied to its port side. The sailor was having a very hard time and almost hit several other boats in his attempt to find a safe place to anchor for the night.

When Tom saw his trouble, he quickly jumped in one of our kayaks and paddled over to offer assistance. By then, the man, named Brian, had dropped anchor, albeit way too close to several other boats. Tom offered to help him pull up anchor and relocate to a spot with more swinging room, but he was too exhausted and frazzled to do so.

In talking with Brian, Tom found out that he had problems with his transmission linkage cables right after he came through Dodd Narrows, so he had to drive it all the way into Nanaimo with his dinghy. However, a disaster was averted by quick thinking on Brian's part and help from his friends in the other Nauticat following behind him to ensure he arrived in Mark Bay safely.

Later, Brian dinghied over to thank Tom for his offer of assistance, give us his contact info, and gift us with a six-pack of beer. Wow! That was so nice and totally unexpected! Tom and I often comment that most cruisers tend to be "salt-of-the-sea" kind of folks, helpful and generous to their core.

Brian heads north tomorrow. The other Nauticat folks will also be leaving tomorrow on their own journey to Alaska, so we will most likely meet up again along the way. Safe journey, everyone!

Good Night from Nanaimo - End of Day 2

DAY 3

LAYOVER DAY: NANAIMO

Boardwalk in Nanaimo Harbor

Day three was a planned layover day in Nanaimo. We took the boat taxi from the Dinghy Dock Pub to town to find a topical cannabis cream for my arthritis and to provision fresh vegetables. We went to three cannabis shops before finding a small $60 jar of cream at Kiro's that I felt would meet my needs. I used it in the middle of the night for restless legs, and it worked reasonably well.

Even though cannabis is now legal in Canada, it is illegal to bring any cannabis products across the border. We simply were not going to chance being caught with it and losing our right to travel back and forth across the US/CA border, so we had to find a product that would work to relieve my arthritis, restless legs, and muscle spasms right here in Canada.

While we were in town, we ate at the Noodle Box. The food was good, but we both experienced gastronomical issues throughout the night. It probably didn't help that we ate ice cream at my favorite ice cream shop on the boardwalk and then a pear and cottage cheese salad when we returned home, adding insult to injury to our already unhappy bellies. As much as we both love to eat out, we will honestly be glad to get back to our own home-cooked meals.

After our after-dinner snack, we were able to stream an episode of one of our favorite series using my iPhone as a hotspot. Yea!

We slid under the covers around 10:30 or so, looking forward to a restful night's sleep.

Oh...an added note: The exhaust elbow work Tom did yesterday was successful! So far, so good!

Good Night from Nanaimo – End of Day 3

DAY 4

DESTINATION: CROSSING GEORGIA STRAIT TO BALLET BAY

Home in Ballet Bay / West Entrance

I was at the helm when we left Mark Bay this morning around 7:00 and motored down Newcastle Island Passage to the Departure Bay Gas N Go to purchase fuel and water. I pulled in and side docked the boat, nailing the landing the first time. (Do I sound proud, or what? I may still be a work in progress, but I am definitely progressing right along.)

We arrived at the fuel dock by 8:00, when it was scheduled to open, but the dock guy was 30 minutes late. We fueled and watered up and then were on our way to cross the Georgia Strait. The seas were relatively calm much of the day with rain coming in around 11:00 and continuing the rest of the day. The rain was quite light at first, so we were able to remain at the outside steering station for all but about two hours of the trip.

About halfway to Fox Cove (our original destination), we decided to try Ballet Bay instead, as neither of us had anchored there before. The entrance to the bay is tricky due to a shallow, narrow passage strewn with rocks, but I thoroughly enjoyed navigating through it. We were one of only two boats that anchored there for the night.

Dotting the shoreline of Ballet Bay are notably elaborate homes juxtaposed right next to surprisingly meager ones. The contrasting lifestyles on display here make for an uncommonly unique anchorage.

This would have been an intriguing place to kayak, but it did not stop raining all afternoon and evening, and we just needed to relax, journal, and plan the next few days of cruising.

We prepared a healthy vegetable meal comprised of boiled red potatoes and carrots and steamed cauliflower and broccoli topped with a sprinkling of parmesan cheese. And, of course, a generous amount of butter slathered on top of everything. I know, I know...the added butter pretty much nullifies the healthiness of the veggies, but I simply could not exist without butter.

Tomorrow, we travel to Lund to pick up the new Pollen sweater I ordered a month ago and grocery shop for fresh vegetables and Canadian beer. Overall, we prefer beer brewed in the US (IPAs like Bodhizaffa, Lucille, Elysian, and Tropic Haze, to name a few of our favorites), but at the end of a long cruising day, pretty much any IPA will do.

Good Night from Ballet Bay - End of Day 4

DAY 5

DESTINATION: LUND

Our journey to the little town of Lund was wet, cold, and lumpy as we first motored and then sailed down Malaspina Strait. After we raised the mizzen sail and the jib, Havis Amanda stabilized, providing us a more pleasant ride. After a while, we came inside, leaving the sails up. I am pretty sure this was the first time I had driven the boat from the inside helm station with the sails up. It felt a bit disconcerting for me initially because the sails couldn't be controlled from the inside, but I quickly adjusted and realized I had no reason to worry.

When we arrived at Lund, there was considerable wind as we rounded the corner into the marina. I had intended to dock the boat, but I came in too steep, got scared, and turned the helm over to Tom. This meant I had to be the one to jump off with lines and tie the boat up...in a 20-knot wind, no less. Tom pulled me close enough to step off onto the dock, but the wind blew so hard that I couldn't get the lines tied fast enough to secure and stop the boat. There were bull rails AND cleats, and I got confused.

I should have wrapped the lines twice around one of the cleats or some part of the bull rail to relieve the pressure on the line. Then, I would have been able to hold the boat in place until Tom could get off and help me. Unfortunately, the wind was blowing the boat away from the dock, and I was only able to wrap the line around once.

Tom told me to try and throw the line back to him, but I didn't throw the line hard enough, and it didn't make it back to the boat. Tom had the boat in reverse at that point but was still able to run forward and grab the line so it didn't get tangled in the prop. He backed up and made two more attempts before he was able to dock successfully. That time, I was able to get the midline around a cleat twice and stop the boat. Tom jumped off and secured the bow line first, followed by the stern line. Success at last!

I was a wreck emotionally. I felt so bad that I didn't perform well under these adverse circumstances that I burst into tears. We came inside the boat and, without either of us placing blame, talked through what went wrong and what we both could have done differently. Good talk!

I have found that I am quite hard on myself when I don't perform well under pressure. In the past, I have had situations where there was an emergency, and I freaked out a bit and couldn't think clearly and work out the problem. When that happens, it makes me fearful that the next time I am in a critical situation of any kind, I will panic again, and something bad will happen.

Now, to be fair to myself, I don't freeze up to the point I am helpless, screaming, or useless…I am still trying to figure out what to do...but the fear I feel inside myself is almost debilitating. I do know that over time, the more I practice these things in real-time, in good and adverse situations, the more confident I will feel and the more proficient I will become. Patience, Jandira. Patience.

After our docking fiasco, we kayaked over to the small town of Lund and walked up to the Pollen sweater shop to pick up my new yeti-colored sweater and hat. This will make my third Pollen sweater. They are 100% merino wool, don't itch, and love to be machine-washed and dried. They are pricy, but in my opinion, quite worth it. Sara, the worker bee for the locally made sweaters, and I had a lively conversation about women and boats while Tom and her husband chatted about boats in general.

Nancy's Bakery was next on our to-do list. We purchased carrot cake, shared a beer, and bought a nice loaf of bread to take back to the boat. We were so tired that we just fixed turkey and Swiss sandwiches on our freshly baked bread along with chips and leftovers from the night before.

Sunset in Lund Harbor

Good Night from Lund - End of Day 5

DAY 6

DESTINATION: BIG BAY AND YUCULTA RAPIDS

View of snow-capped mountains from Big Bay, Stuart Island

Before leaving Lund this morning, we needed to get fuel and water. It was important for me to rebuild my confidence and replace the anxiety I felt over my poor performance yesterday, so I elected to pilot the boat and side tie her to the fuel dock. I was a bit nervous, but all went well. In full disclosure, there was no wind or current to speak of, so not as difficult a challenge as yesterday.

Last year and this year too, the water pipes at the fuel dock had burst, and we were unable to water up…so very frustrating. We know now that topping off our water tanks from the Lund fuel dock cannot necessarily be relied upon in the future. Useful information to store away for next year.

Fog and rain traveled with us most of the day, so we drove from the inside steering station. We traveled through Lewis Channel, one of the prettiest places on the Inside Passage, but because of the weather conditions, there wasn't much to see.

I drove through the Yuculta Rapids at slack and straight into Big Bay. The current is always swirly in there due to rapids on both sides of the bay, so docking is pretty much always an issue. I tried three times, and Tom tried twice with no success until we decided to come in starboard side to on the other side of the dock. That way, the wind would push us onto rather than off of the dock. It was so much easier!!! I am not sure why we didn't think of doing it that way from the beginning, but we will certainly remember to do so the next time we venture back into Big Bay for an overnight. You know...hindsight...

About mid-afternoon, the current radically shifted, now pushing us off the dock, so we pulled the lines in closer and tied the boat up tighter. Afterward, Tom made three trips to the potable water faucet on shore to fill up our two five-gallon watering cans and top off our onboard water tanks while I started preparing a dinner consisting of fried red potatoes and steamed broccoli and cauliflower. When he returned from his water run, Tom made nachos for happy hour to go along with our homemade pimento cheese and crackers. So Good!

We were quite tired and hit the sack around 9:45. Tomorrow, more squirrely rapids to transit on our way to Forward Harbor. Woohoo! Theme-park-waterslide-rides coming up!

Good Night from Big Bay - End of Day 6

DAY 7

DESTINATION: FORWARD HARBOR
THROUGH GILLARD, DENT, GREEN POINT AND WHIRLPOOL RAPIDS

Going through Dent Rapids at slack tide

We woke to blue skies after six straight days of rain, clouds, and fog. The sun warmed not only our bodies but our hearts as well and brought clarity to our rain-soaked minds. We were up and on our way around 7:30, as we had four sets of rapids to transit today. Tom had timed them perfectly so we could navigate each one close to slack tide.

We hit each rapid just as Tom had planned, arrived in Forward Harbor (one of our favorite anchorages from last year) around 11:40, and dropped the hook. It was so nice to be at anchor instead of docked in a marina, and we had the harbor all to ourselves. We totally forgot to take a picture of Forward Harbor today so we have included one from last year.

Going through Greenpoint Rapids at slack tide

Going through Wellbore Channel/Whirlpool Rapids at slack tide

Jandira kayaking in Forward Harbor 2021

Tom gathered together all the crabbing gear, squeezed it into his Fatty Knees dinghy, and motored over close to shore to drop the pot. This was the first time we used our new crab pot, so we were excited to see how well it would perform. We used canned cat food and shrimp pellets for bait, as we had forgotten to buy chicken before we left Friday Harbor. We plan to pick up chicken parts (which are one of the better bait choices for catching crab if you don't have fresh salmon heads) tomorrow at Port McNeill.

Around 3:00, Tom dinghied back over to where he had dropped the crab pot but disappointingly, there was not even one crab gracing our brand-new pot. It was a good test, however, to see how he could manage the pot in his very small dinghy and then haul the pot back on board Havis Amanda safely without scratching her hull in the process.

After we ate dinner (a pot full of macaroni, peppers, onions, tomatoes, spinach, canned mushrooms, and lots of seasonings...soooo tasty), we sat out on the back of the boat for a long time just enjoying the sunshine and the beautiful evening.

I was leaning back against Tom, and he quietly said: "Will you marry me?" I immediately said, "YES! Absolutely! Will you marry me?" To which he said, "YES! Absolutely!"

We have been lovingly committed to one another since the beginning of our relationship and have talked many times about getting married, knowing we wanted to spend the rest of our lives together, but Tom had not yet officially asked me to marry him. Forward Harbor, one of our VERY favorite anchorages, certainly was the perfect setting for the most perfect man to pop the most important question! It was simply magical! I love him so much!

I found out the next day that a couple of weeks back, Tom had asked my mom for permission to ask me to marry him but not to tell me. She said, "YES!" too! Good thing we are all on the same page!

Good Night from Forward Harbor - End of Day 7

DAY 8

DESTINATION: PORT MCNEILL

Sunrise in Forward Harbor

Good Morning from Forward Harbor! Our day started with the alarm going off at 5:00 for a 6:00 departure time. We had an eight-hour cruising day down Johnstone Strait, which can be a challenge on the best days, so we wanted to get an early start. The winds were predicted to be 10-20+ knots with rain and current against us much of the way.

The transit was very choppy, with winds upwards of 24 knots, and swells consistently between three and four feet. Even still, we made the day a fun one by listening, singing, and drumming to music as we motored along, while at the same time keeping an eye out for logs, kelp, and, of course…other boats.

We arrived in Port McNeill after a long and tiring day, but no worse for wear. After Tom called into North Harbor Marina to get our slip assignment, we headed for the fuel dock, where we were met by a friendly dock worker named William. He grabbed our lines and tied us up securely before the wind could blow us off the dock. So helpful!

The town of Port McNeill offers numerous amenities (shower, laundry, grocery store, drug store, medical center, hospital, three restaurants, and a marine shop, to name a few), all within walking distance, which we will take advantage of tomorrow.

Havis Amanda moored in Port McNeill Marina

We put the boat to bed and heated up leftovers from last night along with Tom's tasty biscuits and salad. Tom worked on paperwork while I worked on today's journal entry. We went to bed early, wrung out from the long day.

Good Night from Port McNeill – End of Day 8

DAY 9

LAYOVER DAY: PORT MCNEILL

This layover day in Port McNeill was dedicated to accomplishing a number of chores, but even so, it was quite enjoyable.

We gathered together our dirty laundry and made a grocery list. We walked toward town, dropped off our garbage at the top of the port, washed clothes, and shopped for groceries before walking back to the boat to put everything away.

Later, we walked back up into town to find a suitable restaurant for dinner and found a new brewpub called Devil's Bath, named for a huge sinkhole somewhere outside of town called…well, you guessed it…Devil's Bath. It is owned by three brothers and their mother (not the sinkhole…the brewery), all who love beer. We shared an exceptionally good pizza and a kale-based salad and tried out the brewery's IPA. We really liked this brewpub with its indoor/outdoor seating, friendly wait staff, and delightful atmosphere.

Tom paid for our meal and bought a white T-shirt, a hat, and two stickers for our laptops. We are collecting stickers from the places we stay to remember them. The hat ended up too small for Tom, so I am now the proud owner of a Devil's Bath Brew Pub beanie. So Fun! I will be styling!

We had a relaxing evening getting prepared to travel across Queen Charlotte Strait tomorrow. Our plan is to anchor in Skull Cove for the night to stage to go around Cape Caution on Tuesday.

Good Night from Port McNeill - End of Day 9

DAY 10

DESTINATION: SKULL COVE

Crossing Queen Charlotte Strait on our way to Skull Cove

We departed Port McNeill around 7:00 and headed across Queen Charlotte Strait to anchor in Skull Cove for the night. Tom said Skull Cove was a great place to kayak, so we were looking forward to arriving there early enough to do so. There we will stage for our journey to go around Cape Caution on Tuesday.

We had a very smooth and uneventful ride over to Skull Cove. The wind was on our nose (isn't it always?), but we had a strong current going with us, so we were able to maintain a fairly consistent eight knots of speed. There were lots of clouds, a few sprinkles of rain, and a bit of break-through sunshine here and there.

Navigating the entrance into Skull Cove is a bit tricky in that you have to dodge kelp beds and rocks and go through a very narrow opening before entering the anchorage. Once we reached the inside of the cove, the sun came out and pretty much stayed out the rest of the afternoon and early evening. Tom got the kayaks down, and we had a lovely afternoon puttering around all the little islets, looking at the colorations, patterns, and formations of the rocks on the shore. Tom took lots of photos so I could use them as inspiration for my mandala art projects.

Kayaking in Skull Cove

Shoreline in Skull Cove

When we returned to the boat from kayaking, Tom discovered that the Y coupling in the forward head was completely clogged up with years of accumulated crud, making the head inoperable. Now, if you have ever had to work on a head, you totally understand how despicable this job can be and why no boat owner *ever* wants to be faced with this task. Luckily, Tom doesn't use foul language (unless you call muttering "Good Grief!" under his breath using foul language), or the anchored boaters around us would have gotten an ear full. Thankfully, after dismantling and removing the head, floors, and pipes, cleaning them, and putting them back together, four hours later, we had a totally reworked head.

Thank goodness that, along with the trials and tribulations of boat life, we are also blessed with delightful experiences.

We were both exhausted, so we ate sandwiches and salads and dropped into bed around 10:00. Tomorrow...rounding Cape Caution.

Good Night from Skull Cove - End of Day 10

DAY 11

ROUNDING CAPE CAUTION
DESTINATION: FURY COVE

Rounding Cape Caution heading toward Fury Cove

Finally, the day had arrived...the day I had been looking forward to with an equal measure of fear and excitement...the rounding of Cape Caution. You see, even on the best days, Cape Caution can be an uncomfortable crossing due to strong winds and swells that roll in off the ocean opposing one another, and on the worst days, it can be dangerous and even deadly. When you add the currents coming out of Slingsby Channel into the mix...well...you can be in for a rip-roaring ride.

Many factors must be considered before making the crossing. Tom, being the careful, methodical planner that he is, thoroughly examined all these factors days before, getting the most up-to-date information available each day.

He checked out the tides and currents, which consider the moon's phase (spring or neap tide – neap is better), whether the current is flooding or ebbing (flooding is preferred), and when slack water time occurs at Slingsby Channel.

He checked with the NOAA Ocean Prediction Center to make sure there were no dangerous weather systems predicted on the chosen day, looked at wind speed and direction in relation to the direction of our travel, checked out wave height and interval, and monitored trends of forecast conditions.

He also selected duck-in locations all along our route in case of an emergency. We, of course, hope for the best, but we plan for the worst. As you can see, there are many factors to consider before sailing around Cape Caution but don't let that stop you from doing it…the experience is well worth it. Trust me on this.

So, now to how the day unfolded. We got up at 4:45 to meet our previously determined departure time of 6:00. We try to get an early start each morning because the winds in the Pacific NW tend to build in the afternoons, plus leaving early gives us the added advantage of getting to the anchorage early enough to find a favorable spot to drop the hook and enjoy the rest of the day hiking, kayaking, or just resting.

We left Skull Cove just after sunrise and headed into Queen Charlotte Strait to begin our journey around Cape Caution. We experienced a light, drizzling rain for a while, with mostly cloudy skies hovering over us the rest of the day. Only a few breakthrough rays of sunshine popped out here and there as the day progressed.

The rollers/swells coming in off the ocean as we rounded the Cape were quite different from the ones we encountered transiting Johnstone Strait (or other similar passages) in that the wave height was higher and the intervals between each wave longer, so they were less choppy and more like a slow roller coaster ride. We rode the wave up to the crest and then surfed down the other side. It takes a bit of getting used to, but I found the experience way more enjoyable than the choppy ride down Johnstone Strait.

We raised the jib (fore sail) and the mizzen (aft sail), which stabilized the boat and provided us with a more comfortable ride. For approximately the last half of the ride, the rollers coming in on our beam were as tall as the boat (not counting the mast, of course), sometimes even crashing over the bow. I had never experienced waves quite that high, but as I let myself relax, I found the experience less intimidating.

Over my 71 years of living, I have discovered that life is pretty much all in my perspective...in how I choose to frame what I am experiencing at any given moment. I had the choice to frame the journey around the Cape as exhilarating or terrifying, and by choosing to frame it as exhilarating, I could relax and get into the rhythm of the sea, actually finding it quite enjoyable.

I feel fortunate to have had some years of sailing experience under my belt before being thrown into the type of situation we faced today. Tom has said many times that he never wants to knowingly put me in a situation that is too far above my comfort level...stretch that comfort level, yes...but not to the point that I freak out and don't want to experience that again. Of course, I don't want that either. Sailing is a huge part of our lives and will be so for many years to come, and we neither one want anything to negatively affect that.

The sail around Cape Caution and into Fury Cove took approximately five-and-one-fourth hours. One sailboat was already anchored in the area that would provide the most protection from the southwest wind predicted to blow through the next day. Rats! We hesitantly chose an anchor across the bay from them for the first night, but after seeing how fiercely the winds were blowing through the cove the next morning, we decided to pull up anchor and move across the bay to the same side as the other boat. A much better decision.

I prepared a spicy-hot pot of chili and our typical tossed salad of greens, cucumber, cherry tomatoes, feta, shredded parmesan cheese, dried cranberries, and mandarin oranges, and Tom made Red Lobster biscuits, for you see, in Tom's world, a meal is not a meal if bread is not part of it.

It had been a long, exhausting, albeit positive and exhilarating day, so with very full but satisfied bellies, we were tucked in bed by 7:00. Thank you, Angels, for watching over us as we made our way around the infamous Cape Caution. It was most definitely an experience to remember.

Early evening in Fury Cove

Good Night from Fury Cove – End of Day 11

DAY 12

LAYOVER DAY: FURY COVE

Tom and Jandira on the beach in Fury Cove

After 12 hours of sleep, our bodies and minds, thankfully, felt more relaxed and rested. We had been going full steam for 11 straight days and decided to lay over at least one day in Fury Cove to recuperate. We got up around 7:00, had coffee and tea and the first Quiet Time we had had in a few days.

Our Quiet Time, as we call it, consists of lighting a candle, setting positive intentions for the day, and reading something inspirational. Our favorite for over a year now is a daybook of inspirational messages by Mark Nepo called *The Book of Awakening*. I have read this book at least 10 times, and Tom and I are on our second time through it. It is one of those books you can read many times and still get new insights each time. The daily messages often spark very compelling conversations, which have helped us deepen our relationship with one another. We have noticed that when we begin our day in this intentional way, our day tends to play out in a more positive manner.

Kayaking on the outside of Fury Cove

We have also been taking turns reading aloud other books such as *The Alchemist* by Paulo Coelho, *The Way of the Peaceful Warrior* series by Dan Millman, and several books by Mitch Albom (*Tuesdays with Morrie, The Five People You Meet in Heaven,* and others). We have found this to be a good way to pass the time when we are moving from one anchorage to another.

After our Quiet Time, we kayaked for about two hours before coming back for a light lunch. As we were finishing lunch, we noticed the couple from the sailboat across the way dinghying over to our boat. We had a lovely conversation with DJ and Carol about mutual boating topics and their many years of cruising in these waters. We learned they had lived aboard their sailboat for 23 years and had traveled all over Northern BC. They are also world travelers, picking a different country each year to explore. Inspiring!

Later in the day, Carol and DJ came back by with two rockfish and one lingcod they had just caught and gave us our pick. Tom chose the rockfish. I had planned to have leftover chili for dinner, but no one in their right mind turns down freshly caught fish, so of course, we said yes. The chili could certainly wait until the next evening to be eaten.

Kayaking outside of Fury Cove

DJ told Tom how to fillet the rockfish, and in that Tom never meets a challenge he isn't willing to attempt, he brought the two fish into the galley and commenced to fillet them. The first one was already dead, but the second one still had some life left in it and flopped around even after its guts were removed and its head cut off. I am told that is due to involuntary nerve action, but man is it freaky when its headless body all of a sudden jumps out of your hands! Yikes!

In hindsight, filleting the rockfish inside the galley instead of out on the deck was not the best idea as far as the cleanup and the fishy smell were concerned. Oh well...we live and learn. At least that's what we tell ourselves anyway.

This type of rockfish has very sharp and somewhat poisonous dorsal fins, so care must be taken when handling it. A cut by them can be quite painful, but if you are careful, this tasty fish is worth the risk. We had a wonderful meal of rockfish cooked in garlic butter and seasonings, wild grain rice, and salad, then headed straight to bed.

Nighty-Night from Fury Cove – End of Day 12

DAY 13

SECOND LAYOVER DAY: FURY COVE

Jandira log-walking along the beach in Fury Cove

Our second layover day in Fury Cove was relaxing and fun. Once again, we enjoyed tea, coffee, and Quiet Time before getting into our daily activities.

We wanted to thank Carol and DJ for the generous gift of rockfish they gifted us the night before, so I made Tollhouse chocolate chip cookies, and we gave them a container of our homemade pimento cheese spread. We kayaked over to their boat around noon to share our goodies. They seemed pleased. We exchanged contact information with them to keep in touch along our respective journeys.

We also wanted to pick their brains about any cruising, fishing, crabbing, and shrimping knowledge they might have that would be helpful to us on our journey north. We were not disappointed, as they were a wealth of knowledge on many cruising subjects. It is so interesting to meet like-minded folks and share knowledge and stories of our collective experiences.

After talking with Carol and DJ for about an hour, we continued kayaking around the bay, getting off several times to explore the shoreline. When we pulled our kayaks up onto shore (it was low tide and getting lower by the minute), we had to walk through some muck to drag them up far enough to be able to tie them to a rock. We knew the tide wouldn't begin coming back in until around 3:00, so we had plenty of time to get back to them before that time.

White sandy beaches in Fury Cove

The beaches are white here due to all the broken-up clam shells. Unlike other beaches we have explored, where there is often a wide variety of colorful stones, all the rocks here appeared to be the same: black rocks with a spattering of sparkly flakes. As is typical of me, I couldn't resist bringing a few back to the boat.

When we returned from kayaking, Tom worked on the generator starter for a couple of hours while I worked on journaling. We heated leftover chili, made a salad, ate, and went to bed. We have an early morning start tomorrow, so we were in bed by 10:30. Our layover days in Fury Cove had incorporated relaxation, light exercise, connecting with new friends, and fun...a great combination in anybody's book.

Looking from Fury Cove into Fitz Hugh Sound

Good Night from Fury Cove – End of Day 13

DAY 14

DESTINATION: FANCY COVE, HUNTER ISLAND

Sailing up Fitz Hugh Sound to Fancy Cove

I awoke one minute before our 5:30 alarm went off this morning groaning: *"I really don't want to be up this early,"* but as all good sailors know, timing can be everything. We had determined that pulling up the anchor by 6:30 was prudent, in that 20-30-knot winds were predicted to blow straight down Fitz Hugh Sound today on our 41-mile transit to Fancy Cove, and we wanted to get out ahead of it...plus...it was Friday the 13th. Oh dear! We sailors are not superstitious (yeah, right!), but we were not about to test the Gods on this fine day! No siree!

After pulling up the anchor and exiting Fury Cove, we immediately hoisted the jib and mizzen sails. We knew the sails would help to stabilize us as well as give us a push in speed down the channel. The combination of a flooding tide and a beam-to-broad reach sail gave us a smooth six-hour transit, traveling at a speed of seven-and-a-half knots.

We motor-sailed almost the whole way between snow-capped mountains on our starboard and low rolling hills on our port. It was predictably cloudy but quite beautiful. The winds never reached the predicted 20-30 knots, so we had a very calm ride. I read aloud from the Mitch Albom novel *The Next Person You Meet in Heaven* as we sailed along.

Our new friends, Carol and DJ, left about an hour before we did, and we watched their sailboat far off in the distance until they turned off at Goldstream Harbor for the night. The next day, they had a friend's celebration of life to attend at Shearwater Resort. We planned to be in Shearwater on that day as well. Perhaps we will reconnect with them then.

We reached Fancy Cove in a light drizzle, dropped anchor in a depth of 46 feet, and hunkered down for the afternoon and evening. We had intended to kayak, but the rain picked up, and we both fell asleep for about an hour, me on the settee and Tom stretched out on the floor.

Our dinner consisted of a big pot of cabbage, red potatoes, carrots, and onions, served with defrosted sourdough bread from Bakery San Juan. Ahhhh, yes…a delicious taste of home.

After a few hands of cards (YEA! I won this time!), we crawled into bed to watch TV before drifting off to sleep.

Water Totems along the shoreline in Fancy Cove

These reflections occur when the water is dead calm. Can you tell where the rocks stop and the water begins?

Good Night from Fancy Cove – End of Day 14

DAYS 15-16

DESTINATION: SHEARWATER RESORT

The sounds of a pileated woodpecker drilling holes in a nearby tree and the caw of a jet-black crow greeted us on this fine, sun-kissed morning. Thankfully we were able to sleep in until around 7:00...a far sight better, in my mind at least, than the 5:00 wake-up call we have adhered to on so many other days during this trip.

Tom happily wakes up early every morning ready to dive into the day's activities, but I tend to be a bit of a sleepyhead, slower to be excited about the upcoming day. However, once my feet hit the floor, and I have had the first sip of tea that Tom brews for me every morning, I am so happy to be up early enjoying the crisp, quiet morning. I just can't say that I am always *that* delighted when the alarm goes off.

We only had a one-and-a-half-hour transit today to Shearwater, so we decided to leave Fancy Cove around 9:20. It was an easy ride down Lama Passage, and we arrived at the Shearwater Resort around 11:00. This would be the last place to fuel and water up, provision, and do laundry until Prince Rupert.

Our plan was to go to Rescue Cove on Monday and then up into the Fiordland Recreation Area for a few days after that. Instead, we ended up staying another day in Shearwater to set up the group email I would use to send out the daily journal entries to all our friends and family. This turned out to be a bigger challenge than we expected.

After spending hours in front of the computer, by the end of the day, we were brain-dead, so after dinner, we stretched out in bed and zoned out in front of the TV, giving our fried brains a welcome break.

Oh...one last note: Yesterday, a young man knocked on our boat and handed us two large filets cut from a 70-pound halibut his boss, on the mega-yacht anchored there at the marina, had caught earlier that day. We were delighted to be the recipients of their kindness and generosity.

Float plane landing at Shearwater Resort

Good Night from Shearwater Resort – End of Days 15-16

DAY 17

DESTINATION: RESCUE BAY, SUSAN ISLAND

Lighthouse at Dryad Point

We left Shearwater Marina and passed the Lighthouse at Dryad Point this morning, blanketed with sunny skies and a few low-hanging clouds tossed in for good measure...a welcome change from the many rainy mornings we have experienced since we left Friday Harbor. The sun rays on the water looked like millions of fireflies all lighting up at once...shimmery and sparkly. It took me back to my childhood when we caught what we called lightening bugs and put them in a jar with holes punched into the lid so they could breathe. It was simply magical...then and now.

As far as the weather is concerned, Tom and I have learned to embrace whatever weather conditions the Universe gives us and try and find the joy in it all. (Notice I didn't say grind our teeth and just put up with it.) It is, after all, not like we have any real say in the matter, right?

Sailing down Seaforth Channel on our way to Rescue Bay

Einstein said that the definition of insanity is arguing with "what is," so I would say getting all grumpy and shouting at the heavens over a bit of rain certainly qualifies as arguing with "what is." It is simply counterproductive. (In full disclosure, it helps that we have an inside pilot house to steer from and really good foul-weather gear, so bring on the rain!)

We sailed west down Seaforth Channel until we turned north, then surfed down the swells into Reid Passage. The entrance to Reid is strewn with rocks, and the passage through it is narrow and serpentine-like, so we had to be super careful. Tom and I both like the challenge of these routes, as they certainly keep us on our toes. No sleeping on watch in these waters, or we could find our boat aground, and we absolutely do NOT want to spend the night waiting for the Canadian Coastguard to come to our rescue!

From there we sailed into Perceval Narrows, a chokepoint between the swells rolling in off the Pacific Ocean and the entrance to Mathieson Channel. This section can be very dangerous and challenging to transit in certain conditions. Today, we had the luck of the Irish with us. The wind was behind us, blowing between 15-22 knots, and the current was flooding (all of which was in our favor), making the Narrows not so dicey to navigate.

Continuing our transit of Seaforth Channel

As we came out of Perceval Narrows into Mathieson Channel, we were out of most of the large swells and outside winds coming in off the Pacific Ocean. The high mountains on either side of Mathieson Channel helped protect us and were a welcome respite from the lumpy ride of the open channel.

From Mathieson Channel, we rounded the corner into Rescue Bay, a very sweet little anchorage tucked into the northeast corner of Susan Island where Jackson Narrows meets Mathieson Channel. We dropped anchor at 12:05 in 28 feet of water at the southeast corner of Rescue Bay. At that point, we were one of six boats anchored in the cove, but in that 25-35-knot winds are expected tonight and 30-40-knot winds during the day tomorrow, more boats will most likely tuck into this very protected anchorage for a day or so until the weather shifts.

Tom worked on planning upcoming routes while I worked on today's journal entry. He generously did all the cooking today, from popcorn to pizza to a lovely tossed salad with everything but the kitchen sink in it. So Good! And such a good, good man to take over dish duties so I can write each day. I feel so very blessed!

Good Night from Rescue Bay - End of Day 17

DAY 18

LAYOVER DAY: RESCUE BAY

Our Morning Quiet Time

We woke to a light drizzle (again), drank our coffee and tea, and had our Quiet Time. For some time now, our Quiet Time readings have centered around the importance of being our authentic selves, having the courage to ask for what we need from one another, and speaking and listening from our hearts. The readings have prompted many deep and profound discussions and helped us to grow in love and understanding of one another...so very important to both of us.

Later in the morning, we began to plan our route up to the Glacier Bay area, including a stop in the Fiordland Conservancy, provisioning in Prince Rupert, crossing the Canadian border back into the US, several stops in the Misty Fiords, and others. We needed to get a better idea of approximately where we would be when so that Tom's nephew, Brian, and his wife, Gila, could plan where to fly into when they come for a few days to visit the last week of June. In making these plans, we also wanted to consider what types of adventures they might want to experience so that we could select the right places for them to see in the short window of time they would have to spend with us. We are so looking forward to our time with them.

After several hours of sitting with charts and cruising guides like *Exploring Southeast Alaska* and *Waggoner Cruising Guide*, we had a loose plan for June. We had previously planned the month of May, knowing perfectly well that alterations to those plans might have to be made along the way, and now we had a head start on June.

There is a lot of planning that goes into these month's long cruising trips, so having a plan that is doable in the time frame you have, flexible in case of weather changes, boat breakdowns, or illnesses, and that also takes into account layover days to rest, reset, and build your energy level back up, is vital to the success of your trip. We work very hard in the planning aspects of the trip so that we can thoroughly enjoy the doing parts, but honestly, we enjoy all the many aspects of boat life. (Although…having said that…I think I can safely speak for Tom in saying that working on a boat head (toilet) is an aspect of boat life he would just as soon never have to tackle.)

After planning routes all afternoon, we fixed enchiladas for dinner. I have been using a boxed roasted red pepper and tomato soup as my base for the enchilada sauce, which I then doctor up with hot sauces, Worcestershire, and various dried spices (garam masala, parsley, basil, garlic powder, thyme, cilantro, cumin, chili powder, red pepper flakes, and black pepper). We have found we like my concoction way better than the typical canned version.

Later, I worked on journaling while Tom did the dishes. Then we hit the sack, hoping for a decent night's sleep before an early rise for our journey to Kynoch Inlet tomorrow. Sleep tight, everyone.

Fellow boater anchored next to us in Rescue Bay

Good Night from Rescue Bay - End of Day 18

DAY 19

DESTINATION: KYNOCH INLET, THE FIORDLANDS

"WE GOTTA GO!!! WE'RE IN SEVEN FEET OF WATER, AND WE DRAW SIX!!!"

That was how my day started. I was coming up from the aft cabin after getting my foul weather gear on and witnessed Tom frantically scrambling around to get out the door and pull up the anchor. I too had to move fast as I needed to be at the helm to drive the boat quickly away from shallow water as soon as the anchor was out of the water. The tide was rapidly going out, and we were about to be dragging bottom. Within a very few minutes, however, we were in the middle of the channel and safely on our way. Disaster averted! That's certainly ONE way to get our blood flowing first thing in the morning!

Even though it was rainy and a bit cold when we left Rescue Bay this morning, we still wanted to drive from the outside aft-helm station. Yes, it would be physically more comfortable to be steering from the inside helm station where we would be toasty-warm and dry, but honestly, there is a spiritual and emotional element to cruising that we feel can best be experienced while viewing the wonders of nature actually outside IN nature. There is just something vital to the whole experience that is missing when we drive from inside the pilot house.

As we travel I am always on the lookout for rock walls with interesting patterns and colorations to use as inspiration for the mandalas that I create, so I was thrilled with the various hues and designs that I was able to photograph along the way today. These rocks stir something within me that I am at a loss for words to express.

As we motored down Mathieson Channel, we saw several waterfalls, all of which were amazing in their own right, but none more spectacular than Kynoch Falls, a stunningly beautiful waterfall that originates from Lessom Creek and comes into view just after you round the point into Kynoch Inlet. We were able to motor up very close, experiencing the spray and turbulence created by the huge amount of rushing water that cascaded down the mountainside. Initially, just being up close and personal with all that raw power was intimidating for me. I foolishly wondered if we might get sucked into the base of the falls, but that was not the case. In fact, just the opposite...it pushed us away. Interesting.

Rock formations and patterns at low tide in Mathieson Channel

Looking at Kynoch Falls from Havis Amanda

As we entered the inlet, the high snow-covered peaks and vertical granite walls that towered above the water absolutely took our breath away. It rained most of the day, but honestly, we didn't care. The first part of the day, the clouds were high enough that you could see the mountain tops, but after we dropped anchor in 84 feet of water at the head of Kynoch Inlet, the clouds dropped lower in the sky, and the rain picked up...and you know what? We still didn't care! It's simply ALL part of the experience.

We had started preparing salmon, sweet potatoes, steamed Brussel sprouts, and corn when Tom looked up to see our first bear sighting of the trip: a very large, thick-coated brown bear (otherwise known as a grizzly bear) with his nose up, sniffing the air. I thought he just might be catching a whiff of the salmon Tom was cooking on the grill and trying to figure out how to get hold of it for his supper. Sorry, Grizz...not gonna happen.

Unfortunately, we were too far away from the bear to get a good photo. Perhaps we will have better luck tomorrow. Watch this space.

Tom and I are in agreement that this is THE most stunning anchorage we have either one ever experienced. The quiet majesty of this spot is truly awe-inspiring and promotes a sense of peace and well-being. We will definitely spend more than one day in this beautiful anchorage.

Our view of the mountains while anchored in Kynoch Inlet

Good Night from Kynoch Inlet - End of Day 19

DAY 20

LAYOVER DAY: KYNOCH INLET

View from our "back porch" this morning

"HONEY! COME QUICK! THERE IS A MAMA BEAR AND HER CUB OVER ON SHORE! HURRY!!!"

I had been getting dressed and was still barefoot, so I had to scramble to get my slippers on, but it was worth it. They were both just ambling along eating something from the ground…no hurries…no worries...seemingly not a care in the world: no weather to check, no tide or current changes to prepare for, no wind speed to consider, no logs and kelp beds to dodge…just where their next meal would come from. They just seemed so peaceful and content.

But wait…just so you know…I am in no way saying that a bear's life is better than ours. After all, Tom and I could have lawns to mow, gutters to clean out, walls to paint, and roofs to replace. Instead, we get to sail, kayak, hike, and sit on the back of the boat to take in the splendor of nature. It simply doesn't get any better than that.

We believe that our lives are all about choices, and we have chosen to live freely, love fiercely, follow our hearts, and reach for our dreams no matter where they lead us. Sometimes, it feels too good to be true. Thankfully, it's not. We are retired, after all!

So, this morning, we chose to sit out on our "back porch" and take in this incredible view as we enjoyed our morning rituals. We were the only boat in this incredibly beautiful place…until…OH NO! Is that a boat we see motoring in? You mean we will have to share this nature cathedral with someone else? Rats! We love having anchorages all to ourselves, but we also know that good things can happen when you least expect them to, as you will see. Read on.

After our Quiet Time, Tom got the dinghy down, and we motored around the inlet. It was a very low tide, which meant we could see a lot of the colorations and patterns on the rocks along the water's edge. There were hues of orange, black, green and gold striking off in all directions.

Aren't the rocks in the photo below absolutely stunning? I get so excited thinking about the art projects I can create with inspirations from these ancient stones.

While we were out looking at rock patterns and colors, we decided to dinghy over to meet our new boat neighbors, Ryan and Laurel. It's easy to meet new and interesting people on the water, so we struck up a conversation. Nice folks!

Colorations and patterns in the rock formations in Kynoch Inlet

Later we took the kayaks out and paddled to the back of the inlet in hopes of seeing the brown bears more closely. We got off on shore and walked around a bit. Tom was hoping to get a photo of a bear footprint but no such luck. We had our trusty bear spray in hand, so we were prepared, but sadly, no bear sighting this afternoon.

We saw Ryan and Laurel after they had returned from dinghying up into Culpepper Bay and invited them for a simple supper of appetizers, homemade chicken noodle soup, and Tom's Red Lobster Biscuits. We had a pleasant evening talking about boats, Alaska, New Zealand (where Ryan is from originally), and a new Elon Musk Wi-Fi invention called Starlink, which they had recently installed on their boat. We are considering purchasing one as it will give us more streaming capability pretty much no matter where we travel on the boat. They also gave us their password to Starlink so I could send out journal entries from the past few days. Such generous and trusting folks! We hope to meet them again along the way.

Havis Amanda anchored in Kynoch Inlet

Good Night from Kynoch Inlet - End of Day 20

DAY 21

SECOND LAYOVER DAY: KYNOCH INLET

This amazing view greeted us the last two mornings

(I mean, really…why would anyone leave such a sacred, majestic place?)

There are many words one could use to describe this profoundly beautiful place: stunning, awe-inspiring, majestic…but for me, the word that most adequately describes it would be *Sacred*. This truly is *God's Country*.

And this....

And this...perhaps no other words are necessary

It was around 10:30 this morning when we donned our jackets, rubber boots (a must for boating in Alaska), PFDs (personal floatation devices), and cell phones to take photos before heading out to a small snow field at the base of a waterfall here in Kynoch Inlet. We paddled to shore, got out, and pulled our kayaks up far enough that when the tide came in, it would not sweep them away. We usually tie them to a log or rock on shore but knew we wouldn't be away from the kayaks long enough for that to be an issue today.

As we walked the shoreline, we saw a starfish, several sea cucumbers that had washed up on shore when the tide went out, and lots of sparkling granite rocks. Tom says that I could be content looking for interesting rocks for hours at a time...which is totally true...but so often, he is the one who finds the most unique rocks to bring back and add to our collection.

When hiking in the woods or walking a shoreline, we often create what we call Nature Altars or Offerings to Nature. We gather rocks, driftwood, pinecones, berries, greenery...whatever we find that inspires us...and create a sculpture or a medicine wheel as an offering of our deep appreciation to Nature for the beauty with which she surrounds us. We like to picture someone coming upon our creations and feeling blessed, and we hope Nature feels blessed by our offerings as well.

So that is what we did. Tom selected several rocks and stacked them one upon the other, balancing them in a sort of tower. I found two more rocks to lean against the rock tower he had constructed. I saw this as an example of how Tom and I support one another in our day-to-day lives. It felt good to leave a little piece of us there in Kynoch Inlet.

We then scrambled up the snow field to the base of the waterfall and got some good photos. There was a low cave there that Tom got too close to for my comfort...I mean, it could have been a bear's den, for goodness' sake! Then, true to his adventurist nature, he climbed to the other side of the snow field and took a great photo looking through the ice.

He said he had to take the shot from a "groundhog's point of view," but I don't know of any groundhog with such an eye for composition. Honestly, I think this particular photo is one of his most creative. It is just so uniquely Tom. He is an outside-of-the-box kind of thinker, and I think you would have to agree that this photo certainly fits that description.

When we started kayaking back to the boat, we saw many different species of sea life: starfish, sea cucumbers, sea urchins, and some kind of orange, fluffy-looking creatures. The tide was ebbing by then, so we had to paddle hard against the current. We are most definitely building up some upper body strength kayaking, but our legs are suffering a bit from a lack of hiking. We are going to have to come up with a leg-strengthening exercise routine to do on a daily basis, or our muscles are going to atrophy. The landscape here just doesn't lend itself to longer-distance hiking.

When we returned from kayaking, I worked on journaling while Tom finished setting up the shrimp pot, putting the kayaks back on board, and hoisting the dinghy up onto the davit on the stern of the boat. We ate leftover chicken noodle soup, sourdough bread for Tom, and saltines and butter for me—comfort food from my childhood.

Looking through the ice field into Kynoch Inlet

Small waterfall at the top of the snowfield in Kynoch Inlet

Good Night from Kynoch Inlet – End of Day 21

DAY 22

DESTINATION: WINDY BAY, POOLEY ISLAND

Havis Amanda in Kynoch Inlet

As we pulled up anchor in Kynoch Inlet this morning, it was with a mixture of sadness at leaving this majestic, sacred place and anticipation of what this new day would bring us as we headed to Windy Bay, Pooley Island. Although we usually get moving early on travel days, this day was different. We resisted rushing our leaving and instead sat out on the back deck with our hot beverages to do our Quiet Time. On most travel days we do our Quiet Time after we are on our way, but on this day, we simply wanted to take in the beauty of this place for just a little longer.

Motoring back down Kynoch Inlet was a real treat. When we came in three days ago, it was raining with low-hanging clouds, and even though it was beautiful in its own way, the tops of the mountains were not visible. Today, on the other hand, we had blue skies all the way. It was an easy 20-mile day with no issues of any kind.

Colorful rock walls in Windy Bay

When we rounded the corner into Windy Bay, we were delighted to see that we had the bay all to ourselves. We dropped anchor, fixed a quick snack, and headed out in our kayaks. We wanted to paddle over to this small, unnamed islet that was just inside the entrance to the bay and kayak around it. There was a teeny tiny islet next to the little islet that had about 20 harbor seals on top of it stretched out sunning. When they saw us coming, they all slid into the water to avoid contact with us. It wasn't long before their little heads popped back up and off they swam to places unknown. We had rudely interrupted their afternoon siesta.

We paddled all the way around the densely forested bigger islet looking for a place to pull our kayaks up, get off and go exploring. Which we did!

We kayaked back to the boat and sat out on the stern to relax for a while. We stretched out for about ten minutes in the sun, and then Tom put the kayaks back on board and worked on repairing some rope while I began today's journal. Another boat has joined us for the evening, but it's anchored a good bit away, so we will still enjoy lots of privacy.

We ate a lovely dinner of grilled halibut, yellow rice, and butter lettuce salad out on the stern of the boat. We were barefooted and had on short-sleeved tee shirts for the first time since we left Friday Harbor. It was delightful!

Look at this upside-down heart tree! Tom and I look for and find hearts in nature everywhere we go

We sat on this big rock and took in the view of Pooley Island

Good Night from Windy Bay – End of Day 22

DAY 23

DESTINATION: KHUTZE INLET

Havis Amanda anchored in Khutze Inlet

This journal entry is going to be short and sweet, as today was pretty uneventful overall. I spent a long time working on the first "New Insights" entry, which you will see below, and I need sleep. So, here goes...

We left Windy Bay, motored down Sheep Passage to Graham Reach, on to Frazer Reach, and finally through Hiekish Narrows on our way to Khutze Inlet. We had clouds, lots of fog, and some sun. The current was ebbing against us, with following winds and some squirrely waters in the Narrows. We arrived around noon and dropped anchor just past the spit on the south side of the inlet.

As soon as the anchor dropped, Tom noticed a very wooly brown bear grazing grass on the shoreline. We grabbed a snack (for those of you who know our routine of intermittent fasting and not eating until around 4:00 each day...you can tell from the last several entries that we have not been adhering to our fasting regimen very well), quickly got in our kayaks, and paddled toward shore, hoping to get a better look at the bear. He seemed not to notice us at first as we were downwind from him. When he got a whiff of us, he stood up on his hind legs to get a better look. When he saw we were just a couple of tourists and of no danger to him, he dropped back to all fours and ambled into the woods.

We paddled back to the boat, fixed a dinner of halibut, red parsley potatoes, salad, and biscuits, played cards (Tom won...rats!), and went to bed. Unfortunately, we still did not get a photo of Mr. Bear. Stay tuned. Before our trip ends, we will snap a bear photo or die trying! (Just kidding!) Watch this space!

Good Night from Khutze Inlet - End of Day 23

NEW INSIGHTS: SOMETHING TO PONDER...

Journey or Destination?

Tom and I have been gaining so many new insights while on our journey (as well as confirmation on some already realized ones) that we thought we would share some of these insights with all of you from time to time in a separate entry. So, here is our first one.

When Tom and I began our four-month journey North to Alaska, we had some goals that we wanted to accomplish...places we wanted to visit...experiences we hoped to have...but now we are pondering what realizing those goals would accomplish. Is it important to be able to say we have traveled as far as Glacier Bay or Tracy Arm, experienced Warm Springs, visited Ketchikan or Sitka or Juneau? Is the destination the goal or is the goal to take in all the experiences along the way? If we are always looking ahead to the next stop and the next stop and the next stop...checking off the places or events like a to-do list...have we really been able to stay present moment by moment to what we are experiencing? Have we taken the time to talk about how we feel about what we are experiencing and ponder the impact it has had on us? Isn't enjoying each moment for itself just as important as reaching the end goal? Or perhaps more important?

So, destination or journey...which should take precedence? We have come to believe that the joy of the journey itself far surpasses just being able to say we have been to this place or had that experience, and more importantly, how those experiences have changed us, reshaped us, given us a higher perspective on things. In

Tom's words, "The destination has taken a backseat to the journey."

So now, after the first three weeks of our 16-week journey, we have shifted our priorities a bit. Instead of a "Glacier Bay or die" kind of attitude, our new mantra is: "One bay, inlet, harbor, cove, lagoon, sound, passage, anchorage, channel, rapid, narrows, reach, strait, or cape a day"...staying present each moment to what the Universe has in store for us along the way. Our new goal is to make a loose plan to follow, not a hard and fast one, knowing that it really is OK to change our plan on a whim...it IS our plan, after all.

We are at an anchorage in Khutze Bay with no Wi-Fi, so I can't look up the exact quote or the author of the quote, but it goes something like: "The only constant in life is change."

So, it would follow that the ever-present moment is really all we have. All our plans and schemes for the future can change in the blink of an eye, whether by design or something completely out of our control, so Tom and I are going to do our best to go with the flow moment by moment and just see where it takes us.

Each and every day brings with it joys as well as challenges. Our task is to greet each day with an open-hearted acceptance of what the Universe presents to us and develop the grace to patiently learn and grow from each of those experiences. It is what we do. It is who we are.

So, Destination or Journey? We will choose Journey every time.

DAY 24

DESTINATION: BISHOP BAY HOT SPRINGS

Low-hanging clouds in Frazier Reach on our way to Bishop Bay

When my alarm sang to me at 5:45, I was rested and ready to take on the day. We had a four-and-a-half-hour cruising day and were hoping to beat the crowd for the hot springs located at the head of Bishop Bay on the east side of Ursula Channel. I had never experienced a natural hot spring and was really looking forward to doing so.

We pulled up anchor a few minutes before 7:00 and were on our way, navigating around a very shallow spit as we left Khutze Inlet. The day was overcast, with very low-hanging clouds hovering over the water. Tom and I both commented on the sense of peace and calm we felt motoring through the cool, damp morning. It was almost other-worldly.

We encountered a lot of debris in the form of logs and kelp beds along the way, as well as some fog in places, so we had to stay focused and watchful. We drove from the upper helm rather than from inside, even though there was a light mist at times.

We arrived in Bishop Bay and spent a good 15 minutes determining where in the back of the bay would be the safest place to anchor. We had to consider several factors: the lay of the bottom, a ten-foot tide, and a shoal that came out from the shore. We settled on a spot just off the southwest corner of the dock and dropped the hook in 60 feet of water.

There were three other boats in the bay at the time, but thankfully, two of them left. Many fishermen come in during the day to partake of the hot springs and then leave and move on, and this appeared to be the case today.

We quickly put on our bathing suits under our outer clothes, got in our kayaks, and paddled over to the dock. We walked up the ramps to the boardwalk that led to the structure the First Nations band had constructed to enclose the natural hot springs.

Bishop Bay Hot Springs is a funky, unique place, to say the least. There are buoys, wooden plaques, flag insignias for boats, and other various and sundry items that represent the many boaters that have bathed there, all hanging from the ceiling or on the wall. Folks have also written their names, the names of their boats, and other euphemisms on the walls in various colored markers.

Bishop Bay Hot Springs

The water temperature was perfect, and we had a delightful soak looking out over the bay and Havis Amanda. We tried to remember the last time we had soaked in a tub of any kind and determined that it was when we spent several days in Rosario Resort over Valentine's weekend. On our boat, we shower in a combination shower/head, so as you can imagine, soaking in the Bishop Bay hot springs was quite a treat for us.

Happy and relaxed after our Bishop Bay Hot Springs soak

When we returned from shore, Tom worked on the windless while I worked on today's journal entry. Then, he separated and consolidated the garbage for our upcoming stop in Hartley Bay. (Many Canadian marinas require you to separate your trash by category.) While doing so, he punctured his hand with a sharp piece of plastic, so we got to practice our first aid skills. Boat life can certainly be hazardous to one's health!

We prepared enchiladas for dinner as we were out of fresh produce. We have a v-berth full of dry and canned goods but are almost out of fresh vegetables until we stop at Prince Rupert in four to five days to provision. Places to provision for fresh produce are few and far between, so planning is essential.

Sleep called to us both, so we crawled under the covers in our sweet aft cabin and fell asleep watching a movie, the name of which I couldn't tell you even if my life depended on it.

Good Night from Bishop Bay - End of Day 24

SOMETHING TO PONDER:

FUNNY DILEMMA: DRY VERSUS WET

From the photos below of Tom and me, you can see we both have to put on many layers of clothes when it is cold, and when it is raining, we also have the extra layer of foul weather/rain gear. It is extremely important to have really good rain gear, a must for long-distance cruising, but it does create one particular problem for folks our age: Like when we have to pee but put it off because it is just way too much trouble and time-consuming to get out of all those layers...especially the rain gear. So, we wait until we are at full capacity and <u>then</u> run in and hurriedly try to get out of all those layers before we pee our pants. You young folks haven't experienced this yet, but the older you get, the harder it is to hold it.

As Tom very candidly said today, "Peeing with rain gear on needs proper planning at our age. "Do not wait!" has become our mantra."

Coming out of a full set of rain gear, along with all the other layers underneath it, when you have waited too long to go pee, can become a big problem.

As Tom jokingly says, "Instead of the rain gear keeping the wetness out, it may just be keeping the 'wetness' in."

Enough said.

Tom in layers of warm clothes with foul-weather gear on top

Jandira wearing even <u>more</u> layers than Tom, with "foulies" on top

DAY 25

HARTLEY BAY FOR FUEL/WATER/GARBAGE DROP OFF
DESTINATION: COGHLAND ANCHORAGE

"Zebra" rocks along the shoreline coming out of Bishop Bay. I could look at these all day. They pull at my artistic heartstrings.

We both slept like babies last night due, we think, to those amazingly relaxing hot springs. I am so glad there will be more hot springs to experience along the way.

We pulled the anchor up at 7:40 this morning. As we got to the mouth of Bishop Bay, we encountered a lot of logs and kelp, just as we did coming into the bay yesterday.

Thankfully, not far into Ursula Channel, the way ahead became mostly clear of debris. Such a welcome relief!

It can be tricky to navigate around debris, especially when you get to an area where there is a tideline that stretches all the way across the channel. Then, it can look as if there is no way through, but if you go slow and stay focused and watchful, you will find you can weave in, out, and around the debris with relative ease.

Snow-covered mountains in Ursula Channel

After we serpentined our way through the tideline debris, we had a very calm and peaceful ride down Ursula Channel into Verney Passage, across Douglas Channel, and into Hartley Bay, where we would get fuel and water and dump our trash.

Hartley Bay, home to the Gitga'at First Nations Band...population 130...is a friendly little village with no roads in town. Most folks get around by bicycle, ATVs, smart cars, and on foot.

As we were approaching the fuel dock, there was a large houseboat taking up most of the dock, but when they saw us coming, they untied their lines and moved their boat forward to make room for us. A very nice gesture indeed from one boater to another.

We had intended for me to dock the boat, but due to the constrained area coming into the fuel dock and navigating around the houseboat, the docking had the potential to be problematic, so Tom wisely decided to bring the boat in himself. Unlike in Lund, where the wind was blowing us off the dock, the wind was lightly blowing us onto the dock here, so I was able to successfully get off and stop the boat with no problem.

With our boat chores complete, we left Hartley Bay, turned right into Stewart Narrows, then into Coghlan Anchorage for the night. This anchorage is wide open to the south but still somewhat protected. We are here with six other boats, all presumably staging for a transit of Grenville Channel tomorrow. Early to bed tonight to prepare for a long day of traveling tomorrow.

Good Night from Coghlan Anchorage – End of Day 25

DAY 26

DESTINATION: BAKER INLET

Tom planning the Grenville Channel transit

Tom says, *"The thing about traveling in this area is that it requires constant awareness of tides, currents, wind, and, of course, weather. Just as important is the knowledge of When to be Where and When to Beware."*

Every day, Tom consults with paper charts, *Ports and Passages* for tides and currents, and several guidebooks. He listens to NOAA and Canadian Weather Broadcasts, and when the internet is available, he uses weather apps like *Predict Wind* and *Windy* to plan the next day's transit. When he has all the information he needs from these various sources, he then plots our route for the day on our Raymarine Chart Plotter, allowing for rocks, shoals, places of turbulence, and the like. As you can imagine, there is a lot to take into consideration.

That way, when the morning comes, our day is already planned out. We know how many miles we have to go, what time we want to arrive at our next anchorage, what speed we need to maintain in order to meet that timeline, and how the tides, currents, wind, and other weather factors will affect the plans we have set in place. Tom is extremely competent at all of this which creates a deep level of comfort in me.

So, when it came time to plan the Grenville Channel transit, he was again hard at it. Tom explains the transit of this narrow 45-mile-long channel like this: *"When transiting Grenville Channel from the South, we will ride the flood up to Klewnuggit Inlet to catch the ebb the rest of the way toward Prince Rupert. The water in this channel floods north from the south and south from the north and meets in the middle. The ebb does just the opposite, so we will use that to our advantage. Better get this right, as the currents in this channel can run up to six knots on the ebb, and there are not any definitive current tables to go by."*

Most mornings, we don't have time to drink our warm beverages and do our Quiet Time until we are underway, but this morning, we did, as we were timing the tides in Grenville Channel to take advantage of the way they ebb and flow.

One of our daily morning practices is to set positive intentions for the day ahead. For example, we set intentions that our families and friends remain safe, healthy, and happy, and if they are ill, that their recovery will be swift. We set intentions that we will travel safely and use good judgment in the decisions we make along the way. I always set the intention that we will both remain on board the boat unless we choose to get off the boat. (In other words, "Don't fall off!") Obviously, neither one of us wants to go overboard, but in all honesty, it would be better if it were me, as Tom would have a better chance of saving me than I would saving him.

Also, very importantly, we ask the "Debris Dodging Angels," as we call them, to either keep our path clear of logs, kelp beds, and a myriad of other items that are sometimes found floating in the water or alert us in time to make a course correction to avoid them. I can't tell you how many times we have looked up just in time to swerve to miss hitting something. Thank you, Debris Dodging Angels, for keeping watch even when we "fall asleep" at the helm.

So, after Quiet Time this morning, our day began. We left Coghlan Anchorage in the rain at 7:25 and headed up Stewart Narrows, turned right, and rounded Waterman Point into Wright's Sound, then right again into Grenville Channel. We had 43 miles to go today and planned to be anchored in Baker Inlet before 3:00.

Tom foot-steering from the inside helm and watching for logs as we transited Grenville Channel in the rain

Driving in the rain all day can get tedious, especially when we are faced with a lot of debris like we had today, so we were constantly coming in out of the rain when the "coast looked clear," only to hustle back out to the upper helm when going through a debris field. Some logs can be clearly seen, but others play hide and seek from us in the waves and can be missed.

Transiting Grenville Channel

After about six-and-a-half-hours, we entered Baker Inlet via Watts Narrows, a very skinny, winding channel where second-growth trees line the shore. This beautiful little channel is very deep and river-like and is barely wide enough for the boat. The sides are steep, and the rocky shore causes the water to appear to "boil." There can be a great deal of current in there, which can push and pull you all over the place. You really don't want to end up on the rocks, so it is crucial to stay in the middle of the channel.

Tom: *"You have to stay in the middle cause if you get sideways, you will be touching the shore bow to stern...Remember now Honey, you have to stay in the middle."*

Jandira: *"I got this."*

Tom: *"Stay over here!"* (Not sure where 'here' is) *"NO! NO! Over here!"* (Still not sure where 'here' is. Tom is pointing to where 'here' is, but I am not seeing where he is pointing as I am focused on...you guessed it...staying in the middle of the channel. We're obviously still working on our communication skills.)

Jandira: *"I got this!!!"*

Tom: *"Stay to the left Honey...stay...stay...now to the right..."*

Jandira: ***"I GOT THIS!!!"*** And you know what? I did! It was a great ride!

Looking from inside Baker Inlet back through Watts Narrows

After we exited Watts Narrows, we wound our way down Baker Inlet and found a good holding anchorage at the head of the inlet. We were surrounded by tall, snow-covered mountains draped with low-hanging clouds. Absolutely stunning!

This is about as protected an anchorage as you can find, and it looked at first as though we would have it all to ourselves, but later that afternoon, we saw a sailboat (one that had been anchored in the Coghlan area with us the night before) motor into the bay where we were anchored. An older gentleman and a younger one...father and son maybe...dropped anchor across the bay from us. As we watched, the younger man began pulling the anchor back up hand over hand, which I can assure you is no easy feat. We assumed that meant he either did not have a manual or an electric windless, or what he did have was not functioning properly. But this story did not end there.

After he pulled up the anchor, he motored to a different spot and dropped the anchor for the second time, only to pull it back up, again by hand, mind you. But, alas, this tale did not end there either.

Three more times they dropped their anchor, pulled the anchor back up...each time by hand...and moved to another spot to try again. At least two of the times, he seemed to have a good holding anchorage, so we were baffled as to why he would keep pulling up his anchor.

Finally, they pulled up their anchor and left the bay entirely. We speculated as to whether they were inexperienced, had a faulty windless, or just didn't trust the anchorages they had tried, but either way, we felt sorry for them. We knew it had been a long day for them. It was getting dark, and they still had not found an anchorage that suited them. We have both experienced our very own "boat rodeo" more times than we care to mention, so no judgment here. We just hoped they found a safe place to put the boat and themselves to bed for the night. On the positive side for us, we once again had this beautiful spot all to ourselves.

We prepared and ate spaghetti and marinara sauce and got in bed to watch a movie. We almost never get through a whole movie without one of us falling asleep. Is that what happens when you get old?

Nighty Night from Baker Inlet - End of Day 26

DAY 27

LAYOVER DAY: BAKER INLET

Baker Inlet: quiet, cozy, serene, protected

Yea! We got to sleep in this morning! (Well...if you call 7:45 sleeping in.) Tom commented that it is not so much what time we get up as it is the peace of knowing that we don't have to get up at a certain time and go anywhere on layover days...we can lay in bed as long as we want. The problem is that we are so programmed now to get up early and get moving across the water, that we wake up and find it hard to go back to sleep. Well, in reality, Tom finds it hard to go back to sleep. I, on the other hand, can fall back to sleep at the drop of a hat.

After our morning rituals, Tom got in the dinghy to go check the crab pot he had dropped yesterday afternoon and found we had one very large male. (Females cannot be kept, and the males must be at least six and a half inches from point to point across the top shell.) He put the pot back down in the water, crab and all, hoping that the one lonely crab he had caught just might attract a crab friend. We would check it again later in the day.

We have learned how to move quickly in the morning, even on layover days, so we were in our kayaks moving through the dead calm water around 9:45. We both love to putter around the shorelines in our kayaks looking for interesting patterns, colorations, and formations of rocks. It seems that almost every anchorage we come to is quite different in these respects. We like to imagine what the glaciers must have done to create such varied rocks.

Rocks along the shore in Baker Inlet

I know I have mentioned this before, but these rocks and the surrounding trees, roots, moss, and grasses inspire my mandala art pieces like nothing else in nature has to this point. I do a very abstract interpretation of the photos we take using ink pens and colored pencils. I have been so into the writing of the journal entries for this trip that I haven't worked on any mandalas since we left. I am thinking wintertime would be the perfect time to focus my energies on my art again.

More unique and colorful rocks in Baker Inlet

After we kayaked around for a couple of hours, Tom went back to pull up the crab pot. There was still just one male crab, but he was a big one, so we decided to cook him up and share him for happy hour dipped in drawn garlic butter.

Before our trip began, we had purchased a new crab pot, all the accessories you need to fish for crab, a heavy-duty burner, and a large pot to boil them in. Today was our first time to try out the burner and new cook pot, and everything worked great except that the cooker legs got really hot. Tom worried that they might damage the teak decking, so he had me bring potholders to put under each leg, and he poured cold water on them to keep them from burning the deck.

Tom said that next time he would cook the crab on the bow of the boat where the anchor-wash-down is located, so he could keep water poured on the legs during the cooking process. The learning curve in boat life can be steep, but thankfully, this time, there was a simple solution.

I do believe this pic says it all! Yum!

Good Night from Baker Inlet - End of Day 27

DAY 28

DESTINATION: PRINCE RUPERT

Looking back through Watts Narrows

Our day began at 5:15 this morning as we needed to hit Watts Narrows at slack tide going back out of Baker Inlet. We got ready early and were able to leave at 6:11. Departing at this time meant we would arrive at the Narrows just a little past 6:30, when the tide would turn from ebb to flood. A power boat that shared the anchorage we were in last night left about 20 minutes before we did, so we had to wait for it to go through first.

If you remember from two days ago, when I drove through the Narrows into Baker Inlet, it can be really squirrely if hit at a strong ebb or flood tide. Because we reached the entrance to the Narrows a bit earlier than we had planned, we didn't have to go into the Narrows at the start of the flood. I piloted Havis Amanda through with ease, thanks to doing so at slack tide. Piece of cake!

Coming out of Watts Narrows into Grenville Channel

We had been told that Baker Inlet was teeming with wildlife, including bears and wolves, but after two days there, we neither saw nor heard any wolves and only saw a black bear grass-grazing on our way out of the inlet. Finally! We got a photo of a bear, and we didn't have to die trying! Such a relief!

Black bear spotted as we exited Watts Narrows

Our transit today took us up the north end of Grenville Channel, into Arthur Passage, across Chatham Sound, to finally round the corner into our destination: Prince Rupert Harbor. It was a calm, rainy day with few boats coming or going until we got closer to the harbor. This is a thriving west coast seaport, with cruise ships, container ships, fishing vessels, and pleasure boats coming in and out of the harbor all through the day.

When we were in VHF range, we radioed into the harbor to get our slip placement as we were planning to stay on the dock for two nights rather than anchoring. They placed us on the outside of the breakwater, which, needless to say, is not the most ideal moorage. All the rocking and rolling caused by the wakes of so many boats passing by can make for an uncomfortable stay.

As I made my approach, the wind was lightly blowing me onto the dock. I was still able to dock the boat (with a few words of "encouragement" from Skipper Tom) with relative ease. I obviously prefer to be blown onto the dock rather than off the dock if I have a choice.

We had just gotten the boat all tied up when Zeke, a dock worker, came down to tell us we could move to a spot on the inside of the breakwater as another boat was leaving. Great News! And, that meant I would have the opportunity to try and dock Havis Amanda for the first time ever between two side tied boats.

On the inside of the breakwater, the wind was blowing me off the dock, and as I was coming in, I turned a little too quickly. I didn't get the boat quite close enough for Tom to easily jump off to tie her up, but I was able to back out, turn around and try it again, this time nailing the landing. Practice really does make "almost" perfect!

But our moorage story is not over. The harbor master caught us coming back from an early dinner of hamburgers and fries at the Breaker Pub and told us there was a mix-up in reservations and that tomorrow, we would have to moor on the outside of the breakwater again. Grrrr...

On the positive side of things...this would give me the opportunity to practice docking again in very tight quarters. Maybe this time, practice really will make perfect.

Our day ended with a nice hot shower, reading aloud to each other in bed, and then off to sleep.

Good Night from Prince Rupert - End of Day 28

DAY 29

LAYOVER DAY: PRINCE RUPERT HARBOR

Prince Rupert Harbor

No sleeping in on this layover day, that's for sure! In fact, we didn't even get in our Quiet Time. As I explained yesterday, we were going to have to move Havis Amanda to a spot on the outside of the breakwater due to a mix up in reservations. There was a spot on the inside corner of the outside breakwater, and Tom wanted to grab it before anyone else did, so we hurriedly untied the lines, and Tom drove the boat to the new position. Usually, being on the breakwater can be pretty dicey, but today, the seas were calm, and fewer boats were out and about, so we had very little roly-poly action.

We had plans to go up and do laundry at the facility provided by the port, but alas...Max, one of the port office staff, told us that the laundry machines were broken down. A bit irritating for sure, but we are only two days away from Ketchikan where we can do laundry and other provisioning.

Thankfully, we have neither one run out of clean underwear yet, so all is well!

We walked up into town to get groceries and some plumbing supplies to create a saltwater faucet for rinsing and washing dishes and found what we needed. When we returned, Tom set to work to do what he thought would be a simple alteration, but of course, in that it's a boat we are talking about here, simple is not often a word that fits the situation. Without going into tedious detail, Tom worked for the next couple of hours to fix the problem, and true to Tom-form, it worked like a charm.

I can't tell you how many times I have heard the expression: "Well...it's a boat after all," spoken by someone who has had to do more than their fair share of boat repair work over their lifetime. It seems to be true that there is always something to repair, recondition, or simply throw overboard (just kidding) when you are fooling around with boats. It is what you knowingly sign up for, after all.

When the plumbing repair work was finished, Tom and I went back up to the Breakers Pub for fish and chips and, of course, BEER as a reward for our hard work...well...actually...Tom's hard work...if we're being honest here.

After we came home, Tom worked on planning our route to Ketchikan, Alaska, tomorrow. We hope to cross over the border from Canada back into the US before noon, so we will get up at 4:00 to leave at 5:00. Leaving this early will also potentially enable us to beat any swells that could make for a very lumpy ride across Dixon entrance, so I will sign off now and crawl into my warm, comfy bed for a short night's sleep. Catch up with you tomorrow after we enter Alaska.

Good Night from Prince Rupert - End of Day 29

DAY 30

DESTINATION: FOGGY BAY

Motoring up Chatham Sound

You know that expression that goes something like: When man makes a plan, God laughs? That is exactly what happened this morning. Last evening, Tom planned out the whole day today, including going through Venn Passage (a very narrow, winding, shallow section of today's journey), up Chatham Sound to Dundas Island, and then across Dixon Entrance to Foggy Bay for the night.

But guess what? The Universe laughed! We woke to dense fog that didn't lift until later in the morning, which resulted in a delay in our start time. We have a great radar system, but going through Venn Passage in dense fog, no matter how good your radar is, would simply be foolhardy.

So...we waited. This would mean an arrival time of approximately 7:00 tonight. Sense we had been up since 4:00, this made for quite a long day, but that is just the way of it sometimes. Sailors truly are at the mercy of Mother Nature, and you disrespect her at your peril. On the positive side, we will catch an ebb tide for most of the day.

We "set sail," so to speak, around 11:00. The wind is almost always on our nose up here in the PNW, so in all actuality, we motored rather than sailed across Prince Rupert

Harbor and into Venn Passage. We had timed the tide correctly (the current was with us on an ebb), but we had to stay on our toes due to the layout of this passage. We motored through with relative ease and out into Chatham Sound, which was overcast and somewhat breezy but basically calm for most of the way.

At the confluence of Chatham Sound and Dixon Entrance, we passed a beautiful combination lighthouse/weather station. We found Dixon to be choppy and somewhat uncomfortable but didn't encounter anything we couldn't handle.

About halfway through the Dixon Entrance crossing, we called into ROAM, a Trusted Traveler program for cruisers that Tom and I had signed up for last year, which enables us to check in with the US Border Patrol by phone without having to get off the boat. It was simple and straightforward, and we breathed a sigh of relief when the officer in charge passed us on through without a hitch. Even though we didn't have anything to hide, it would still be very disconcerting to have the Border Patrol board and search our boat. Thankfully, we have never had that happen.

Later, I went down into the galley to prepare salmon for grilling, but when the choppy seas made me nauseous, I decided to postpone dinner preparations until we reached Foggy Bay.

Foggy Bay is a well-protected stopping place between Prince Rupert and Ketchikan. We drove all the way to the inner cove and found a sweet anchorage in the back right-hand corner. We were completely exhausted, so we fixed a quick supper of grilled salmon, rice and steamed broccoli and then went straight to bed. We will lay over here tomorrow to rest.

Lighthouse/weather station at the confluence of
Chatham Sound and Dixon Crossing

Good Night from Foggy Bay - End of Day 30

DAY 31

LAYOVER DAY: FOGGY BAY

Foggy Bay at 7:00 this morning

This was the scene from our anchorage here in Foggy Bay at 7:00 this morning...a welcome change from the cloudy, rainy, cool days we have encountered most of our trip so far. We were so excited to get the kayaks out and get on the water to enjoy this warm, sunny, blue-sky day, but...

Then...at 7:10, the Universe laughed aloud at our plans again, and two days running, patience was required of us again (as you can see from the photo below). So, we had our coffee/tea/Quiet Time, did some route planning for the next few days, and had a homemade pimento cheese sandwich on pumpernickel bread with Kirkland brand chips. By the time we were through with that, the fog had mostly lifted, and we could prepare again to go kayaking.

Foggy Bay at 7:10 this morning

So, we had to wait a few hours for the sun to come out and burn off all that pesky fog...so what? We survived this minor inconvenience and had a wonderful afternoon out on the water, feeling the warm sun and the cool breeze on our faces. I am just not sure it gets any better than that.

So, what's a little weather delay in the grand scheme of things? I have come to the conclusion that the art of patience is one of the lessons we humans most need to learn. It certainly seems that the Universe is more than happy to oblige us with all kinds of situations to test our patience on a daily basis, like the person walking through a crosswalk texting on their phone while cars are backed up waiting (Tom's personal favorite) or having to wait in the grocery line while the customer ahead of you carries on a long conversation with the checker (my personal favorite). Why are we, as a society, always in such a hurry?

Tom and I have just finished reading another Mitch Albom novel called *The Time Keeper*, which addresses human's obsession with time. This fable is one of Tom's personal favorites. Check it out. We think you'll like it.

After kayaking, I worked on journal entries while Tom planned routes and did research on some of the places we wanted to stop along our journey.

Nature's sculpture floating in Foggy Bay

Later, I prepared and cooked a noodle dish that is one of Tom's favorites: egg noodles covered with pesto, sautéed onions, peppers, mushrooms, sun-dried tomatoes, and parmesan cheese. Afterward, we sat out on the back deck to take in the quiet. Another absolutely amazing day!

Tomorrow, we head to Ketchikan, a town of 8,200 people on the southeastern coast of Alaska. It is known for its many totem poles on display throughout the town and the historical area of Creek Street. We can't wait to explore this unique community and plan to spend a couple of days here.

Kayaking in Foggy Bay in the late afternoon

Good Night from Foggy Bay - End of Day 31

DAY 32

DESTINATION: KETCHIKAN, ALASKA

Leaving Foggy Bay on our way to Ketchikan, Alaska

We pulled up anchor and motored out of Foggy Bay this morning at 5:40. There was fog out in the channel but almost none in Foggy Bay itself, so we felt comfortable navigating the skinny, shallow passage out of the bay and into Revillagigedo Channel, followed by Felice Strait and finally through Tongass Narrows into Ketchikan. This historic town is generally the first Alaskan stop for boaters heading north, as it is a check-in point for travelers coming in from Canada.

When we arrived in Ketchikan, we called into Bar Harbor for a slip assignment and were told to go to Dock 10, Slip 17, a port side to slip. For non-boaters out there, the port is the left side of the boat, and the starboard is the right as you're facing forward. A port side to slip simply means you come in and tie up on the left side. Tom docked Havis Amanda with ease, and I tied her up.

After we went to the harbor master's office to pay for a three-night stay, we had a quick snack and then called a cab to take us to Petro Marine, a commercial marine supply store. We needed a new starter battery and had to call three places before we finally found what we required. Afterward, we walked to a hardware store nearby to purchase plumbing supplies for a saltwater sprayer for rinsing and washing dishes. Using a saltwater sprayer in this way will help to save our potable water, which is important when you travel long distances between fill-ups.

When we returned from shopping, we showered before catching another cab to town for dinner. Most boaters can't wait to get into a marina so they can take a "real" shower, but we are just the opposite. By the time we drag all our toiletries, towels, hair dryer, clean clothes, etc. up to a marina shower, that may or may not be very clean, we could have showered twice in our combination head/shower on the boat...and...we *know* that it is clean! A nice hot shower did wonders to soothe our tired, achy bodies and clear out the cobwebs of our salt-fried brains.

I want to speak for a moment about boat life...especially live-a-board boat life. From the outside looking in, you might think that living aboard a boat is a lot harder than living in a home...and, honestly, you would be right. It is not for the faint-hearted! I have lived aboard one boat or another for over 17 years, and it takes some getting used to.

For example, we must water up the boat once or twice a week to have water for dishes, showers, toilet flushing, etc. Our potable water tank holds 120 gallons, so the number of fill-ups we require depends on our water usage that week. It is imperative to conserve water, especially when you are cruising for several days in a row with no stops at a marina to top off the water tanks.

During this trip, Tom connected the anchor wash-down system to our galley sink, which now allows us to pre-rinse and wash dishes in salt water and then do the final rinse in hot potable water. This solution has greatly helped us conserve water and alleviated our worry of running out of water between stops.

Laundry is another challenge for live-a-boards. We have to drag our dirty clothes up to the port laundry and pay anywhere from $30-$40 dollars every couple of weeks to have clean clothes. This means that if our favorite shirt is dirty, and we want to wear it that night...well...it's simply not going to happen. We don't have the luxury of throwing in one or two items like in a home washer/dryer, we have to wear a different shirt and wait until we have accumulated enough dirty clothes to justify full loads at the laundry mat.

And then there is the whole aspect of storage...where will we store all our STUFF?!? This is especially difficult for a woman. We have a lot of STUFF, and there is only so much room on board to store all our STUFF.

Thankfully, there are a lot of hidey-holes on our boat where we can squirrel stuff away. The challenge is that we tend to "hide" things so well that we can't find them later. Case in point:

Tom, *"Honey, do you remember where we put _____? I can't find it anywhere."*

Jandira, *"No, Sweetheart. I've got no idea. Have you looked_____?"*

At which point, all activity stops while we commence a 20-minute search of all the places where it might make sense we would have "hidden" it. It is embarrassing how often this happens. Organization? Hardly.

Getting used to a boat head can be another challenge. I mean, you don't just push a handle down to flush the toilet, you pump the pee, poop, and as little tissue as possible down, each time hoping you haven't stopped up the works. Believe me, I have been the person responsible for stopping up a boat head, and you don't ever want to be that person...but that is a story for another time.

And then there is the galley...I have prepared meals in four different galleys on four different boats, and each one had its own set of challenges. Due to limited cabinet and counter space, smaller stoves, and way smaller refrigerators than most of us are used to, kitchen work can be challenging. These conditions, however, have made me a more proficient cook. I have learned to operate efficiently in tiny spaces, cook on a two-burner stove, and organize the top-loading fridge down to the inch.

Ok, so yes, there *are* many challenges to living aboard a boat, but honestly, from my perspective, the positives far outweigh the negatives. I absolutely LOVE being a live-a-board! It is a slower, simpler lifestyle overall, and it has forced me to be more conservative about water, fuel, propane, and electricity...a good thing for the environment all the way around.

I have also found that I am a good deal closer to my boat neighbors than when I lived in a subdivision on land. As live-a-boards, we love and support one another, watch out for each other's boats, and sit out on the dock for happy hour almost every night during the summer months. It's a great life! Granted, not everyone's cup of tea, but if you are adaptable and enjoy the simpler lifestyle, it just might be for you.

I realize I have totally digressed from the "what we did today" narrative...I do have a slight tendency to go off on tangents at times.

But, back to the daily narrative: There were three cruise ships moored right here earlier today, and you know what? I wouldn't trade the way we are experiencing Alaska on our sailboat for doing so on a luxury cruise ship for all the tea in China. When cruising on our boat, we are the orchestrator of our journey, not some cruise director. We plan our days to suit us, not an arbitrary schedule set by someone else, and we love the freedom this allows us.

OH! I almost forgot! We saw our first whale of the trip today! It was all alone as we rounded Ham Island, but too far away to get a good photo. Hopefully, the next sighting will be more profitable.

So, other than eating out at Bar Harbor Ale House for dinner (Tom's halibut fish and chips were good; my pulled pork sandwich was mediocre), the rest of the evening was uneventful. We will stay here through Thursday and then be off to the Misty Fiords.

Good Night from Ketchikan - End of Day 32

DAY 33

LAYOVER DAY: KETCHIKAN

The sun shimmers low across the water as we relax on our boat in Bar Harbor, enjoying this beautiful evening. Two watchful eagles are perched high on pilings across the fairway from us, waiting patiently for fish scraps from local fishermen. It is a quiet evening, and I feel a deep sense of peace as I sit down to write to you about the day's happenings.

Tom and I have been reflecting on the generosity of the people we have met along our journey so far. There was the couple, Carol and DJ, who gave us two rockfish they had caught that very afternoon. They still communicate with us as they follow their path around Northern BC.

There was the mega yacht owner who didn't know us from Adam but gave us over $100 worth of freshly caught halibut. So very generous!

Then there were Ryan and Laurel, who took beautiful photos of our boat in Kynoch Inlet and let us use their Starlink Wi-Fi system to connect with all of you.

And, just a few minutes ago, Melody and Verge, a live-a-board couple we met on the dock today, came over and brought us a frozen piece of halibut they had caught and some kind of fishing contraption to help us get started learning how to fish for halibut. They also recommended some of their favorite anchorages for us to try as we continue our way north.

These random acts of kindness came out of nowhere. None of these folks expected anything in return. They just gave from their heart center. We feel so blessed by these folks and look forward to finding ways to pay it forward along the way.

Now, taking you in an entirely different direction, I have a weird story to tell you about our time at the local laundry facility this morning. This marina, like many marinas in

Alaska, does not offer extra services like a laundry mat (or even Wi-Fi, for that matter), so Tom and I had to drag two carts filled with our dirty clothes about a half a mile or so up the main highway to the local laundry mat. It was 11:30 but already packed with locals, cruisers, and fishermen. (God love those fishermen [and I do because I sure do love seafood], but when they come into the laundry mat after a month or more of being offshore fishing, the smell that wafts in with them and their laundry will literally knock your socks off.)

Tom was outside the building talking to his brother, Bobby, while I was inside watching over the clothes in the dryers when these two women came in to do their laundry. The skinny one of the two began nonchalantly talking as she was Spray-N-Washing her blood-stained clothes, *"I've got blood all over my clothes from the fight last night. I didn't mean to break her neck, but she shouldn't have come after me like that. You know, my hands are like lethal weapons."* What?!?

She nonchalantly went on to describe how her grandfather had recently murdered his daughter...all of this about three feet away from me, mind you... and I gotta tell you, this put me just a wee bit out of my comfort zone. I actually felt cold chills crawl up my spine.

It took me back to the days when one of the grooms, Jimmy, in the riding stable where I kept my hunter-jumper and trained, told me stories about his clan who lived up in Marble Creek, Kentucky. He said they would cut your ear off just for looking at 'em cross-eyed or burn your house down for some simple grievance. He warned me not to ever go up into that neck of the woods without him going along to protect me. What he didn't realize was that I wouldn't have been caught dead up in those hollers, with or without him. I knew better than to venture into that area of the county. That was over 50 years ago, and I must admit I wonder what infamous Marble Creek is like these days.

As I sat in the Ketchikan laundry mat today listening to that woman talking about breaking another woman's neck, like it was as common as folks in the hollers in Kentucky drinking moonshine, I felt like I was back in those very hollers in some kind of weird time warp. It's been a long time since I have been around folks who approach life like the Hatfields and McCoys. It reminded me of stories I have been told of Alaska in days gone by. I guess I just didn't expect to encounter such behavior in today's Alaska. I obviously lead a very sheltered life.

Later this afternoon, we walked up to a marine store to purchase an Alaskan flag to go on our mast. I found some warm socks for Tom and me and an extra eyeglass holder so I won't lose my glasses overboard. We had also been looking for a different type of hand cart and found just the one we were looking for. Yea! Persistence pays off!

We ate dinner at Ocean View, a combination Italian/Mexican restaurant about a mile down the road from the marina. We ordered a nice Greek salad and a pizza to share. It was quite good and a fair sight better than last night's meal.

Back on board, Tom cleaned out the shower sump while I finished the journal entry for today. Now, we are heading to bed.

Sorry no photos today. I promise to send some of Ketchikan tomorrow.

Nighty-Night from Ketchikan - End of Day 33

DAY 34

SECOND LAYOVER DAY: KETCHIKAN

Bar Harbor – the main cruising boat moorage in Ketchikan

This is our third and last day in Ketchikan. We are laundered-up, watered-up, and squeaky clean from our onboard shower. We shopped at local marine and hardware stores for needed boat items and the Safeway Market to reprovision, and we now have a full and overflowing fridge of fresh veggies and fruits. Yea! We were both GREEN-VEGGIE-HUNGRY!

After grocery shopping, we took a cab uptown to Creek Street. This infamous section of town used to be the largest red-light district west of the Mississippi. Now, it is full of smart boutiques and restaurants where many First Nations shops sell their art, jewelry, carvings, and other Native wares. Some of the shops are high-end, but many others cater to the cruise ship folks and are more touristy in nature.

We stopped in this small First Nations shop called Crazy Wolf Studios, where the owner, Ken Decker, AKA Crazy Wolf, was busy carving an oil bowl. He was a fine carver and loved to talk about his work. He seemed to be the local storyteller, regaling us with stories of plane crashes in the mountains around Ketchikan...one as far back as 1943 during World War II. Ken was quite an interesting fellow.

We asked around and found a shop called Stony Moose that sold topical cannabis. I was looking for a lotion, cream, or balm, but I only found a cannabis oil called "Siren's Secret with Rose Oil." I was pleased to find that the ratio of CBD to THC was 420 to 420, which should make for a strong healant. I am going to try it out before bed tonight in hopes it will take some of my arthritis pain away and allow me to sleep more soundly.

We took a cab back to the boat, and while I began working on today's journal, Tom rinsed the salt water off Havis Amanda and carted garbage up to the top of the port. He had a nice conversation with another boat neighbor, Dave, who was cleaning his boat up to sell. Tom said he didn't see how in the world Dave could possibly sell his boat for the $150,000 he is asking considering the poor condition it is in presently. He invited Tom over to see his clothes washer, which he says he has used for over ten years with no problem. I have been told over the years that most marine washers/dryers are not worth the money, but Dave seemed to have a different take on the matter. He also gave Tom some much-needed advice on halibut fishing, which we hope to put into play soon.

I bought a rotisserie chicken from Safeway and made a big lettuce salad to have along with baked sweet potatoes. We sat down to eat in the Beer Parlor/Pilot House just as a light rain began to fall. We have a 90 percent chance of rain tomorrow as we head up into Misty Fiords, but honestly, we are so used to it now that it hardly factors into any decisions we make. Wind, on the other hand, always factors in.

Tom is finishing up the route for tomorrow on the GPS while I write, then a hot shower and off to bed we go.

Oh...one final thing...the couple that gave Tom the halibut last night gave him a fishing pole this morning to help him get started fishing for halibut. Such good people!

Tom is planning our route to Misty Fiords

Good Night from Ketchikan - End of Day 34

DAY 35

DESTINATION: SYKES COVE

Motoring up Behm Canal on our way to Sykes Cove

We were up at 5:45 and "out the door" by 7:00. We wanted to arrive at the fuel dock a little past 8:00 in order to fuel up with diesel and propane before it got crowded with fishing and cruising vessels. Well...that didn't happen. We motored right on by the fuel dock by accident and had to turn around and backtrack. I drove the boat in for a side tie and landed her right in front of the fuel tanks. Sweet. The dock folks were quite busy, so we were there about 30 minutes before heading back up the channel.

Tom was at the helm for most of the day, as I was trying to get in touch with Island Peace Health concerning my mom, Polly. She had a doctor's appointment yesterday with her primary care physician and had some tests run as she has been experiencing extreme tiredness and weakness. All her blood work was in the normal range, but the doc thinks she may have some heart issues and wants her to have an echocardiogram on the island and a nuclear stress test in Anacortes. In that I am in Southeast Alaska, I obviously won't be by her side for the tests, but I am working with the

Village where she lives to get her transported to these appointments. I also have four caregivers lined up to assist her if needed, so hopefully all will be well.

At one point today I had gone in to use the restroom when I heard Tom yelling that there were Dall's Porpoises riding the bow of the boat. I ran out to see about ten porpoises crisscrossing in front of the boat. I have only seen this happen in film, so I was quite excited to see this beautiful water dance in person. I wondered aloud as to why they do this. I am going to guess that it is quite simply for the sheer joy of it. They stayed with us for about 10 minutes. It was truly a mystical experience!

According to the *Waggoner 2022 Cruising Guide*: *"Most boaters won't have any trouble finding Dall's Porpoises; this species will most likely find you. They actively seek out vessels that are underway and will charge toward a boat to bow ride the wake. They are extremely fast and agile, reaching speeds of up to 35 mph. They frequently swim in a zig-zag pattern with fast, steep-angled turns as they ride a bow wake, then come to the surface with a slow or fast roll. Dive times are short at 2-4 minutes. The Dall's Porpoise creates a fan-shaped splash called a "rooster tail" when swimming at high speeds through the water, and boaters will no doubt see them coming."*

These mystical creatures led us right up to the entrance of Sykes Cove, a tiny one to two boat anchorage right off Behm Canal. After we dropped anchor, Tom took off in the dinghy to set out the crab pot. We put raw chicken legs and leftover chicken parts from the rotisserie chicken we had the night before in the pot as bait.

While we were letting the crab pot "soak," we took a kayak tour of the island, getting off and walking the beach at the head of the cove. Tom loves to search for sea glass and other interesting objects that might have washed up on shore, and together we collect rocks and driftwood to create small nature offerings or medicine wheels. Sometimes we bring rocks home to Friday Harbor to add to our medicine wheel out at Briggs Lake (in the Mount Young area), and other times we create nature offerings right where we find the objects. Today we did both.

We had a jovial banter back and forth about how many rocks Tom was going to "allow" me to bring back on board the boat:

Tom: *"You can only take three rocks. If you keep bringing rocks on board, we will sink before we can get back home."*

Me: *"What? Really? Are you managing me Thomas? I'm not leaving any of these rocks here...they're all just too pretty. I'm taking them all!"* I said, as I laughingly walked back and forth placing ALL the rocks I had selected into my kayak.

I simply smiled mischievously, knowing I had already won this rock tug-o-war. Victory is so very sweet.

Finding multicolored stones to create nature art

We circled the cove in our kayaks, just puttering around the shoreline. We speak often of the denseness of the woods in this part of the Pacific Northwest. Because of this, there are very few man-made trails except around towns. I would venture to guess there are many places not even a bear or mountain lion has ever set foot, much less a human.

After kayaking Tom went back to check the crab pot, but this time there was not even one lonely crab swimming around in this sea-bottom prison. We saved the bait and plan to try again when we get to Punchbowl Cove tomorrow. Perhaps we will have more luck there.

We prepared and ate a fine evening meal of fresh grilled halibut that our boat neighbors, Verg and Melody, gave us. Along with yellow rice and steamed broccoli, butter was slathered, and parmesan cheese was sprinkled on top. Simply delicious and so nutritious! (Do I sound like a food commercial, or what?)

Good Night from Sykes Cove - End of Day 35

DAY 36

DESTINATION: PUNCHBOWL COVE, MISTY FIORDS

Motoring up Behm Canal toward Punchbowl Cove

We experienced between 10-20-knot winds in Sykes Cove throughout the night. Our anchor held well, and we slept soundly, knowing the anchor alarm would alert us if the anchor drug.

When we got up at 6:15 this morning, the skies were overcast with low hanging clouds. It was truly beautiful. I know I have mentioned this before, but Tom and I both have learned to appreciate whatever weather we are given each day. I am by nature a sunshine girl: I want the sun, need the sun for my frame of mind, but I have learned to see the beauty in all kinds of weather, and more importantly, not to let the weather affect my moods like it used to years ago. The weather forecast for the last two days called for rain, but thankfully we only had a sprinkle or two during the day today.

We motored with light wind on our nose and very calm seas up Behm Canal. My son, Rupa, who has spent a good bit of time in India, says a common saying of theirs is,

"_____ is as calm as a cow in India." As you are probably aware, cows don't have a care in the world in India as they are protected by the Hindu religion. We had no weather cares either.

We passed New Eddystone Rock, an iconic 230-foot landmark that rises straight up out of the sea bottom right in the middle of Behm Canal. Simply stunning! Although not nearly as large and grand, it reminded me a bit of Haystack Rock in Seaside, Oregon, which also jutes up from the sea bottom.

Once we passed New Eddystone Rock, we were not far from the entrance to Punchbowl Cove. When we turned the corner into the cove, we saw the majestic 3,000-foot granite wall (one of the most dramatic sights in Misty Fiords). Right at that very moment, the sun popped out and graced us with its presence for the rest of the afternoon. Simply glorious!

New Eddystone Rock in Behm Canal

We generally prefer to anchor, but the anchoring is limited in Punchbowl Cove, so when we saw that no one was on the one and only mooring ball, we took advantage of our good luck. There were two other boats ahead of us, but both were anchored as they were too large for the mooring balls. Two more boats came in later but didn't find an anchorage that suited them, so they motored back out of the cove to bed down for the night somewhere else.

Entrance to Punchbowl Cove

After we dropped anchor, Tom got the kayaks down, we ate a small snack, and then took off to cruise along the shoreline to see what we could see. There were some pretty spectacular rocks and several cascading waterfalls created by melting snow run-off from the tops of the mountains.

We came back from kayaking and sat out on the back deck with a beer to enjoy the sunshine before beginning to prepare dinner. The temps were in the low 70's. It was heavenly!

We had two pieces of halibut left from the large piece that Verge and Melody gave us, so Tom grilled it out, and I made fried potatoes and a nice big salad with lettuces, cucs, tomatoes, grapes, dried cranberries, sliced apples, and feta and parmesan cheeses. Tom likes poppyseed dressing and I chose blue cheese. We chose ice cream sandwiches for a light dessert.

Tom did dishes while I finished the journal entry for today, and then we sat out on the back of the boat once again to watch the sunset...obviously one of our favorite pastimes no matter what time of day it is.

We will stay in Punchbowl Cove tomorrow and do a one-mile scramble up to Punchbowl Lake, which is said to be utterly beautiful.

Good Night from Punchbowl Cove - The End of Day 36

DAY 37

LAYOVER DAY: PUNCHBOWL COVE

Beginning of hike up Punchbowl Lake Trail...AKA.. "Never-to-be-walked-again-by-me-trail!!!"

We began the one-mile hike (a piece of cake, right?) up to Punchbowl Lake with bear spray in hand, thinking that a face-to-face with a grizzly was the most challenging situation we would face today (which, of course, if that had happened, would most definitely be a "monstrous" challenge), but about halfway back down the trail from the lake, I was mentally begging a bear to come and eat me to get me out of my misery.

This trail is reported to be a poorly maintained scramble, which totally understates the difficulty of this hike. It is mostly made up of very wet, very slippery rocks, roots, and moss. There are broken down boardwalks with large nails sticking up everywhere and downed trees with sharp stobs sticking out just waiting to catch, trip, or stab you...which one did Tom...right in his left leg. Ouch!

It is said that if you endure this trail, you will be greatly rewarded by a large, cascading waterfall on the way up and a gorgeous alpine lake set in the midst of towering granite rock walls rising above it at the top. All of this may be true, but the splendor of the waterfall, the granite walls, and the alpine lake were not worth the difficulty of this hike for me. I think they actually named a song after this trail called "Slip Sliding Away." Everywhere we stepped, we were either slipping off of a rock or root, stepping up past our shoelaces in mud, or navigating across slick, mossy boardwalks with loose, slanted boards or no boards at all, just holes where boards once existed. And to top it all off, gnats constantly buzzed around our heads. These pesky critters even crawled up under my baseball cap! ARGH! I was being dive-bombed by an army of flying insects, and they were winning!

I love a fun challenge, but this was not fun for me and was beyond my comfort zone. It wasn't long into the hike that I was worried less about a grizzly bear attack and more about falling and breaking a hip, spraining my ankle, or sliding off one of the broken-down boardwalks into a bear's lair! Yikes! (Obviously, my imagination was in overdrive.)

I have always liked to stretch myself physically, mentally, and emotionally, not usually shying away from sensible risk-taking: like horse jumping in competition, rock climbing a 5'9" pitch, or learning to dock our 44-foot sailboat. And then there were the two separate occasions that I spent four days and nights alone in the Ozark Mountains with no tent, no food, and almost no water to experience a Native American Vision Quest. And yet, somehow, this trail put me over the edge.

The constant focus on trying to keep my footing for three hours gave me a sense of not being in control, and I am not comfortable if I don't feel I have at least a measure of control over things going on in my life. It felt like I was "slip sliding away" with no safety net in place. Unsettling.

Punchbowl Creek Water Fall on the way to Punchbowl Lake...Yes, yes, I have to admit...it was incredibly beautiful.

I am pretty sure we all feel this way at times. It is human nature to want to be in control of our lives and what goes on around us, but how much control do we really have over anything? How much of what happens to us, do we orchestrate (whether consciously or unconsciously) by our thoughts and actions? How much is the Universe/God/Spirit/Source giving us a challenge like a "gift" for our spiritual growth? And, how much is just pure dumb luck? Or maybe a combination of all the above? I am really not sure, but I am constantly searching for answers to all my deeper questions.

I am more of the belief that what I put my attention on, whether positive or negative, tends to out-picture in my life, so it is important to me to focus on the positive. The hike today was a real test for me in this arena, and honestly, I didn't "look on the bright side" (as Tom likes to say), see the higher perspective, or rise above my discomfort as much as I would have liked. Today was a trial by fire for me, but I did come away with some personal insights.

The first insight was that I had a choice of seeing myself as a limited 71-year-old woman unable to perform at the level I did even five years ago and beat myself up about it, or I could choose to see myself as a brave 71-year-old woman who attempted and succeeded to hike a trail that many half her age would not have even tried. So, instead of seeing myself as limited, I am choosing to look realistically at the capabilities I have now and adjust my expectations to meet those capabilities, not compare myself to my 66-year-old self and come up lacking.

The second insight centered around me having the courage to be my authentic self, to admit to myself and to Tom that even though I love to hike, I really don't like to hike the kind of trail we did yesterday.

It has taken me most of my life to realize that I don't have to try to be someone that I am not, not even for Tom, who would never ask that of me anyway. I get to be unapologetically me, no matter the circumstances, no matter the opinions of others.

Punchbowl Lake is truly beautiful, but Tom and I agree that the views in Punchbowl Cove, where we are anchored, are just as spectacular, so we never need to walk this trail ever again!

The above account was my take on the day. On the other hand, Tom had a completely different view of things. For him, the hike today was a joy to experience. He loved feeling his lungs expand and contract, his heart pumping, his legs burning from the exercise of going uphill.

Punchbowl Lake

He loves challenges of this nature and meets them with vigor, excitement, and a sense of adventure. He approaches them with a "We can do this! Let's go and have fun!"

Of course, Tom would like for me to feel this same way, for both of our sakes, but thankfully, it's more important to him that I have fun doing what I like to do, not try and cajole me into doing what he likes to do. He commented that he had learned a few things in his old age on that subject!

We love doing everything together: cooking, dishes, shopping, hiking, kayaking, errands...everything...so not doing an activity together doesn't feel good to either one of us. But, having said that, we also don't want to stop each other from doing what makes each of us happy, even if the other person doesn't find the same joy in the activity. We choose to honor each other in this way and will continue to do so in the future.

So, all in all, it was a good day. We both gained insights into ourselves and each other, and we will be better for it.

I came back so exhausted from the hike, that I took a two-hour nap. Tom came in to wake me up, and we fixed dinner together. Afterward, we talked about the day and how it had affected us both, which helped to inform my writing of this entry. We are so grateful for our ability and willingness to share our true selves with one another. We feel blessed to have found each other at this time in our lives.

Kayaking in Punchbowl Cove

Good Night from Punchbowl Cove - End of Day 37

DAY 38

DESTINATION: WALKER COVE, MISTY FIORDS

Entrance to Walker Cove from Behm Canal

Today began with a short jaunt of 19 miles to Walker Cove. It was a dry, windless day, so we piloted the boat from the upper helm the three hours or so that it took us to get there. We traveled through beautiful snow-covered mountains on both sides of us with waterfalls of all different shapes and sizes everywhere we looked. Once we turned into Walker Cove Inlet, the mountains funneled a light breeze down the narrow, winding fiord that leads into the cove. The mountains, towering above us so majestic and proud, gave us a sense of being young, insignificant, and small in comparison to their ancient wisdom, longevity, and grandeur. We felt quiet, peaceful, and serene, that all was right in our little piece of the world, at least in that moment.

Wendy and Grant, a couple we met in Punchbowl Cove yesterday, were already tied to the one mooring ball. We generally prefer to anchor anyway, so we looked for a good spot to drop the hook.

There is a creek here in Walker Cove that comes out and creates a shoal. Because of this, anchoring can be a bit tricky as the ocean floor quickly drops from shallow shoal to 150 feet deep. On our first attempt to drop anchor, we bumped Daythe bottom and had to turn and move further out in the cove to try again. On our second try, we dropped 250 feet of rode in about 90 feet of water, almost a three-to-one ratio. The anchor held securely in the mud bottom.

As soon as our anchor was down, Wendy and Grant hailed us on the VHF radio to tell us that a grizzly bear was on shore digging for clams. We quickly grabbed our binoculars and took a look. Sure enough, a very big, very dirty, very scruffy-looking male (or so we surmised) was calmly pawing the mud to search for his clam lunch.

The photos we took were too far away to clearly see him, and by the time we thought about getting the kayaks down to paddle over and get a better look, he had ambled back into the woods from which he came.

But a little while later, we looked up to see a smaller, seemingly younger, cinnamon-colored grizzly bear chomping on grass. This time, we were ready. We hopped into our kayaks and very quietly paddled over to where she was. We assumed this one was a female—not sure why, really—just a hunch from her size and demeanor.

Cinnamon-colored grizzly bear resting on a rock

At first, she moved away and galloped a few strides to put distance between us, not so much in fear but seemingly just being a bit wary of us and what we might be up to. She climbed over a fallen tree, crawled up on top of a good-sized rock, laid down, and put her head on her paws as if to take a nap. She let us get within 50 feet or so, just calmly watching us from her perch on the rock. We three stayed that way for 15 minutes or so, just quietly observing and being in each other's presence. It was quite a spiritual experience for us. We felt honored that she allowed us to share space with her for so long.

Finally, we paddled away from her and over to the shore where we had seen the male grizzly earlier, as Tom wanted to see if he could get a photo of a bear paw print. He didn't have to search long before finding several different sizes of prints, one of which is pictured below.

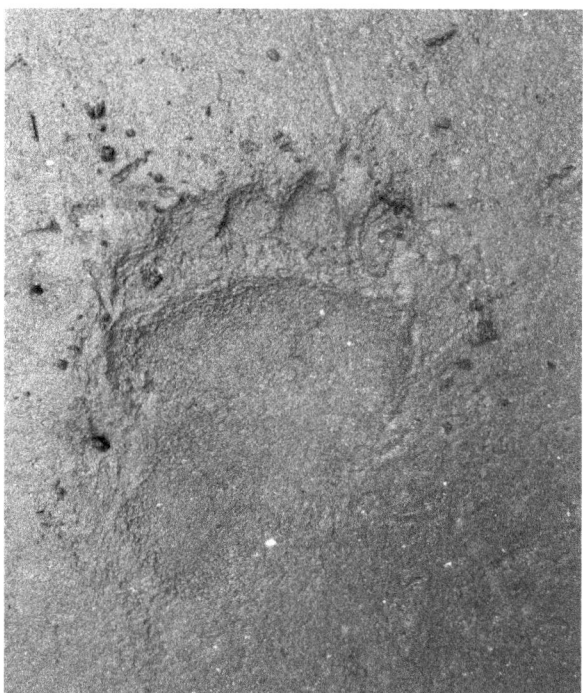

Grizzly bear paw print on the shore in Walker Cove

We saw a rainstorm coming and started paddling back to the boat, but not before the wind picked up and made it very difficult to paddle against. The waves were beam-on to our kayaks, which made for a very rough and wet ride back. It is amazing how fast the wind can come up and conditions change out on the water, especially in the afternoon.

Later, Tom fixed nachos for happy hour, then together we made a light supper of boiled potatoes and carrots, a fresh tossed salad, and asiago cheese bread. I wrote, Tom washed dishes and then we crawled into bed to watch a movie.

View from inside Walker Cove

Good Night from Walker Cove - End of Day 38

DAY 39

LAYOVER DAY: WALKER COVE

Walker Cove mountains dwarfing Havis Amanda

The above photo certainly puts things into perspective, doesn't it? How small and insignificant we appear in comparison to the grandeur and splendor of these majestic mountains. I like to imagine what these mountains have seen and experienced over their very, very long lifetimes.

The photo below depicts the scene looking out our starboard side window this morning: thick, fluffy clouds hovering just below the mountain tops and a skinny ribbon of mist just above the water. Incredibly beautiful!

Can you pick out the sideways face in the photo below? Big white eyes, oval face, open mouth? Tom calls them Water Totems. They occur when land is reflected in very still water. We have heard it said that Native People were inspired to create totem poles from seeing these and other mirror images in nature.

Water Totem in Walker Bay

We love these layover days! We sleep a little later; I putter around in my house slippers and Tom in his bare feet. We take longer for our Quiet Time together, with no rush to get on the move because of wind, tide, current, or getting to an anchorage early to grab the best anchor spot or mooring ball. We breathe slower, relax more deeply, and take in our surroundings in ways we don't on transit days.

Don't get me wrong, we love transit days too! We get excited to travel to new places, and we move in a quick and seamless way that we have established over time with one another. We have learned to honor and respect each other's rhythms: mine is more methodical, and Tom's more fast-paced. The differences in our rhythms have helped us both to become more balanced and to meet one another in the middle instead of always trying to change each other's pace to be more like our own. Today, we both chose to have a quiet, reflective day. It was divine.

The evening is now closing down around us, and we have a decision to make: Do we stay in this serenely gorgeous cove for one more day or pull up anchor and travel to places yet to be explored tomorrow? I know, I know, such tough decisions we are faced with every day...but hey...we <u>are</u> retired! We earned this time in our lives, right?

So, we will make that determination after dinner when our bellies are full, and our minds have settled. I guess you will just have to wait until tomorrow to find out! Sleep well, all!

Good Night from Walker Cove – End of Day 39

DAY 40

SECOND LAYOVER DAY: WALKER COVE

Cloud ribbons hovering just above the water in Walker Cove

Last night, it rained (we love sleeping in the rain), and this morning, we woke to cloudy skies with patches of blue, low-hanging, wispy ghost clouds, calm waters, and a slight breeze. As you can see, we chose to stay in Walker Cove one more day. This has to be one of the most stunningly beautiful places on the planet, and we just haven't had enough of it yet.

We had planned to kayak yesterday, but when Tom took the dinghy out to drop a crab pot to soak for a few hours, it wouldn't idle and kept stopping on him. He wondered aloud (he does that a lot) if it might be starved for fuel. Tom absolutely cannot stand to put off repairing something that is broken, so, true to his nature, he immediately tackled this latest boat challenge. He tore the carburetor completely apart, cleaned it, and put it back together, but it still did not function properly. He then took the spark plug out, cleaned it, adjusted the gap on it, put it back together, and **Voila!** It works like a charm now! He is crossing his fingers that that will do the trick.

I seriously don't know how boaters who do not have the skills and/or who are not willing to learn what they don't know survive on a long journey like this. More often than not, we are in remote areas with no Ace Hardware or West Marine stores right around the corner to buy parts from when something breaks down. Knowing your boat's systems and how to repair them, carrying extra parts, pumps, filters, and tools can literally save your life. Thankfully we are in Tom's capable hands.

Today, we were determined to get in our kayaks and go exploring, so as soon as Tom checked the oil, let the genset run for a bit, and pumped the water out of the dinghy from last night's rain, we jumped in our kayaks and headed out. We had been wanting to explore a waterfall and a small, fast-moving creek there in the cove, so we set off in that direction.

Tom and I paddled our kayaks right up to the waterfall and positioned ourselves on either side of it so that the eddies would hold us in place and keep the force of the waterfall from sweeping us back and away. This is about as up close and personal as it gets! It was magical! Of course, I found a beautiful rock to mark the occasion.

Waterfall in Walker Cove

Small creek in Walker Cove

We then tried to paddle up the small creek, but the current was too strong and kept pushing us back, so we turned around and rode the current back along the shoreline. We realized the wind was picking up strength with some pretty strong gusts pushing against us. The tide was ebbing out and we almost got stuck on a wide, shallow shelf, so we had to paddle against the wind way down and around the shelf to get back to the boat. This was actually to our benefit as the wind then pushed us home toward Havis Amanda.

I was pretty wet so I changed clothes and sat down to write today's journal. It was then that Tom noticed the scruffy-looking grizzly bear was back digging for clams. Both times we observed him there were 10-12 crows hopping all around his paws. We surmised that they were picking up scraps left over from the bear's foraging, but the interesting thing was this: the grizzly paid the crows no mind. Bear and crows seemed to be co-existing in a sort of dance with one another...a symbiotic relationship, if you will...not fighting with one another over the same piece of land but sharing the same space in peace. If only we humans could be so generous with one another.

I think for me personally, I have probably learned more by watching nature and nature's creatures, than I have ever learned from another human. Yes, nature can be brutal, which brings to mind a scene in Gary Paulson's juvenal non-fiction book, *Woodsong*, which graphically describes a pack of wolves that chase a deer and take her down. But the wolves had no hidden agenda like we humans so often do. They took the deer down purely for the survival of their pack.

Tom and I love to look for examples in nature that can teach us a kinder, gentler way of being, like the bear and the crows. Another example would be the many different species of trees that co-exist in a forest together, letting their root systems intertwine to support one another and keep one another strong. Then you have the tide flooding into this bay bringing food from the ocean to feed the bears, seals, otters, seagulls, and loons and then ebbing back out to do it all over again...a dance of survival for all.

Well now...I do believe I will end today's journal entry on that note. It has been an incredible day in an incredible setting. We know this anchorage will be one of our favorites for years to come.

Sunset in Walker Cove

Good Night from Walker Cove - End of Day 40

DAY 41

DESTINATION: FITZGIBBON COVE, MISTY FIORDS

Leaving Walker Cove

After an amazing layover, we left Walker Cove this morning with a great deal of sadness. We had had it all: sunshine, rain, clouds, fog, wind, waves, waterfalls, fast-moving creeks, majestic snow-covered mountains, bears, loons, seals, seagulls, eagles, and martins—simply everything!

We had an easy four-hour transit up Behm Canal to Fitzgibbon Cove. It was sprinkling rain when we left Walker Cove, so we had donned our rain gear, but the rain stopped not long after we turned right into Behm Canal and did not start up again until around 4:30 later this afternoon.

Islets in Fitzgibbon Cove

Fitzgibbon Cove is a sweet little anchorage with a few small islets that we kayaked around after we dropped anchor and split a turkey and Swiss cheese sandwich with chips. It is extremely quiet, and once again, we were the only boat in the cove. We have not laid eyes on another human or boat for three days now. It is like having the whole universe to ourselves—so serene, so peaceful, so us.

We did, however, briefly share the anchorage with a grizzly, but he didn't stop to chat. Tom said he walked purposefully straight back into the woods from whence he came right after we dropped anchor.

As we were kayaking around today, Tom and I were talking about the many differences and similarities in the places we have anchored on this trip. For example, in Kynoch Inlet and Windy Cove, there were tons of purple and orange starfish and burnt red-orange sea cucumbers, but in Fitzgibbon Cove today, there were none to be found of either species. In Sykes Cove, there were lots of starfish but no sea cucumbers.

Some bays have what we call Zebra Rocks, some have rocks in shades of pink, red, gold, and brown patterns, and still other anchorages have rocks with almost no colorations at all.

Some inlets have bears and eagles, while others have none to be seen. It is truly amazing the diversity that is found in this part of the country. We never grow tired of traveling and seeing new places, as each place has its own uniqueness.

Some might say, *"If you have seen one mountain* (or rock, or tree, or cove, or bear, or sunset, or, or...), *you've seen them all, right?"*

And we would answer, *"Absolutely not! Every rock or tree or mountain, cove or bay or inlet has its own beauty, energy, and uniqueness, and we love exploring and experiencing them all."*

And just think...we are just getting started! We have the rest of our lives to explore and experience whatever our hearts desire (and our wallets can afford, ha-ha), and we are looking forward with gratitude and joy to every moment to come.

Kayaking in Fitzgibbon Cove

And, I can tell you what else I am grateful for right now in this present moment of time: Tom voluntarily takes over dish duty every night while I finish up the daily journal entry. In the past, he washed and I dried, and we enjoyed the time spent together, but now, Tom washes and dries while I write. It works out well as we both tend to finish at about the same time, so we can enjoy the rest of the evening playing cards, watching a movie, or reading aloud to one another. Such sweetness there is to our very simple but very rich life!

Tom's nightly dish duties

Good Night from Fitzgibbon Cove - End of Day 41

DAY 42

DESTINATION: YES BAY

Islets outside the entrance to Fitzgibbon Cove

We arose this morning at 5:45 in order to pull up the anchor by 7:00 and be on our way to **Yes Bay**. The name of this bay has special significance to Tom and me for a couple of reasons.

First of all, we love Jason Mraz's *Yes* album. It is almost as if the whole album was written with us in mind. We discovered this album early in our relationship, and it has remained one of our favorites. We play it often, sing along, and drum to the beat as we move through the water, going from one anchorage to another.

The second reason we are looking forward to being in **Yes Bay** is that Tom asked me to marry him on this trip, to which I answered a resounding, *"YES!!! Absolutely YES!!!"* So you see, **Yes Bay** just might hold a special significance for the two of us. We shall see...watch this space...

Well...as it turns out, **Yes Bay** did not hold a special significance for us. When we turned from Behm Canal into the small channel that leads into **Yes Bay**, we radioed the resort to see if we could pull up to the dock to get fuel and water and to see if the restaurant was open for business yet. Unfortunately, the answer to all three questions was a resounding **No**. Rats! From this day forward, we will think of this bay as **No Bay.**

We decided on the spot to turn around and go right back out into Behm Canal and continue on to Helm Bay for the night.

All in all, we are glad we "sailored-on," but there was a small craft advisory for that area which made for a rough transit day. With 24-knot winds on our nose, we were in for a lumpy, choppy, bumpy ride. Several times, the seas were rough enough to almost bury the bow in the waves.

"Yee-haw!!! Ride 'em cowboy!!!" was Tom's fun-loving, fearless attitude.

"Oh God!!! We're gonna die!!!" was mine.

Tom: *"Come up on the bow, Honey! You'll love it!"*

Jandira: *"No way! I will not love that!"*

Tom: *"But Sweetheart...you don't know what you're missing."*

So I cautiously made my way up to the bow, clinging to the handrail for dear life. Did I love it, as Tom said I would? Nope! Not even a little! I couldn't wait to get back to the stern of the boat where I felt at least some sense of safety.

Tom, *"The seas were just off our nose until we had to turn down into Helm Bay, which meant turning down-wind with heavy following seas. Turning across those waves made for an "exciting" ride and lots of commotion in the v-berth where we store much of our food. A lot of our food bins ended up on the floor during all that commotion, so after we arrived, Jandira did a refit of the v-berth. I guess our food storage was not as secure as we thought. Another project!"*

The part of the bay we planned to stay in for the night required navigating between two underwater rocks before mooring starboard side to at the Alaskan state-owned dock. A 20- knot wind blew us off the dock, making what would have been a reasonably easy docking in calm conditions very difficult.

On Tom's second attempt, he was able to get in close enough for me to get off and tie up the mid line, then the bow line, while he jumped off to tie up the stern line. When all three lines were tied, we still had to work against the 20-knot wind to pull the boat in tight enough to secure her for the night. Unfortunately, we could not attempt to tie up on the windward side, where the wind would have pushed us onto the dock, because that side was too shallow at low tide.

This was a very challenging day, but we worked as a team every step of the way. We are tucked in for the night, all safe and sound.

Good Night from Helm Bay - End of Day 42

DAY 43

WEATHER LAYOVER DAY: HELM BAY

Havis Amanda tied up to an Alaska state-owned dock

Tom and I had planned to leave for Myers Chuck today, but we woke early to high winds and lots of rain. The rain wouldn't have stopped us, but the wind conditions just might have. It rained, the wind blew, and the sky was dark all day long, so we chose to hunker down and ride it out.

So, this became a boat maintenance day for Tom, a writing day for me, and a rest for us both. Tom worked on several small boat projects, the first being to secure the food bins in the v-berth by stretching an adjustable cord around them and securing the cords with hooks screwed into the walls. Excellent! No more food bins crashing to the floor in lumpy seas!

Then he put plastic Velcro on my altar objects so I wouldn't have to secure them every day before pulling up anchor.

And...oh...I forgot to tell you that Tom figured out a way to catch rainwater for potable usage last night. He cleaned out the troughs on the pilot house roof and put one five-gallon bucket on either side with funnels in the openings to catch the rainwater. He then poured the collected rainwater into the large water tanks on the boat. The only problem was that in the strong winds last night, one of the funnels got blown away. Thankfully, Tom had an extra one, so to prevent this from occurring again in the future, he tied the two funnels to the potable water cans. A simple fix.

While Tom worked on boat projects, I worked on sending out the eight journal entries I had written since Ketchikan, catching up on emails, and talking to my mom.

Later, Tom and I worked on preparing dinner: egg noodles topped with sauteed green peppers, onions, black olives, canned mushrooms, sun-dried tomatoes, and pesto sauce, along with a simple green salad. Tom made Red Lobster cheddar cheese biscuits because, to Tom, a meal is not a meal without bread of some kind. Delicious as always!

After that, I finished today's journal entry and got ready for bed. An uneventful but pleasant catch-up day for us both.

Good Night from Helm Bay - End of Day 43

DAY 44

DESTINATION: MEYERS CHUCK

According to *Exploring Southeast Alaska*: *"Meyers Chuck is a tiny, salt-stained fishing settlement on the Cleveland Peninsula on the east side of Clarence Strait, about 40 miles north of Ketchikan. It has about 50 houses and a dozen year-round residents, most of whom are fishermen or retirees. There are no roads and no local government. It has a school house but no students (they all grew up!). 'Main Street' is a narrow footpath... Meyers Chuck has no store. Groceries are ordered by phone from Ketchikan and arrive on the weekly mail plane. The isolation is an attraction for the independent souls who choose to live there, but is also the reason there are so few of them."*

The "chuck" part of the name comes from a Chinook word meaning an inlet that fills at high tide. Tom and I can attest to that, as we saw first-hand how the opposite can occur at low tide...when the tide can ebb out and leave once navigable waters a tidal flat...where once accessible inlets become landlocked "chucks."

When we arrived here, after a smooth transit down Behm Canal into Clarence Strait, we found a sleepy little community with houses dotting the shore, a tiny post office, and a dock for several boats to tie up to.

After we anchored and ate a snack, we kayaked over to the dock to take a short hike along a gravel path that meandered along the shore, through the woods, and around several homesteads.

Homesteads in Meyers Chuck

Sculpture of a blue heron along the trail

Rock formations we saw as we kayaked around Meyers Chuck

The islets below were barely showing when we anchored today, and now they are completely uncovered. Amazing the power of the moon and tides.

Islets on the south side of Meyers Chuck at high tide

We had read about Cassy (a long-time resident of Myers Chuck) and her famous cinnamon buns, found her number on a bulletin board on the dock, and called her to order six buns and a dozen oatmeal cookies to be delivered to our boat the following morning at 7:30 sharp. Now that is what I call service! We will have breakfast for the next three mornings and desserts for the next three nights. Yea! Homemade sweet treats!

Good Night from Meyers Chuck - End of Day 44

DAY 45

DESTINATION: BERG BAY

"Ahhhh...warm rolls," was Jack Nicholson's last line in *As Good as It Gets.*

Well, this morning, Tom and I were saying, *"Ahhhh...warm cinnamon buns,"* when Cassie, the local Postmaster and baker extraordinaire, dinghied out to Havis Amanda at 7:30 to deliver our order of six cinnamon buns and a dozen oatmeal cookies fresh out of the oven. After partaking of these rolls, I can assure you this truly is...As Good as It Gets!

Cassie in her cinnamon bun delivery "truck"

Cassie shared with us that she had lived in Meyers Chuck for 60 years with her husband who tragically died in a boating accident back in February of this year. I said she must have loved living here to have stayed in this tiny, remote community all those years, but she said her husband loved it more than she did, that she would have liked to have been closer to their children who live on a neighboring island. She told us she didn't know if she could make it through another winter living here without him. Who knows if the next time we come to Meyers Chuck Cassie will still be here, delivering her famous cinnamon buns to boaters passing through. We certainly hope so!

Meyers Chuck at low tide

Do you remember the photo of Meyers Chuck at high tide I sent out yesterday? Well, the photo above is the same area at low tide. As you can see, you can walk across the bay from one side to the other. Incredible!

We wove our way out of Meyers Chuck's tiny, narrow, rock-filled entrance this morning, motored through Ernest Sound, turned right into Bradfield Canal, then left into Blake Channel, which led us straight into Berg Bay.

Motoring through Ernest Sound on our way to Berg Bay

Our transit today was six-and-a-half hours of totally calm waters, tall, snow-covered mountains off in the distance, rain the last 30 minutes of our journey, and almost no wildlife to be seen or heard. Where are the whales we were promised we would see?!? Calling all whales!!!

Tom and I had a lovely time steering from the upper helm all day. While he and the Log Dodging Angels kept watch, I read aloud from the Mitch Albom book we are presently reading called *Have a Little Faith*. This book is a true story about a Rabi and a Christian minister and the way they both influenced, taught, and inspired Mitch Albom and their respective congregations. His books have sure given us a lot to ponder.

The photo below was taken from the bow of Havis Amanda looking forward at the one other boat anchored in tiny Berg Bay. This is a serenely quiet anchorage with Swiss-Alps-looking mountains in the background.

Beautiful Berg Bay

We had hoped to kayak today, but it drizzled all afternoon and into the evening. We love the rain, so it was a pleasant, restful afternoon for us both. We went to bed early to prepare for an early morning wake-up call.

Good Night from Berg Bay - End of Day 45

DAY 46

DESTINATION: WRANGELL

Water Totems in Berg Bay this morning

When we woke this morning there were Water Totems on all sides of us in Berg Bay. The water was calm and still and the tide was very low which is what creates them. They never fail to amaze me.

We traveled to the town of Wrangell today, a 20.5-mile/3-hour transit. When we left Berg Bay, we turned back into Blake Channel and transited it through The Narrows to the Eastern Passage, which led us to the top of Wrangell. It was a lovely ride in calm waters, and we enjoyed steering from the upper helm and taking in the beautiful mountains and other amazing sights. You always hear that everything is bigger in Alaska, and I can attest that this is true.

According to the *Waggoner 2022 Cruising Guide*, *"Wrangell was founded by the Russians, who began trading furs here with the Natives in 1811. Baron Ferdinand*

*Petrovich Wrangell was put in charge of government affairs.
Around 1840, the Hudson Bay Company leased land from
the Russians. The Tlingits resided here thousands of years
before the arrival of the Europeans, as evidenced by the
petroglyphs found along Petroglyph Beach located on the
edge of town."*

Tom and I had planned to hike out to Petroglyph Beach
to see the petroglyphs today, but after our early morning take
off, our transit here, walking into town for groceries and to
the hardware store, we decided we were just too tired. And
Tom had to plan our route through Wrangell Narrows
tomorrow, which is quite a big deal.

Tom explains the Wrangell Narrows like this: *"A 21-mile
narrow, winding channel whose current, which tomorrow
will reach six plus knots, floods north from the south end and
south from Petersburg. The current meets just north of the
mid-way point and then ebbs in the opposite direction. There
are over 60 channel markers and five ranges. All that, along
with recreational and commercial traffic added to the mix,
makes for a challenging and interesting day! The current
around Petersburg runs heavily through the marinas, so we
are trying to time our arrival at slack. No accidents, please!
I think I better go back and check my math one more time...*

Oh My Goodness!!! While Tom was writing the above
explanation for me, these two little brothers, one about two
and the other maybe four, were running up and down the
dock with their grandfather in tow, obviously babysitting.
We spoke to them and were watching them play when, out
of the blue, the older boy pushed the younger one into the
water. Thankfully, they both had their PFDs on, but this
water is 51 degrees, and hypothermia can set in quickly. The
grandfather got down on his knees to try and reach the little
boy, but he was floating away from the dock, and he couldn't
catch him. Tom rushed out the side door of our boat and got
there just in time to grab the child by the back of his PFD
and haul him out of the water. I ran in and got a towel, and
Tom dried him off, soothing him and telling him what a
brave little boy he was. Disaster averted!

I would say that is enough excitement for one evening, and so...on that note...we say

Good Night from Wrangell - End of Day 46

Tom relaxing on the stern of Havis Amanda in Heritage Marina

DAYS 47-48

THROUGH WRANGELL NARROWS
DESTINATION: PETERSBURG

DAY 47 Our day started at 6:30 this morning with coffee/tea, the last two cinnamon buns made by Cassie from Myers Chuck, and Quiet Time on the back of Havis Amanda. It was a beautiful, sunlit morning without a cloud in the sky.

The daily reflection that we read from Mark Nepo's *The Book of Awakening* centered around the times in our lives when we have pretended to be less than who we are in order to be loved. I mean, who among us hasn't, at some point, chosen to hide who we are beneath our outward exterior in order to be accepted? I know I have.

I have personally struggled throughout my life to be all of who I am...to allow the world to see me as the unique, special, one-of-a-kind person that is me. I have learned not to compromise who I am, what I value, or my integrity just to please others, and mostly, nowadays, I succeed.

As I have gotten older and hopefully wiser, I am more able to be my authentic self without worrying what others think of me, my choices, or my lifestyle, and, oh my goodness, what a freeing feeling that is!

Tom and I have deep, reflective conversations during our Quiet Time each morning that, more often than not, carry over into the rest of our day. One of the things we have most come to value during the long hours we spend on the boat, motoring or sailing from anchorage to anchorage, is the time to really talk...to share the deepest parts of ourselves...and therefore grow in understanding and acceptance of one another.

After our morning rituals, we set off to the fuel dock to fill up with diesel. There was another boat already in one of the docking spots, so I side docked Havis Amanda in front of that boat with no problem...good practice for me to come into a docking situation where I have to navigate around other boats.

After fueling up, we motored (there was no wind to speak of) across Sumner Strait for about three hours before entering Wrangell Narrows. The transit through the Narrows was very technical and challenging but loads of fun. Navigating through over 60 channel markers and six range markers forced us to stay completely focused and on point for a good three hours. It was mentally exhausting, but there was not even one boring moment. We kept the red markers always on our right or starboard (red, right, return from the sea) and the green markers on our left, or port.

The Narrows are serpentine-like, and the currents can be quite tricky. We also had other boats coming and going with which to contend. Tom had calculated the transit perfectly, timing each channel and range marker and checking them off as we passed them to keep track of where we were at all times. It was quite an experience. We tried to take photos, but none of them accurately represent the challenge of navigating these narrows.

When we arrived in Petersburg, we called the harbor master for a slip assignment and were given slip #98, with a very nice view of the mountains. This marina mainly caters to fishermen over pleasure craft. It is our understanding that it is often hard for a pleasure craft owner to get parts and labor as fishermen are given first consideration.

We went up and paid for two nights and got a recommendation for dinner: Inga's Galley, a very small place with only outdoor seating that features Thai and local seafood entries. We both had fresh halibut fish and chips. Quite tasty.

North Harbor Marina in Petersburg, Alaska

On our way back down to the boat, we ended up in conversations with three different folks: a First Nations man named Ross from the Tlingit Clan and his dog, Raven Warrior, a lady from San Diego working for the summer at OBI, a fish processing plant, and another Nauticat owner, John, from Southern California, up here in Alaska for the summer. What should have taken 15 minutes to walk back to the boat took us the better part of two hours, but it was very interesting and fun to meet and make new friends along our way.

DAY 48 Today was chore day, so not much to tell. It went like this: up the dock to do laundry; while the laundry was washing, we hurried to the next block to Wells Fargo for cash and to the hardware store for...well...hardware stuff; back to the laundry to transfer the wet clothes to the dryer; while the clothes were drying, we went grocery shopping and hurried back to the boat to put the groceries away (we found Tillamook ice cream bars...yum!); then back up the dock to get the clothes from the dryer, fold them, and bring them back to the boat to put them away. All of this at low tide, mind you, which means the ramps up from the dock were very steep. Oh, my sore and aching legs!

Fishing boats moored in North Harbor Marina in Petersburg

We then did some route planning, ate a small snack, and went back up the ramp (three times now) to do some more shopping at the local hardware store for Tom and browse through local shops for me. I couldn't find anything I couldn't live without, so no purchases today. After shopping, we ate at Inga's Galley again, this time getting fried rice, stir-fried veggies, and egg rolls. Another delicious meal.

When we came back to the boat, Tom worked on designing and making a rainwater catchment system, so that we are not solely reliant on marinas for our water, especially when there are long periods of time between marina stops.

We talked again to John, our Nauticat neighbor, and he asked if he could be on the list to receive the journal entries. He wanted to share them with his wife, to help her to feel more comfortable on the boat. Of course, we said yes! We would be delighted to add them to the email list to receive our daily journals.

Ok...enough for now. Tom is almost finished with his rainwater catchment system project and wants us to sit out on the back of the boat and enjoy the evening.

Tomorrow: Thomas Bay! I wonder...did they name this bay after our Tom? This is the location of the little book called, *The Strangest Story Ever Told*, so we just have to go and check it out.

Good Night from Petersburg - End of Days 47-48

DAY 49

DESTINATION: THOMAS BAY, RUTH ISLAND

Leaving Petersburg

We left Petersburg around 10:20 this morning, right before slack tide. The current rips through Wrangell Narrows, and it is suggested to wait until slack tide to come in or go out of this marina. This morning, it was rushing through there at about six knots, so we wisely waited until there was little to no current when we left. Tom untied us from the dock, and I was going to back her out of the slip, but the current was pushing us into the boat next to us. Tom jumped in and took over but later apologized, saying he knew I would have handled it just fine.

With snow-capped mountains all around us, we motored up Frederick Sound and talked about two things: how important honest communication is to a relationship in general and specifically how crucial it is when working as a cruising couple on a boat together.

The second topic we discussed was that when we make a mistake, to simply own the mistake and say we are sorry, and if someone else makes a mistake that affects us negatively in some way, to not play the blame game or store it in our memory to use against them at some later time...but to share how that makes us feel, talk about how it can be handled differently next time, forgive, and move on.

Sharing Frederick Sound with a fishing vessel

This came up because Tom had apologized for jumping in and taking over when we were backing out of the slip this morning instead of letting me handle it. This type of situation had come up before, so we had already discussed it at some length. Tom explained that he had single-handed his previous boat (a 24-foot Dana) for so many years that it was difficult at times for him to confidently turn this boat over to someone else. He added that sometimes it was difficult to explain to me in the moment what to do in a way I could understand quickly enough to avert "disaster" (my word, not his), and that it felt easier and safer to just do it himself.

I don't get upset when he jumps in. I get it. I know that he has way more knowledge and experience than I do, so I readily defer to him. He, however, doesn't want me to defer to him...he wants me to feel confident enough to say, "Relax, I got this," like I did when we were coming through Watts Narrows. The problem is that sometimes I am also not sure that "I got this," so when he jumps in, I second guess my abilities, and then it is simply easier to just let him take the helm. I guess we both have some work to do on this issue.

The good thing is that we are both willing to detach from our egos, speak and listen from our hearts, and not get defensive with one another. This is where honest, heartfelt communication is so valuable.

Changes to our basic nature are not always easy to accomplish. And we're old...old habits die hard...but Tom and I are committed to staying open to learning and practicing new ways of communicating with one another. Yep...these two old salty dogs are determined to learn new tricks!

But back to the goings-on of the day. After our transit of Frederick Sound, we entered Thomas Bay, enthralled with the snow-covered mountains all around us. It seems that almost everywhere we go up here in Alaska, there is "big beauty" to behold. Everything seems to be on a grander scale than in Washington state or Canada...not necessarily better...but definitely grander. The mountains are taller, the channels wider, and the distances between anchorages longer, giving everything a more expansive feel to it.

Thomas Bay is just around the corner

We hadn't been anchored long when a couple from a boat anchored nearby rowed over in their dinghy, came aboard, and chatted for about an hour. The deer flies were out in force, and this couple spent the whole time they were on our boat swatting and killing them. I'm not sure which was more annoying, the deer flies or the couple.

After they left, we kayaked for about an hour, then grilled out salmon and added steamed broccoli and rice. I tried to work on the journal entry for today but couldn't keep my eyes open. Tom was having the same problem working on routes, so we decided to bag it and lay over another day. Tom would work on boat projects and plan routes, and I would work on the journal entries and assist him when needed. Good plan!

Night-Night from Thomas Bay - End of Day 49

DAY 50

LAYOVER DAY: THOMAS BAY

View of Thomas Bay from Havis Amanda

Today was to be a work/catch-up day, so after our morning rituals, Tom worked on making screens to go over the two side doors that lead into the pilot house to keep the bugs out. After we were inundated with deer flies last night, we knew it was time to tackle this issue. Tom renamed this anchorage, Deerfly Bay...no need to explain why, right? These buggers relentlessly bit us and left us scratching like crazy. One bit Tom behind the ear while he was working, so out came the Benadryl itch cream. Agh!!! So annoying!!! (Do I sound bitter? That would be an emphatic "YES!")

I have been taught for years that "what we resist, persists"...that where we focus our attention expands and grows...and I must tell you...that proved to be true today. The more I resisted these pesky little critters, the more they hung around to test my resolve to walk my talk. Knowing that, according to Einstein, the definition of insanity is arguing with "what is" ("what is" being the annoying deerflies in this case), you would think it would have behooved me to focus on the positive side of things as much as possible, but that didn't really happen here today. I guess

I still have a ways to go in this department, because by the end of the day, I had a plastic bag full of dead deer flies. (And, yes, I am definitely still bitter!)

Before we left on this journey, Tom had gathered all the items needed to construct detachable screens for both of the pilot house doors...all that is...except for a boatload of teeny-tiny hinges that the dealer promised would be delivered before we left. Well...we left on a Saturday, and the hinges were delivered on Monday! Not so perfect timing!

So, Tom tried to do a temporary fix and actually worked on it all day, but without the hinges, it didn't work effectively. A bit disappointing, for sure, but from the perseverance of another Thomas...Thomas Edison...we have learned that every "failure" has the potential of teaching us what doesn't work, moving us along the experimental path to finding what will. And knowing Tom, he will go to bed tonight and wake up tomorrow morning working and reworking this problem until he finds a solution.

After Tom put his tools and supplies away, he put the dinghy down, and we went for a row. It was a lovely afternoon, and we allowed ourselves to relax, breathe deep, and let the frustration and disappointment of the failed screen-door project and the irritation of those "mean-spirited" deer flies ease right out of our bodies.

The water in this bay is a pale, opaque-green color that is created by glacier runoff. It was so dense that we couldn't see the bottom even in very shallow areas. I had never seen anything remotely like it. As we dinghied along the shore, we observed interesting rock colorations made up of parallel stripes that were consistent all the way across. We wondered, *"Are they tide lines or are they minerals of some kind inherent in the rocks?"* Below is a photo to better express what I am describing.

A bit of history: Thomas Bay, known to some as the Bay of Death due to a massive landslide in 1750 that killed 500 Alaskan Tlingit, is also known as Devil's Country because of the devil-like-four-foot-tall creatures that were reportedly seen here in the 1900s by four prospectors. Read *The Strangest Story Ever Told* for more details. It will send shivers up your spine. I even thought I heard these creatures howl around dusk tonight. Mercy!

After our dinghy ride, Tom worked for a while on the dinghy motor. He is still trying to troubleshoot the problem. Because it was so late, I prepared a light supper of turkey and Swiss cheese sandwiches and a tossed salad. I am off to bed now. Tomorrow, Cleveland Passage.

Good Night from Thomas Bay - End of Day 50

DAY 51

DESTINATION: CLEVELAND PASSAGE

Motoring up Frederick Sound

"Hi, Honey! We're Home!" is what we say to one another after we drop anchor each day. Because we live aboard our boat, wherever we travel on her *is* Home. Yes, of course, Friday Harbor is homebase to us. Our friends and my mom are there, and it feels like Home to us. However, Georgia and Kentucky still hold a sense of Home for us as well, as many of our family members and friends still reside there.

What is the definition of Home? To Tom and me, Home is wherever we are together...whether that be on the water, on the road, or in the sky. When we hike trails, climb rocks, or paddle the shoreline...we are Home. Even when we do everyday chores like running errands, grocery shopping, or doing laundry...we are Home because we are together.

When my mom asks, *"When are you coming Home?"*...my first thought is that no matter where we are, we are already Home. So, when we traveled out of Thomas Bay and turned into Frederick Sound today...we were Home; when we rounded Cape Fanshaw into Stephens Passage...we were Home...and when we tucked into Cleveland Passage to drop our anchor for the night...we were Home.

You've heard it said, *"Home is where the heart is?"* Well, our hearts are with each other. We are each other's Home.

Looking back at Frederick Sound from the stern of Havis Amanda

Good Night from Cleveland Passage - End of Day 51

DAY 52

DESTINATION: TRACY ARM COVE

Motoring up Stephens Passage on our way to Tracy Arm Cove

Chilly temps, light drizzling rain, and low-hanging clouds pretty much describe the weather conditions this morning when we left Cleveland Passage to head up Stephens Passage into Tracy Arm Cove. I call this *"hot-soup-curl-up-under-a-blanket-with-a-good-book-in-front-of-a-crackling-fire-weather-kind-of-day.* In all actuality, it was a *"hot-tea-wool-sweater-two-coats-under-full-raingear-gloves-hat-rubber-boots-weather-kind-of-day."* But that's perfectly ok with us...it's <u>all</u> good!

Humpback whales today!!! No drizzly, overcast day can take away the magic of a whale sighting. We witnessed them all along the way, moving in rhythm with the sea, currents, and wind. These sea mammals are poetry in motion, plain and simple. They move mindfully with intention and purpose but never seem to get in a hurry. I guess we humans could learn a thing or two from these incredible creatures. It is awe-inspiring to be in their presence.

Misty low-hanging clouds in Stephens Passage.
The towering mountains were so beautiful we
didn't even wish for the sun to come out and play.

You see, humpback whales don't consult with *Ports and Passages*, *Navionics*, *Predict Wind*, or the *Marine Weather Station* before they take off for places unknown each morning like we humans do. NOPE! They just instinctively and intuitively know where to go and how to get there.

Whales don't cram-pack their day with so many tasks that they can't even come up for air. NOPE! They know perfectly well when they need to emerge from the deep to breathe and do so with a very emphatic blow. YEP! They breathe in rhythm with the sea.

Furthermore, they aren't on any kind of arbitrary schedule, running around like worker bees attempting to get their daily chores done by a specific time. NOPE! They simply go with the flow of things.

Maybe we humans could learn a thing or two from our whale brothers and sisters and simply slow our lives down to a manageable, less stressful pace. We do have a choice as to what tasks we pack into our days, and Nature gives us many examples of how to live our lives in a more natural, more intuitive, and rhythmic way—if we are willing to slow down, watch, and learn.

Our very first iceberg sighting!

So, watch and learn we did as we played "dodge-berg" this afternoon coming into Tracy Arm Cove. These turquoise-in-color floating blocks of ice are stunningly beautiful. Now, these icebergs, they too go with the flow, but unlike the whales, they don't move with intention, intuition or purpose...they are moved along by the whims of the sea they float in. Wherever the wind, current, and tide go, so go the bergy bits.

As we motored along today, I began to think about how sometimes I move through my life like the whale...with intention, intuition, and purpose...going with the flow of things...while at other times...I allow myself to be pulled and pushed and prodded by society's expectations, the latest tragic world event, negative politics, prejudice, and intolerance. When that happens, I react more like an iceberg...I allow myself to be affected and influenced in a way that is not emotionally or physically healthy for my well-being. I give away my choice.

I don't want to be the iceberg...I want to be the whale.

So, I intentionally choose Peace. I intentionally choose Joy. I intentionally choose Unconditional Love for myself and others.

And, maybe...just maybe...as I set these lofty intentions for myself...I will be granted the strength and courage to follow through with them. We shall see. Watch this space.

Good Night from Tracy Arm Cove - End of Day 52

DAY 53

DESTINATION: JUNEAU

Low-hanging clouds hovering over Tracy Arm

Change of plans: We woke up at 4:00 (the alarm was set for 5:00), looked out at the mountains and the low-hanging clouds, and decided not to travel up Tracy Arm today, as we knew the clouds would prevent us from adequately enjoying the beautiful views along the way. Tracy Arm is a narrow, winding 24-mile fiord with deep water and towering granite walls. At the head of the arm, two tidewater glaciers, North Sawyer and South Sawyer, generate the turquoise and white bergy bits that are floating in the fiord. It is helpful to have three to four people on board to watch ahead and fend off these floating bergs so they don't damage your boat, and in that, there were just the two of us, that was a consideration as well. Also, many tour boats, pleasure crafts, and even sometimes cruise ships come and go, so there can be a lot of boat dodging.

We discussed all these issues and decided to wait to experience Tracy Arm until Tom's nephew and his wife flew in to meet up with us for a few days on the boat. So, we motored to Juneau today and docked at Douglas Marina for the night. We will meet up with Brian and Gila in the morning.

After we got to Douglas and settled in, we walked to the top of the dock to catch a bus to Costco. The bus only takes you so far, so we had to walk about three-fourths of a mile both ways to pick up a few items. Thankfully, we had a cart to carry stuff in, so it wasn't too labor-intensive.

You know that expression, "What goes around comes around?" Well, that happened to us today. We were the only people on the bus when Tom looked down and saw a dollar bill on the floor of the bus. He picked it up and turned it into the bus driver.

Then when we were walking back to the bus stop from Costco, Tom noticed two five-dollar bills folded up and laying on the side of the street. There was not another living soul around to give the money back to, so we thought, *"Well, we returned the dollar from the bus and gained 10 dollars in return."* We will take that kind of karma any day!

When we got back to the boat, we fixed tuna melts and a tossed salad for a quick and easy dinner and hit the sack.

Good Night from Juneau - End of Day 53

DAY 54

LAYOVER: JUNEAU

Tom and I connected with Bryan and Gila late in the morning and rode the bus into town. We took the tram ride to the top of a mountain, did a short hike while there, checked out the gift shop, rode the tram back down to town, looked around some of the tourist shops, and then ate at The Hanger, a local pub. After that, we walked down to IGA and picked up provisions for our four cruising days out with Bryan and Gila.

I bought way more food than we can probably eat, but like the squirrel, I like being prepared. I have never been a "less is more" kind of person, strongly leaning toward "more is more." Like, more peanut butter on the bread (and spread it all the way to the edges, please), more seasonings on my food, more layers of clothes when it is cold...more, more, more is my motto.

Tom, on the other hand, is a classic "less is more" kind of person: less honey mustard on his turkey sandwich, little to no dressing on his salad, muffins without butter...less, less, less is his motto.

The town of Juneau is host to five or so cruise ships coming in every day, so the streets, shops, and restaurants are jam-packed with tourists. I have been on four different cruises over the years and have seen a lot of shops that are located right off the cruise ships and cater to tourists. Shop owners or their staff are standing outside their doors trying to entice tourists to come in and drop a wad of cash in their establishment. It has been my experience that the majority of the shops are jewelry-related. I have loved jewelry all my life, but not gold, diamonds, rubies, or emeralds...I prefer interesting stones or crystals set in silver.

Over the past two years now, I wear jewelry less and less. In fact, a couple of months ago, I culled my jewelry stash and consigned over half of it to a local consignment shop.

This decision was due to huge lifestyle changes I have made since meeting Tom and to no longer working part-time.

We spend a lot of time participating in outdoor activities, where jewelry could be a hindrance, and I rarely get dressed up now, so my need for jewelry is minimal these days.

What I do need are warm sweaters, warm turtlenecks, warm jackets, gloves and hats...the operative word being warm. The Pacific NW can be cold, damp, windy, and wet (and I really don't like to be cold), so my wardrobe is more practical now. I really love the idea that my clothes are more functional and less me trying to make a fashion statement. (So, I purchased no jewelry today. Yea! Good will power!)

After puttering around town for a while, we came back to the boat, hung out, and talked. Bryan and Gila had bought some taro-flavored bubble tea (also called Boba tea) from the gift shop on top of the mountain. Gila says Boba tea originates in Asia and is based on the tapioca root, which is boiled and turned into tiny bubbles. All the tapioca bubbles fall to the bottom, turn jelly-like, and are sucked up with a straw.

The Bubble Tea kit they bought was somewhat different than the one they were used to, and there was a lot of discussion as to the "correct" way to make the tea. There was a lot of laughter and frivolity during the making of the bubble tea and the partaking of it afterward. We all really liked the flavor of the tea, but sucking up the jelly-like bubbles in the straw was just a bit too weird for my "texture taste." A very interesting experience all the way around.

Bryan and Gila Making Bubble Tea

Afterward, we got Bryan and Gila settled into the v-berth, where they would sleep and keep their belongings. We showed them how to use both heads (toilets) and where the snacks were and explained how important it was to conserve water while out cruising. Bryan has boating experience, but Gila is new to it all, so there will be a steeper learning curve for her. It is evident already that she is a fast learner and open to new adventures.

We all hit the sack, looking forward to our transit to Tracy Arm Cove tomorrow to stage for our journey up Tracy Arm the following day.

Good Night from Juneau - End of Day 54

DAY 55

DESTINATION: BACK TO TRACY ARM COVE

Transiting Gastineau Channel to Stephens Passage

Tom, Bryan, Gila, and I left Juneau around 7:00. We were a bit sleepy but excited to be out on the water together. It was a partly sunny but chilly day, so we were layered up. Gila and Bryan took turns being at the helm. Bryan has taken sailing classes in hopes of one day buying a sailboat of his own. Gila has not had much boating experience but was excited to learn and get a feel for what boating life was all about.

The seas were calm, with little to no wind coming down Gastineau Channel, but as we entered Stephens Passage, we unexpectedly had wind that was a broad reach. Tom and Bryan put up the mizen and the jib sails, also called the jib and jigger, and we had about 30 minutes of nice sailing before we were in the lee of islands on both sides and lost the wind. Nice while it lasted, though. We are always thrilled when there is wind not squarely on our nose and we can motor sail, because so much of the time here in the Pacific Northwest, that is not the case.

Gila trying her hand at being at the helm

Bryan receiving instruction from Tom

When we arrived at Tracy Arm Cove, we found a suitable anchorage in about 50 feet of water. Bryan worked with Tom on the bow to experience dropping and setting the anchor, while Gila learned about being at the helm during this process.

We prepared dinner then sat out on the stern for an informal concert from Bryan. Such a lovely ending to a perfectly lovely day.

An impromptu concert by Bryan

Good Night from Tracy Arm Cove - End of Day 55

DAY 56

DESTINATION: TRACY ARM/NORTH AND SOUTH SAWYER GLACIERS (FINALLY!!!)

Magnificent floating glacier sculptures in Tracy Arm

We began our day filled with excitement. Finally, our anticipated journey up into Tracy Arm would be realized. Looking back over the day, I must admit that I am at a loss for words to adequately describe the grandeur we encountered as we motored past towering granite mountains, cascading waterfalls, icebergs, and literally thousands of bergy bits on our way to view the North and South Sawyer Glaciers today, but I will do my level best.

I know that: "A picture is worth a thousand words,"...but honestly...this was one of those: "You had to be there to believe it" experiences. This fiord definitely lives up to its reputation.

These magnificent ice sculptures are floating all through Tracy Arm, along with thousands of bergy bits. There are places where there are so many bergy bits that you have to weave your way through them slowly and carefully so as not to bump into them. Even the smallest ones can damage your boat, so carefully maneuvering through and around them is a must.

Dodging these bergy bits is challenging but loads of fun. It does, however, help to have someone on the bow to watch for them and alert you to turn "hard to starboard" (right) or "hard to port" (left) in order to miss them, so that became Bryan's and Gila's job, as you can see in the photo below.

It is tradition to capture a small bergy bit, chop it up and keep it in your freezer to use for ice in your cocktails, or whatever beverage you choose. This requires caution and some dexterity. Tom and Bryan took on the challenge and were quite successful.

Tom pulled the boat alongside a bergy bit, put the boat in neutral, grabbed the boat stick, and guided the bergy bit to where Bryan could scoop it up. The chunk of ice was a bit too big to fit in Bryan's bergy-bit-bucket, so he took a hammer and broke off a piece that would. Success!!! Tom and Bryan were so proud!

Bryan and Tom determined to wrangle a bergy bit

Bryan with his prized 10,000-year-old bergy bit

Motoring down Tracy Arm

The photo above and the one directly below were taken motoring further into Tracy Arm. It is hard to adequately describe the beauty that surrounded us today, but even harder to express the emotional impact it had on me. In general, being in nature soothes my soul in deeply profound ways, bringing me a sense of peace and serenity that helps put the day-in and day-out challenges in my life into perspective, but the majestical beauty we were blessed to be a part of today, took it to a whole new level for me.

The majesty of Tracy Arm in full display

The photo below shows the South Sawyer Glacier at the end of the fiord and the one below that the North Sawyer Glacier. The bergy bits at the base of the South Sawyer Glacier can close in around you when the tide starts ebbing out, so we were constantly looking back to make sure we didn't get trapped in that area. It was quite exciting *and* intimidating to be so close to these enormous glaciers, especially when they were calving (which is when chunks of ice break off at the terminus, or end, of a glacier). Ice breaks because the forward movement of a glacier makes the terminus unstable. These resulting chunks of ice are called icebergs. When the center of gravity of the chunk is high enough, it can even flip over. Thankfully, we left in time to avoid being held captive by the bergy bits or buried under a massive monster of calved ice. Whew! That was close!

South Sawyer Glacier

As we motored back to Tracy Arm Cove for the night, Tom and I agreed that the day we spent transiting in and out of Tracy Arm (there are no anchorages in which to overnight) was our favorite day so far. The majesty of this amazing place is almost indescribable, but I truly did my level best to share a bit of the magic with you.

When we got back to Tracy Arm Cove, we prepared rockfish and ling cod on the grill and had yellow rice and steamed broccoli and cauliflower to go with it. After dinner, we played Flip 8, a card game that our friends Colin and Lynda taught us, and then headed to bed with visions of Tracy Arm in our heads. Pleasant dreams, everyone! Zzzzzz...

North Sawyer Glacier

Good Night from Tracy Arm Cove - End of Day 56

DAY 57

LAYOVER DAY: TRACY ARM COVE

The day began with Tom, Bryan, Gila, and me having coffee and tea, reading from The Book of Awakening, and sharing our thoughts on the daily message. Then, we all split off in different directions.

Bryan and Gila took off in the kayaks, paddled over to the shore, and spent several hours exploring that side of the bay on foot, with bear spray in hand, of course. As they were kayaking back to the boat, they realized they were quite close to a floating bergy bit, so they paddled over to it and got the photo shown below. Very Cool! (Literally and figuratively!)

Gila getting up close and personal with a floating ice sculpture

I stayed on board to catch up on journal entries while Tom took the dinghy out for a row and checked the engine. The engine ran well...until it didn't. Sigh...

Tom was working on it when a couple about our age pulled up in their dinghy to introduce themselves and tell Tom that his Fatty Knees dinghy was the cutest one they had ever seen. As they chatted, Tom realized they had a wealth of knowledge from their 30 years of traveling in Alaska and began peppering them with questions. Ron and Jo invited us over to their boat later that evening to share with us which anchorages were their favorites and which ones to avoid.

So, after dinner (shrimp, squash, zucchini, peppers, cauliflower, and onion skewers, with a side of buttered noodles topped with parmesan cheese), Tom and I dinghied over and boarded their power boat. Ron got out his tablet with the *Navionics* navigational program on it and began to share his recommendations with us.

As Ron was trying to explain things to us, Jo constantly interrupted him to tell a story about that particular anchorage. It was a bit funny, but we could tell that Ron was getting quite annoyed with her constant interjections. Tom took notes so that he could use their suggestions when he plotted the next part of our journey.

When we returned "home," we got ready for bed. What a lovely layover day, with each of us doing exactly what we needed and wanted to do.

Good Night from Tracy Arm Cove - End of Day 57

DAY 58

DESTINATION: BACK TO JUNEAU

We awoke to a beautiful, sunny day, but still needed our cold weather gear. Thankfully, as the day progressed, the temps warmed up, and we were able to shed a few layers...such a relief after weeks of mostly cold, wet, windy, cloudy days. We had fun looking at all the large and small bergy bits of ice floating all around us, including the one carrying a row of seagulls shown below.

Bryan and Gila took turns being at the helm and learning other important boating skills. They are looking for a sailboat suitable for a family of four, so this time out on the water with us will give them first-hand experience of what boating life is all about.

As we neared Juneau, Gila piloted Havis Amanda, staying away from very shallow areas on her port, as well as navigating around some logs, kelp beds, and boats large and small coming and going. She asked good questions and is a quick learner. I think she will make a very good captain to her Skipper Bryan when they have a boat of their own.

Passing an "aircraft carrier" on our way back to Juneau

Gila at the helm motoring up Gastineau Channel

As we got close to the entrance to Douglass Marina, Bryan took over the helm. He very smoothly and capably docked Havis Amanda. There was a light wind blowing us onto the dock, which aided the docking process.

After we "put the boat to bed," Tom and I showered, and we all took the bus into Juneau to do a bit of shopping and eat dinner at a small, cozy Italian restaurant. The food was good, but Tom was not happy with the pizza crust as it wasn't homemade. One of his favorite foods on the planet is pizza, so he definitely knows his pizza dough.

Afterward, we walked to Foodland for some breakfast provisions, called a cab, and headed back to the boat. We hit the sack around 9:30 or so. It had been a very long and tiring day, and I was beyond ready for sleep.

Good Night from Juneau - End of Day 58

DAY 59

LAYOVER DAY: JUNEAU

Bryan and Gila hiking the Treadwell Gold Mine Trail

We woke to another beautiful day: clear, sunny skies and warm temps. Eagles, ravens, seagulls, and crows were out and about, chattering and chasing one another.

Bryan and Gila will catch a late afternoon flight back to Virginia. We wanted to have one last adventure with them before their departure, so we decided to take a hike.

We walked up the dock and across the street to the Treadwell Historic Mine Trail and found the self-guided hiking trail. This trail is well maintained with informational plaques all along the way and a few structures that have been restored. Treadwell Gold mine was, in its time, the largest hard rock gold mine in the world, employing over 2000 people.

After hiking, we came back to the boat, and Bryan and Gila packed up to leave. We all caught the bus into Juneau, and at the grocery store stop, Tom and I said goodbye. They were going to shop for gifts for their boys, have some lunch, and catch a late afternoon flight. We will miss them.

After provisioning at Foodland, Tom and I took a taxi back to the marina. Once again, I bought more food than we could carry, so a taxi ride was the best option.

When we arrived back at the boat, Tom stripped the v-berth where Bryan and Gila had slept so we could turn it back into our pantry/storage area. Our v-berth acts like a storage unit for us, whether we are at home in Friday Harbor or cruising on a long journey, so when guests come, we find all kinds of hidey-holes to stow away all the stuff that usually lives there. It is surprising how much storage space there actually is on a boat, but, unfortunately, much of it is not readily accessible for daily use. And, truth be told, we squirrel some things away so well that they are never to be seen or heard from ever again.

While Tom was route-planning the next five days to Sitka, I spent the rest of the afternoon re-organizing the v-berth and then preparing a one-pot dinner of cabbage, potatoes, carrots, and onions with cornbread. The cornbread mix was a good many months old, but I didn't realize it until after I had mixed it up, so it didn't rise properly. It was edible, but that is about all that can be said about the matter.

After dinner, we took a short walk, came back, and enjoyed a relaxing glass of wine on the back deck. It was a lovely evening with little to no bugs buzzing around us. Such a relief! We went to bed early, watched a movie, and fell asleep.

Night-Night from Douglas Marina - End of Day 59

DAY 60

SECOND LAYOVER DAY: JUNEAU

Tom and I decided to stay moored an extra day in Douglas Marina so that I could catch up on writing and he could do maintenance on Havis Amanda. After Quiet Time, Tom dropped down into the engine bay to change oils and fuel filters and do other mid-trip maintenance chores while I got started on journal entries 57-59.

I was happily writing entry #58 when I inadvertently deleted days #57 and #58. It was late in the afternoon, and I still had to do day #59. I tried every way I knew to recapture them, but alas...they were gone. I was on a time schedule as I wanted to finish them and then walk up to the local library to send them out before they closed at 8:00. At that point, there was nothing to do but start over. I spent another two+ hours rewriting them but finished in time to take them to the library before closing time.

This was one of those days when I struggled to walk my positive talk, accept "what is," and find the blessing in the midst of my frustration. I learned a valuable lesson, though: stay focused and mindful and don't get in a hurry. Lesson learned.

I was pretty brain-fried by that time, so Tom and I made a big, tossed salad and warmed up some bread for dinner. We had eaten a late lunch, so we weren't very hungry. I called my mom and chatted for a while to catch up on her upcoming medical tests. She and one of her caregivers had worked out all the details, so she was in good spirits. I went to sleep feeling confident she was in good hands.

Good Night from Juneau - End of Day 60

DAY 61

DESTINATION: COOT COVE
INLET IN FUNTER BAY

Motoring up Stephens Passage on our way to Funter Bay

It was our plan to untie the lines and take off for the fuel dock at 7:30 this morning until we realized that today was a minus tide, and we would not be able to get out of the marina until around 9:30 (when the tide would begin to rise) without bumping bottom and possibly running aground.

So, we waited. We ate a light breakfast of warm cranberry bread, did our Quiet Time, and took the garbage up the dock. On our way back to the boat, we stopped to talk to our new friend, Tom, who is planning to single-hand his boat across the Gulf of Alaska and on up to Kodiak in a couple of weeks. That is either one brave or one crazy man!

A light wind was blowing us onto the dock, but I had no trouble backing Havis Amanda out of the starboard side to side tie into the fairway to leave Douglas Marina. We got to the fuel dock only to discover that it was closed, so we called another fuel dock down the way a piece to find that they were indeed open. In order to get to the other fuel dock, we had to motor under a bridge, but thankfully, it was low tide, so our mast didn't hit the underside of the bridge. Whew! Close! But because it was low tide, we bumped bottom at the fuel dock. Sailors say if you haven't run aground, you haven't been anywhere. So, I guess in that we have bumped bottom twice on this trip, we have definitely "been somewhere."

After filling up the boat with 134 gallons of diesel fuel, we headed back up Gastineau Channel to turn right into Stephens Passage, then a left turn into Saginaw Channel, and finally another left turn into Funter Bay. We anchored in Coot Cove for the night in about 45 feet of water. It had been a very long day, and we didn't arrive in Coot Cove until after 7:00. Thankfully, we had leftovers from our pot of cabbage, potatoes, and carrots from two nights before, so we didn't have to prepare dinner from scratch.

Oh! I almost forgot! When we were in Stephens Passage today, there were whale-watching boats surrounding what appeared to be one solitary humpback whale. We both felt that the boats were too close to the whale for the whale's comfort and protection. I don't know what the Alaskan laws are regarding the distance you must keep between your boat and the whale or even if they have any regulations, but I felt sorry for the whale. Sometimes, I think I am too empathetic for my own good. It is very hard for me to see animals in the wild, who are simply minding their own business and going about their day, being exploited for the almighty dollar.

Motoring in Lynn Canal/Icy Strait area

Good Night from Coot Cove Inlet - End of Day 61

DAY 62

DESTINATION: PAVLOF HARBOR, FRESHWATER BAY

Little islet outside of Funter Bay

Today we officially headed back south. Hoping to arrive around noon, we motored down Chatham Strait on our way to Pavlof Harbor, which is located in Freshwater Bay, for the night. This is our second day of five enroute to Sitka, which we hope to reach on July 3rd, allowing us to enjoy the festivities there on July 4th and maybe even see fireworks.

But to backtrack just a bit, last night, as I was working on yesterday's journal entry, I started to feel unwell: body aches, headache, and a stuffy nose. I promptly drank Emergen-C+ with Echinacea added in, used Zicam nasal swabs, and took Tylenol. I slept poorly, used Zicam nose swabs in the night, and woke up no worse. I started the healing regimen all over again and drank some herbal tea for congestion. We had been in and out of the town of Juneau for three days, and there were lots of tourists there from the five cruise ships, so perhaps I picked up a cold bug from one of them.

Tom and I talk often (well, brag, really) that neither of us has had even the whiff of a cold, much less COVID, in about three years. I have heard it said that pride cometh before the fall... hmmmmm. But then so does stress and long, cold, exhausting days...in all kinds of weather...out on the water.

Normally, our bodies are strong enough to resist colds and flues. We eat well, exercise, and keep as positive an attitude as possible, which I believe greatly contributes to our overall good health. I truly think that a healthy mental and emotional mind set can stave off a lot of bad stuff coming into our lives, illness being one of them.

After we pulled up the anchor, Tom sent me inside out of the wind to rest. I worked on today's journal for a while and then went back to bed. I semi-slept for about two hours with the engine droning in one ear while the other ear listened intently in case Tom needed me.

At about 12:00, I got back up to be at the helm when we anchored in Pavlof Harbor. After we dropped the hook and ate PB&J sandwiches, Tom went for a kayak ride. We decided I needed to stay in and rest, so he went alone with bear spray in hand. He promised to get some good photos for the journal entry today, so it's all good.

In late July, the salmon run up this stream (see the fish ladder on the right of the falls in the photo below) which normally brings out lots of bears. We did not see either one today, as it was too early for the salmon.

There were, however, two eagles who hung around all day, especially after they spied a big, fancy power boat that had come in with freshly caught halibut. An elderly gentlemen stood out on the stern cleaning the halibut, while the eagles eagerly waited for him to throw some fish heads or guts overboard. What the eagles didn't know was that the man was also a crab fisherman and was probably saving the halibut scraps for crab bait. Sorry, eagles. No fish dinner for you tonight. Maybe next time.

Waterfall and fish ladder in Pavlof Harbor

It was such a pleasant evening that we sat out on the back deck for a while before going in to prepare enchiladas and steamed spinach. Yes, I know, those two foods don't seem to go together, and they don't, but spinach is one of Tom's favorite vegetables, and I needed room in the refrigerator, so enchiladas and spinach it was. I was still feeling the effects of a head cold, so after I finished the journal entry and Tom finished the dishes, we turned in, watched a movie, and got to sleep early. We have a 6:00 leave time in the morning for a long 40+ mile day, and I really do love my eight hours of sleep.

Good Night from Pavlof Harbor - End of Day 62

DAY 63

DESTINATION: APPLETON COVE, BARANOF ISLAND

Coming into Peril Strait from Chatham Strait

Five o'clock came way too early for my taste. I had a difficult night with restless legs, muscle cramps, and a stuffy nose and didn't fall asleep until after 2:00. We pulled up anchor at exactly 6:00, headed out of Pavlof Harbor, back into Chatham Strait for a six-hour ride to Peril Strait and into Appleton Cove.

At around 8:00, Tom sent me inside to get me out of the wind and to take a nap. While I was sleeping, several porpoises rode the bow of Havis Amanda and Tom got a few still photos and a video. He chose not to wake me up but to let me rest. Good call.

Peril Strait connects Salisbury Sound to Chatham Strait and separates Chichagof Island from Baranof Island. This strait is used by most vessels that navigate to and from Sitka. It must be navigated carefully as strong current, reacting with the wind, can create large "square" waves which result from the intersection of two seas. This is especially true during southeast gales that blow through Peril Strait from east to west.

Porpoises bow-riding Havis Amanda

As we entered Chatham Strait from Pavlof Harbor, we had the current and the wind in our favor. This enabled us to maintain seven knots of speed all the way to the entrance to Peril Strait, where the current was in our favor once again. Though we had the wind on our nose, which made for a choppy ride (wind against current), we were still able to maintain an acceptable speed.

We arrived in our six-hour window, dropped anchor in Appleton Cove (which is in Rodman Bay), on the north shore of Baranof Island. We ate some lunch and Tom worked on tomorrow's route while I worked on the journal entry for today.

Unfortunately, Tom was now experiencing cold symptoms, so at 2:30, we bagged it, went to bed, and slept for a couple of hours. It felt good to rest with nowhere to go and nothing to do.

Afterward, we heated up leftover enchiladas and together made a nice salad for dinner. It will be an early night for us both. Perhaps a good night's sleep will aid our healing process, and we will feel better tomorrow. Sending some good healing thoughts our way would be very much appreciated.

Good Night from Appleton Cove - End of Day 63

DAY 64

DESTINATION: BABY BEAR BAY, BARANOF ISLAND

Hoona Sound in Peril Strait

Thankfully, our transit today was short, about three and a half hours, compared to six hours yesterday. We left Appleton Cove at 9:00, later than we like to start our day, but with both of us down with a cold now, we slept in. I am on my third day of symptoms and beginning to feel better. Tom, however, is only on his second day and even ran a fever this afternoon. We are both full of various types of cold medications, which help with the symptoms, but as you all know, a cold just has to wear itself out. We are both hoping that happens soon.

After leaving Appleton Cove, we transited further up Peril Strait and through Hoona Sound. It was a sunny morning with a few low hanging clouds, calm seas and light winds. As I mentioned before, Peril Strait can live up to its name and be quite...well...perilous, but that has thankfully not been our experience on this trip. We have thankfully had mill-pond-like seas both days we transited this strait.

The entrance to Baby Bear Bay is narrow, intricate, circuitous, and full of rocks, so it takes a lot of focus and careful navigation. We normally love these types of routes, but with both of us feeling poorly, we took turns at the helm.

Drinking cold-remedy tea

Turning into Hoona Sound

Before turning into Baby Bear Bay

Entrance to Baby Bear Bay

After dropping anchor, we ate grilled cheese sandwiches, took more cold medications, and went straight to bed. We slept most of the afternoon, woke up long enough to watch a movie, and then fell back asleep again afterward.

Later, I fixed egg noodles tossed with butter, seasonings, and parmesan cheese, along with baked bread for a light supper. I journaled, Tom finished the movie he was watching, and then we went to sleep, hoping to feel better by morning. Our plan is to travel to Sitka tomorrow for a three-day layover.

Good Night from Baby Bear Bay – End of Day 64

DAY 65

HEALTH LAYOVER DAY: BABY BEAR BAY

Tom in route planning mode

"I feel like death warmed over," said Tom as he planned routes for the next few weeks.

Be adaptable. Be flexible. Don't fight the current...go with the flow of what is. These are mantras that we use often. There are, of course, times to persevere, to "sailor-on," to stay strong and fight through whatever challenge presents itself to us as a "gift." These times give us the opportunity to test our mettle, face our fears, and find the inner strength we might not know we possess until we are challenged.

And then, there are times that the most prudent choice is not to "sailor on" but to "drop anchor," drop our agenda, settle in, stay put, and accept what is: we are still ill and need to rest, regroup, and recharge so that we can "sailor on" with more vim and vigor after we are well. And that is exactly what we chose to do today.

Gone are the plans to reach Sitka before the Fourth of July to partake in the holiday festivities and see fireworks. In their place are very sensible, health-conscious plans to rest, plan our routes for the next month, prepare homemade chicken noodle soup "for the body and soul" and just BE for the next couple of days.

Along with simply not feeling well enough to travel, we considered that many folks descend on Sitka over the Fourth of July weekend, and in that our immune systems are already compromised, it would probably not be the best idea to be around that many people. Nor did we want to "share" our cold germs with anyone else. So, we will wait to leave for Sitka until the fifth of July and lay over two to three days there to sightsee, provision, and do laundry.

A couple of days ago, I wrote that we would appreciate any good healing thoughts and prayers you might send our way. But then I realized that by the time you get these journal entries, we will probably already be on the mend. However, if you still choose to do so, we will just "bank" those good healing thoughts and prayers into our "health escrow" account for future use. Many thanks in advance! We will take all the prayers we can get!

Baby Bear Bay at dusk

Good Night from Baby Bear Bay - End of Day 65

DAY 66

SECOND HEALTH LAYOVER DAY: BABY BEAR BAY

Looking out from our anchorage in Baby Bear Bay

Since we have been laid up for a few days in Baby Bear Bay trying to feel well enough to "sailor-on," we have started to plan our trip back south. What places do we want to revisit? Which ones were merely over-nighters and held no particular interest for us? Are there places we might want to stay longer than one night? What new anchorages do we want to experience?

When we started our journey north on April 30th, the plan was to make our way up through Northern British Columbia during the month of May, cross over into Alaska by the first of June, and arrive in Juneau no later than June 30th. We would then start back south during the month of July, cross back over into Canada by the first of August, and finally travel back to Friday Harbor by the first week of September. So far, we have managed to meet each benchmark with time to spare, thanks to Tom's expert planning.

We know there is not enough time to see all there is to see in our lifetime, not even in ten lifetimes, so our goal for this trip was to try out lots of places to see which ones we liked the best so that when we come back through the next time, we will know where we want to stay longer. In other words, on our next trip north, we can focus on fewer places and stay longer in those places that held the most magic for us, like Forward Harbor, Kynoch Inlet in the Fiordlands, Misty Fiords, Baker Bay, Tracy Arm, and Kwatsi Bay. And, of course, leave time to explore a few new places as well. This will definitely not be our last trip north into Alaska. This journey has been life-changing for us both, and we can't imagine not continuing our exploration of this amazing part of the world.

We want to be like the elderly couple, Hank and Carolyn, who we met in Petersburg. They have been coming up to Alaska every year since 1997...and they are now in their 80's! Hank still putters around doing boat chores, busily cleaning all his boat fenders one early morning. Honestly, I can't remember the last time we washed our fenders, if ever. He and Carolyn were such an inspiration to us both.

Tom and I have talked often about what it takes to successfully live aboard a boat with another person, and one thing is for sure: not only do you need to REALLY LOVE the person you are sharing space with on board, but you better REALLY LIKE them as well. All of the live-a-board couples we know seem to have two things in common: a healthy love and respect for each other and a wide range of compatible interests. Fortunately, Tom and I deeply love and respect one another and thoroughly enjoy spending time doing the same types of activities, so we feel blessed in both of those areas.

But living in a 'hallway" can be challenging even for the best of us. It is not like we can just go to another part of the "house" to get away from one another if we have a disagreement...there is no other part of the house to escape to.

So, being willing to sit together, deeply listen, and share our most vulnerable feelings with one another is crucial to peacefully living together in close quarters. We have learned not to let feelings fester but to share any frustrations or misunderstandings we might be experiencing with one another in an open, honest, respectful, loving, and timely way. Our morning Quiet Time has been the instrument for this sharing many times, giving us an opportunity daily to bring up and work through any issues we might be having. We credit this morning ritual for the continued deepening of our relationship. We absolutely swear by it!

Ok...enough for tonight. We are hoping to feel well enough to leave for Sitka in the morning bright and early, so time to say good night.

Good Night from Baby Bear Bay - End of Day 66

DAY 67

DESTINATION: SITKA

Leaving Baby Bear Bay

Today was to be an eventful day. We were still getting over our illnesses, and we had to navigate through a bunch of tight, rocky areas, keeping the green markers on our starboard and the red ones on our port this time. About 25 minutes after we came out of Baby Bear Bay, right at low water slack, we went through Sergius Narrows. The rest of our route included transiting through Kakul Narrows, down Neva Strait, past Whitestone Cove, across Kestof Sound, through Olga Strait, across Nakwasina Sound, and down Middle Channel into the popular town of Sitka. Whew!

It was another day of staying on point and focused. As I have said before, we like these kinds of challenges, but with both of us still recovering from being ill for almost a week, it was challenging in a different way.

Upon arriving in the Sitka area, we tried to contact the Harbor Master at Eliason Harbor, but he couldn't hear our transmissions on our inside radio at all. Even inside the breakwater, right next to the marina, he couldn't hear us. Uh-Oh...

Finally, the harbor master gave us a phone number to call from our cell phone, and we were able to get through at last. He gave us a slip assignment: dock 8, slip 13, and I was able to smoothly navigate Havis Amanda right into it slick as a whistle!

It was great to be safe and sound and in Sitka for the next few days, but knowing something was wrong with one of the radios dampened our spirits a bit. After much time and considerable effort, Tom was able to reach the Vesper radio folks and order another one to be shipped to the harbormaster here in Sitka, hopefully by Friday. They will thankfully replace it for free.

After we got the boat tied up and picked up (we always have stuff to put away: coats, hats, gloves, PFDs, coffee, and tea paraphernalia) and everything turned off (radios, chart plotters, autopilot, etc.), we took a long-awaited shower. Because of our unexpected illness-layover days, we had been conserving water more diligently than usual and had not showered in several days. We are fortunate to have an aft head/shower combination, so we don't have to hike up someplace with coins and toiletries in hand to do so. I'm telling ya', nothing washes away the day quite like a nice hot shower!

Afterward, we walked up the dock and into town to find a place to eat. The harbormaster had given us the names of several eateries to try, and we chose the Sitka Hotel Restaurant. We had crabcakes as an appetizer (decent but not great) and freshly caught halibut fish and chips. The halibut was lightly breaded and really, really good. I thoroughly enjoyed mine, but upon taking the first bite of his, Tom noticed he had lost all sense of taste and smell. Oh dear! When we realized this, we also realized we probably had not had the common head cold like we thought, but more likely COVID. Thankfully, we are well past the contagious stage.

After dinner, we wandered around to familiarize ourselves with the town proper. We plan to come back tomorrow when the library opens to send out the last several journal entries.

We returned to the boat and took up our nightly position on the stern. We watched eagles and ravens as they sat high on the masts of fishing vessels, hungrily waiting to grab the remnants of today's cleaned and fileted fish. Lucky eagles...they don't have to "sing for their supper," they can just "sit by the dock of the bay, and watch the tide roll away..."

Eliason Harbor in Sitka, Alaska

Good Night from Sitka - End of Day 67

DAY 68

LAYOVER DAY: SITKA

Edgecumbe Volcano, Sitka, Alaska

The above photo of Mount Edgecumbe was taken right off the stern of our boat here in Eliason Harbor. Until May 2022, this was considered to be a "dormant volcano." Since then, it has been reclassified by the Alaska Volcano Observatory as "historically active." Interesting.

Today, we walked up to the library so I could email the journal entries. We also hit a few hardware-type stores for Tom to browse through, but he didn't find anything he couldn't live without. Afterward, we went to the grocery store to pick up a few items for dinner. It was a nice store with everything we would need to tide us over until we get back to Ketchikan in a couple of weeks. We will make more complete provisions on Friday for our Saturday departure as long as the new radio comes in that day.

When we got back to the boat, I worked on journaling (well...after a 30-minute nap, that is) while Tom rinsed the salt water off Havis Amanda. He then made us pizzas on naan bread topped with sundried tomatoes, mushrooms, black olives, and pesto as toppings. Scrumptious!

As Tom and I were walking the docks looking at boats tonight, we just happened to run into John, the Nauticat boat owner we met in Petersburg a couple of weeks back. This time, he had his wife, Michelle, with him. The two of them had been cruising on their boat for a couple of weeks. She wanted to see Havis Amanda, so we planned to get together at some point tomorrow afternoon for her to do so.

When we returned, I called and talked to my mom. The assisted living community where she lives has had a COVID outbreak over the last several weeks, but thankfully, Mom hasn't been infected. She is extremely careful, always wearing her mask when she is out of her room.

Later, we watched two ravens fly into the crow's nest of the fishing boat next to us and proceed to groom one another around their necks. Tom said that is probably the only place they can't reach for themselves. I have seen other creatures (gorillas come to mind) groom one another, but never ravens or any other type of bird. It was so interesting to watch them and to listen to all of their many and varied vocalizations. We also observed the resident eagles again as they quietly waited for the fishermen to throw out scraps, hoping that sitting on the dock of the bay this evening would not be a waste of their time.

Well, that's about all of the "exciting" news I have to relay today, so until tomorrow...

Good Night from Sitka - End of Day 68

DAY 69

SECOND LAYOVER DAY: SITKA

Typical workday for fishermen in Sitka

We woke this morning to a light sprinkling of rain. It soon stopped, but the clouds remained. We enjoyed a very comfortable 60 degrees, which I know for those of you in Tom's native state of Georgia is not what you wanted to hear in that you're dealing with upwards of 100 degrees today. Have mercy! Sure wouldn't want to be you guys right now!

After sleeping in and our Quiet Time, we gathered up our laundry from the last three weeks and walked it up to the Sitka Laundry Services. We have two different carts that we use for hauling stuff, and Tom wanted to try out the new one that we bought recently in Ketchikan.

Tom explains, *"I had strapped all the laundry onto this brand-spanking new, upright cart that is supposed to hold 150 lbs., and on its maiden voyage, carrying only about 35 lbs., it started to wobble like one of those unbalanced, rogue trailers that you see bouncing down the freeway behind a vehicle. The hub had broken out of the wheel, and the axle was scraping the ground, all of which happened about halfway up to the laundry facility, mind you."* Argh!!!

There was nothing to do but unpack the four bags of laundry from the broken-down cart and carry them across the street to the grocery store, where I would wait with them while Tom walked back down to the boat to retrieve the other cart (this after calling around to several local hardware-type stores to locate another one to no avail).

While I was waiting for Tom to come back, Michelle, John's wife (they who own the other Nauticat), came into the grocery store to provision for their departure tomorrow morning. We chatted awhile and set up a time for them to come over to see our boat around 4:30 today.

Michelle and John had been receiving my journal entries for a few weeks now, and she shared with me how good it was to read sailing stories from the perspective of another woman. I was glad to hear they had had a positive impact on her own sailing experiences of late.

Tom returned then, and we transferred the laundry into the old cart and headed on up to the local laundry facility. On the way, I asked him what became of the broken cart. (Since we would be headed back to Ketchikan in a few days, I thought we could return it and get a refund. I had paid $65 dollars for it, after all.) I was completely flabbergasted when Tom said he'd thrown it in the dumpster. Wait! What?!? I was dumbfounded (astonished, bewildered, shocked, stupefied, and...and...) until I remembered that Tom despises returning items, no matter what he pays for them. I, on the other hand, am the polar opposite, so I was beyond taken aback by his actions. I mean, who does that?!? (Well, Tom, I guess.)

To say I was peeved (irritated, annoyed, exasperated, aggravated, steamed, and...and...) puts it mildly. You better believe this was a topic that was thoroughly discussed during Quiet Time the next morning! OK. Enough said. Well...almost. To be fair...Tom paid me back in full, so all is forgiven.

After the wash cycle, as we were moving the clean clothes over to the dryer, Tom raised up and banged his shoulder into the open dryer door. Ouch! Needless to say, "swimmingly" would not be a word Tom would use to describe his day so far.

While the clothes were drying, we walked across the street to the local McDonald's to use their free Wi-Fi to send yesterday's journal entry and to get some of their amazing fries. I mean, who doesn't love McDonald's fries?

Later in the afternoon, John and Michelle came over to see Havis Amanda and partake in happy hour with us. We really enjoyed swapping Nauticat and cruising stories and hope to meet up with them again someday.

Thankfully, there were no more breakdowns or bruised shoulders or anything else that might qualify as a small catastrophe the whole rest of the day.

Good Night from Sitka - End of Day 69

DAY 70

THIRD LAYOVER DAY: SITKA

Sitka raven dumpster-diving for food

Yesterday was laundry day. We absolutely could not wait to have clean clothes and especially clean sheets. Now, to be clear, we were not out of clean clothes; we were just out of our favorite clean clothes. Have you ever noticed that you have a few items of clothing that are always your go-tos? I tend to wear the same three to four pairs of pants even though I have 12-15 pairs to choose from. Same with t-shirts, sweaters, and jackets. I guess when you get right down to it, we humans are simply creatures of habit.

Today is provisioning day, so after cereal and a banana, we trotted off to do just that. First, though, we checked with the harbormaster to see if the UPS package (our replacement radio) had been delivered yet. It had not. Darla, the staff worker, who Tom and I agreed was the spittin' image of our harbormaster, Tami, told us that the UPS lady was coming back before the end of the day. It was such a relief to know we would not have to lay over another day waiting for the new radio.

We decided to walk to the hardware store first to look for a filter Tom wanted (we, unfortunately, couldn't find one), then back to McDonald's to send two more journal entries (and, of course, get more fries), and last to provision with groceries and other needed items for the next 11 or so days. While we were at McDonald's, Darla called to say our package had arrived. Excellent! We swung by and picked it up on our way back down to the boat.

I put groceries away while Tom hooked up the new wireless radio. He then checked oils, filters, etc., so we would be ready first thing tomorrow morning to head back to Baby Bear Bay for one night. The day after, we will travel to Dead Tree Island, which will be our last anchorage in Peril Strait, before starting to head back south.

We are presently trying to decide whether to eat out tonight or cook in. It is amusing to me that the simplest decisions can create the most chaos in our lives, like whether to eat out or cook in and where to eat if eating out (pizza, Thai, Italian, seafood, a pub). We both tend to say, *"It's up to you,"* or *"I don't really care one way or the other...you decide."* All of this back and forth is, I think, an attempt on both our parts to defer to the other...to be kind and considerate of what the other might want. The problem with this strategy is that we could starve to death by the time one of us finally takes the lead and makes the decision. I will let you know tomorrow what we decided. Watch this space!

Good Night from Sitka - End of Day 70

DAY 71

DESTINATION: BACK TO BABY BEAR BAY

Somewhere between Sitka and Baby Bear Bay

This morning began at what Tom thought was 7:00. I had not looked at my phone, which is almost always right beside our bed, but Tom had looked at his. We had planned to get up at 7:00, have our Quiet Time, leave the dock by 8:30, get fuel then be on our way back to Baby Bear Bay. However...

Tom, *"Honey, what time does your phone say?"*

Me, *"6:00."*

Tom, *"My phone says 7:00, but all the other clocks say 6:00."*

Me, *"Are you telling me I could have slept another hour?!?!"* Peachy...Just peachy!

As it turns out, Tom's phone settings somehow got changed to Washington time, which is an hour ahead of Alaska time. You better believe I will be checking my phone each morning from now on to verify the proper time before I crawl out of my toasty-warm bed on Tom's say-so alone!

On the positive side, since we had a whole extra hour to play with this morning, we had a nice, relaxed, Quiet Time.

At 8:30 sharp, I backed Havis Amanda out of our slip and headed over to the fuel dock. It was very crowded, but we found a spot to side tie on the back side of the dock. Tom docked the boat and a couple of nice young men grabbed the mid and bow line for us while I jumped off and tied up the stern line.

I thought perhaps these young men were dock workers, but they had no uniforms on, so I wasn't sure. I asked and they said that no, they were working on a fishing boat for the summer and had also stopped for fuel. One of them was a newbie this year, and the other was in his third year. They both said they really enjoyed the fishing life. The captain of their boat walked up after having paid his fuel bill of $4000. Holy Moly! They sure would have to catch a "boatload" of fish to offset those fuel costs!

After fueling our own boat (thankfully, nowhere near the $4000 the fisherman spent), we were on our way. It was a gray, low-hanging cloud day, so none of my photos turned out very well. Sorry...take your complaints to the Weather Gods...not my fault!

We were basically going to retrace our steps right back the way we came five days ago, including transiting Sergius Narrows and weaving our way back into the tricky entrance to Baby Bear Bay. The ride itself was basically uneventful until we discovered that the brand-spanking new radio would not transmit. We could hear, but no one could hear us. We discovered this because we tried to hail Wild North, the boat owned by our new friends, Laurel and Ryan, but they couldn't hear us. Remember them? We met them in Kynoch Inlet, and Laurel is the photographer who took that amazing photo of Havis Amanda that everyone raved about.

We had seen Wild North on our AIS and realized they were coming toward us down Olga Strait. We both pulled into this teeny tiny bay to chat for a few minutes and to try and figure out what was wrong with the new radio, but we didn't tarry long as we had to hit Sergius Narrows at low-water slack.

Tom worked on troubleshooting the radio issues while I drove the rest of the way to Baby Bear Bay. It was fun navigating the Narrows, and in that we hit them right at low-water slack, it was super easy.

After we dropped anchor, I started to make dinner (spaghetti with marinara sauce, salad, and oven-warmed croissants) while Tom worked on the radio problem. He read every manual and tried everything he knew to try, but he still couldn't figure out the problem. Bummer!

Thankfully, we still have two other radios to rely on until we can troubleshoot the new one with the Garmin dealer when we get back in cell range in Ketchikan...10 days from now.

We saw several landslides along the way. Can you imagine seeing this happen in real-time?

As all boat owners have said at one time or another, "It's a boat," simply meaning that there is always something to be fixed when you own a boat...always. I try not to see it that way, as I generally try and view things from a positive point of view, but I have to admit, this old adage seems to be true more often than not.

And on that note...I will say:

Good Night from Baby Bear Bay - End of Day 71

DAY 72

DESTINATION: DEAD TREE ISLAND
(Truncated to Appleton Cove)

Eagle is on the left, and raven is on the right

As many of you know, the Eagle and the Raven are very special to Tom and me...Tom is the Eagle to my Raven and the Sun to my Moon. We even had a Canadian artist paint two rock necklaces for us: one with the Eagle and the Sun on it, and the other the Raven and the Moon. Of course, there is a story behind this.

On Tom's first trip north into the Broughton's, he and Colin, a fellow buddy-boater, anchored their boats one evening in Clam Bay, a First Nations community. Sometime after dinner, a First Nations gentleman rowed up to Evening Star (Tom's old boat) to sell his wood carvings. Tom looked through them, but most were too big to fit on his 24-foot Dana. Then he found one that was of an Eagle and a Raven facing one another in the shape of a heart. He knew it would fit on his boat, so he bought it on the spot and hung it on the wall of Evening Star.

Fast forward about ten months when Tom and I were out hiking the Jakle's Lagoon outer trail and saw two eagles and a flock of ravens. I shared with Tom that the eagle and the raven held a special significance for me. It was then that he told me about the wood carving he had purchased many months before, long before he had even met me.

After that, it seemed that every time we walked, we either saw or heard the eagle, the raven, or both. It was as if they showed up just for us. Even still, to this day, and especially on this trip, they appear to us almost every day, either leading us into an anchorage or guiding us out.

But wait, there is even more to this story. When we were in Ketchikan earlier in our trip, we found out from a First Nations carver that the eagle and the raven were considered the Love Birds. We saw several pieces of silver with the eagle and the raven carved on them, and they were almost always facing one another. We have not researched this yet, but since then, we have heard the same story from others.

All along our journey, we have been searching for a First Nations artist who we might commission to create wedding bands for us with the eagle/raven/sun/moon symbols on them. We have asked in each town we visited for recommendations, but so far, we have not found an artist who would be a good fit for us. We are not worried, however, as we know that we will find the right and perfect artist when the time is right.

So, now, to the events of today. We pulled up anchor at exactly 8:00 and maneuvered Havis Amanda back out of the tricky entrance to Baby Bear Bay that we came through yesterday. There was a lot of kelp to weave around on our way down Peril Strait, but we did so with relative ease.

When we came out into the main part of Peril Strait, the wind and wave height kicked up considerably. After about three hours of being kicked around in 25-knot sustained winds with 30-knot gusts and four-foot seas, we decided to truncate our route and duck into Appleton Cove for the night instead of going on to Dead Tree Island. We were so glad we did! The anchor space is limited in this cove due to so many commercial crab pots, but we thankfully were able to get one of the better spots before two more boats ducked in to also get out of the weather.

The rest of the day was fairly typical, except that we ate like starving hippos all afternoon. We had leftover spaghetti for lunch, nachos for happy hour and enchiladas for supper. By the end of the day, we looked and felt like beached whales. Not a pretty sight, I can tell you.

Several hands of cards and a movie rounded out our day. Tomorrow...Takatz Bay.

Good Night from Appleton Cove - End of Day 72

DAY 73

DESTINATION: TAKATZ BAY
(Truncated to Dead Tree Island)

Looking out from our anchorage in Appleton Cove

One thing is for sure about the cruising life: flexibility and the willingness to change your mind when the weather changes its mind is a must. There is no arguing, pleading, or bargaining with the weather that will change its course of action, so you just might as well accept and go with the flow and direction that the weather dictates. After all, what other choice do you have?

So, that is just what we did this morning when, once again, the weather had a mind of its own. It paid no attention to the different weather forecasters' predictions but instead laughed in apparent glee in their collective faces. Instead of the wind dying down overnight as predicted, it continued to blow a very consistent 20-30 knots right through the morning and into the afternoon and evening.

It almost had us fooled, though. When we woke at 6:00, it was dead calm back there in Appleton Cove, and not until we tuned into the VHF radio weather station from NOAA did we realize that out in Peril Strait, a different story was unfolding. There was much static on the radio, and it kept cutting in and out, so it was a solid two hours before we could get a clear weather picture for the next few days. There was a small craft advisory for this morning, but the wind was predicted to lay down as the day went on. In that we had already "lost" part of a day by ducking into Appleton Cove yesterday, instead of going on to Dead Tree Island as planned, we decided to stick our noses out into Peril Strait to see for ourselves. We knew that a couple of hours up the strait, we could duck behind Dead Tree Island if the wind and waves were too choppy for a comfortable ride to our next destination: Takatz Bay.

So, we poked our nose out into Peril Strait and decided to give it a go, trusting the weather predictions that the wind would die down as the morning progressed. It did not. With the current against us at two-and-a-half knots and 25-30-knot winds on our nose, we decided not to fight it for the next five hours. Instead, we ducked behind Dead Tree Island into Hanus Bay and dropped anchor in Portage Arm. A power boat was already anchored there, but with plenty of room in the bay for multiple boats, that was not an issue for us at all.

Throughout the afternoon, the weather continued to defy all the predictions to the contrary and did not die down one little bit. The sun began to peek its head out, but the wind still persisted. We were glad we had decided to get in out of the wind and choppy seas and hoped tomorrow would be a better travel day. Perhaps by then, the weather will have listened to NOAA and will cooperate with the predictions. We shall see.

When we arrived in Portage Arm, I prepared a can of Campbell's chicken noodle soup, a hot turkey and Swiss cheese sandwich, and chips for a light lunch.

Afterward, we talked about changing our route back down south to not include going through Rocky Pass. It will be a full moon with a minus tide of four feet at low tide. The dredged channel is only four feet at low tide (we draw six feet), so we decided it would simply not be worth trying it during the spring tides. Maybe next time.

At 3:30 this afternoon, the wind was still howling. Go figure. We will just have to wait to see what tomorrow brings. Watch this space.

I took a 30-minute power nap while Tom refigured our path back south. Then, he worked on the saltwater pump while I journaled. Tonight, we will eat left over enchiladas, play cards, then hit the sack.

Good Night from Dead Tree Island - End of Day 73

Skipper Tom at the inside helm on a rainy, windy,
lumpy day

DAY 74

DESTINATION: TAKATZ BAY

Jandira on watch in Chatham Strait

Well, finally, the weather and the weather forecasters were on the same page and speaking the same language today. The seas were calm and quiet, just as predicted. We traveled four and a half hours down a perfectly flat Chatham Strait to get to Takatz Bay by 12:30. We had heard how beautiful this bay was, but like Kynoch Inlet, Walker Cove, and Tracy Arm, we were not really prepared for its beauty. Tall, towering granite walls, two cascading waterfalls, and opaque, blue-green glacier water gave us plenty of nature's beauty to photograph. The many different shades of green leaves, as depicted in the photo below, simply took our collective breath away. Everywhere we looked, our eyes feasted on incredible beauty.

As soon as we arrived, Tom got the kayaks down so we could explore the shoreline. We had not been in our kayaks since we came down with Covid a couple of weeks ago and were both itching to be paddling. We saw many different patterns and colorations on the rocks, as well as a large variety of trees. We commented on this, as so many of our previous anchorages have consisted mostly of evergreens. The many different deciduous trees growing side by side in this bay created an intricate kaleidoscope of various shades of green leaves too varied to adequately describe.

Colorful rock formations in Takatz Bay

And then, you have the blue-green glacier water whose color is truly indescribable except through photos.

And, of course, what iconic nature scene would be complete without a cascading waterfall? We anchored right beside this one.

After two hours of kayaking, we came back on board and prepared shrimp and veggie skewers on the grill with yellow rice for dinner and then did the dishes together. Afterward, I sat down to write while Tom watched a movie in bed. We have decided to stay here another day so we can kayak the rest of the bay tomorrow. This is an anchorage we would definitely want to return to on our next trip north to Alaska, so make no mistake,

WE'LL BE BACK!!!

Good Night from Takatz Bay - End of Day 74

DAY 75

LAYOVER DAY: TAKATZ BAY

Pastels in bloom in Takatz Bay.

It took Tom and I a mere five minutes yesterday to decide we were going to layover in Takatz Bay for an extra day. There was simply too much to see and absorb in one day...even in multiple days really. Just take in the beauty of the photos all through today's journal entry. The various colors of leaves, hanging mosses, and tree bark juxtaposed above the sea-green glacier water, as well as the colors, shapes, patterns, and textures of shoreline rocks, all combined to stir up my creative juices. Even the dead tree limbs and roots have a rustic appeal all their own. I never tire of looking at them, photographing them, and dreaming of turning them into art pieces.

Between the two of us, we snapped over 100 photos just today alone! We agreed that Takatz Bay had earned a solid place on our list of top five anchorages during this trip so far.

After Quiet Time this morning, we did something we rarely do...we cooked breakfast. On transit mornings, there is no time to eat, much less cook before we pull up anchor. But, in that it was a layover morning, we scrambled eggs with cheese and had oven-warmed bread. I scrambled my eggs and cheese first, as I like my eggs to be light and fluffy. Tom, on the other hand, cannot eat an egg unless it is scrambled extra hard with loads of cheese...and...there can't be any white showing on his eggs...and...he wants his scrambled eggs between two slices of bread. (Maybe because he can't stand to look at his eggs while eating them?) Needless to say, we each prepared our eggs the way we liked them best. Good way to keep the "egg peace."

After breakfast, we donned our rain gear, jumped in our kayaks, and took off to explore and photograph the shoreline. There were so many incredible photos from yesterday and today that it took me over 30 minutes to pick the ones to include in today's journal entry.

240

Our hunger to be up close and personal with
shoreline nature was certainly satisfied today

Good Night from Takatz Bay - End of Day 75

DAY 76

DESTINATION: WARM SPRINGS

Leaving Takatz Bay, headed to Warm Springs

It occurred to me this morning that Mercury must be in retrograde. You see, when Mercury is in retrograde, communication on all levels is affected throughout the Universe. Now, honestly, what I know about astrology, you could put in a thimble, but Tom and I have had several different issues with our communication systems of late, so I figure something, somewhere out there in the great cosmos, is awry. Seriously.

I have spoken about the VHF radio that had a faulty transmission button and how the company shipped us a new one that arrived in Sitka before we left on Saturday. Then I told you how the new radio was not working correctly either. It would do everything but transmit. That issue was resolved by downloading a software update for the new handset. So far, it seems to be working.

Then, this morning when we were leaving Takatz Bay, either the Navionics chart plotting software or the chart plotter itself was acting very erratic in its route presentation. I drove at the upper helm for the better part of an hour, while

Tom fiddled down below with the system until it seemed to magically reset itself. Go figure.

All of these electronic issues had to do with communication equipment, so, maybe Mercury really is in retrograde. I don't have Wi-Fi at the moment, but I will be asking Google about this when we get to Petersburg on Saturday. I'm serious about this.

After approximately one and a half hours, we arrived at the entrance to Warm Springs Bay, hoping to get on the dock. We normally like to anchor, but it had rained steadily all day and didn't appear to be letting up anytime soon, so we thought it might be more pleasant to be on the dock than to have to dinghy or kayak over in the rain to take a dip in the hot springs. Unfortunately, the dock was completely full, so we picked an anchorage just to the left of the giant, 100-foot waterfall and right across from the dock.

After eating a bowl of raisin bran and almond milk, we hopped into the kayaks and headed for the hot tubs located just up from the dock. Three large private bathing tubs are fed by the natural hot springs half a mile up the hill and offer a magnificent view of the falls. We had debated about whether to experience the natural hot springs or just use the private ones. We decided to use the private ones, but then to hike up to the natural ones to check them out as well.

The natural hot springs are situated right beside a roaring waterfall. It is an incredibly beautiful setting, and had we not already bathed in the private ones, we would have donned our bathing suits and hopped right in. Also, another couple was already enjoying the springs, and we didn't want to intrude upon their privacy. Maybe next time.

Warm Springs (natural hot springs) next to waterfall.

Lake Baranof located up above the waterfall

We hiked up above the waterfall a bit further to see Lake Baranof. We were very impressed by the condition of this trail from start to finish. Most of it consisted of well-maintained boardwalks, and, unlike that horrible trail we took up to the lake in Punchbowl Cove that I said I would never, ever hike again, this trail was quite easy and mostly flat. It definitely deserves repeating the next time we are here, but instead of the private bathing tubs, we will definitely try out the natural hot springs first.

After our hike, we kayaked over to a salt lagoon with a very narrow, 15-foot-wide entrance. The water can really rip through there as it carries six feet of water through its fairway at slack on a 14-foot tide. We cautiously went through at slack and puttered around the shore of the lagoon for a bit. When we came back through, the tide was ebbing, so we got a fun ride out and back to Havis Amanda.

We had intended to fix homemade chili for dinner but forgot to put out the hamburger, so we opted for deli chicken and Swiss cheese sandwiches and fried potatoes (one of Tom's favorites). We will make a big pot of chili for tomorrow evening and eat the leftovers the evening after.

Tom did the dishes. I journaled. Tomorrow we travel to Chapin Bay on Admiralty Island. It will be a four-hour transit, so a pretty easy day.

Oh...by the way...Tom just told me that there are underground magnetic disturbances in many areas in Southeast Alaska, where the observance of compass errors can be as high as 38 degrees. Could this be the reason for our electronic problems of late?

So, you decide...local underground magnetic disturbances or Mercury in retrograde? Or maybe both? Or maybe they are one and the same?

It's an unsolved mystery, that's for sure.

Good Night from Warm Springs - End of Day 76

DAY 77

DESTINATION: CHAPIN BAY, ADMIRALTY ISLAND

Looking back to the entrance of Warm Springs Bay

I woke a little before 6:00, but my alarm was set for 6:30. Nice...I thought...as I rolled over and snuggled deeper under the covers...30 more minutes of sleep. Tom was already awake but still lying in bed. He had been checking the currents for our transit of Chatham Strait to Frederick Sound today on the Navionics app on his phone and had decided we needed to leave at 7:00 instead of 8:00. Oh well...that 30 minutes of extra sleep sure was a nice thought...while it lasted anyway.

With the sound of the roaring waterfall off our starboard side and the rushing rapids we had paddled through at slack the day before off our port, we pulled up anchor surrounded by a thick bank of fog.

With Tom at the helm, we dodged an underwater rock and navigated out past rocks on both sides of Warm Springs Bay. As we entered Chatham Strait, the fog seemed lighter at first, but it wasn't long before it was densely socked in everywhere. It was at this point that we noticed the chart plotter/Navionics system had started acting up again.

Tom worked on trying to problem-solve the electronics issues the whole four hours it took to transit across Chatham Strait into Fredericks Sound, which left me at the outside helm. But hey...I LOVE being at the helm, so no problem there, unless, of course, you count the dense fog...the many patches of kelp to dodge...and the rain on my glasses that had to be constantly wiped off so I could see the many patches of kelp I was dodging. These kinds of challenges, where I have to be at the helm making quick decisions without Tom at my side, are good for me. They give me practice in different types of situations and help build my confidence to handle future challenges on my own. And honestly, it's fun. (In full disclosure, I did enlist the Kelp-Bed Dodging Angels to come on board to assist me. Credit where credit is due, after all.)

During our four-hour transit, we passed two sea otters lying on their backs eating their freshly caught fish breakfast, one sea lion, and one humpback whale's tail just before it dove under. Pretty exciting stuff!

The electronics problems did not get totally resolved, but Tom thinks he is on his way to figuring it all out. He thinks it has something to do with the way the new radio is interfacing with the chart plotter and the Navionics app. Unfortunately, only time will tell. Watch this space.

When we reached Chapin Bay, a lovely, peaceful little anchorage on Admiralty Island, we ate grilled sharp-cheddar cheese sandwiches with chips and bread and butter pickles on the side. Afterward, we kayaked around the whole cove, finding 20-30 rocks to bring back for our collection without even getting out of our kayaks. Sweet. One of the projects we will do with the rocks when we return home is to add to the First Nations medicine wheel that we created from rocks three years ago out at Briggs Lake, one of our favorite hiking destinations on San Juan Island.

There is some basic knowledge that is needed before creating a medicine wheel. First of all, a medicine wheel is an honoring of each of the four directions: North, South, East, and West, and depending on which First Nations tribe you are representing (I was taught the Lakota way), there is an animal, a color, a season, a time of life, and an element that represents each direction. East is represented by the color yellow, the eagle and owl, springtime, infancy, and new beginnings in our lives. The color red, the coyote and mouse, summer, childhood years, and our emotional self represent the South, while the color black, the bear, the teenage years, the fall season, and a time of going within to find oneself represent the West. Finally, the North is represented by the white buffalo, the color white, the winter season, our elder years, and the clarity and wisdom that comes with age.

Now, to be sure, there is A LOT more to it than what I have described above, but this is my somewhat limited working knowledge on the subject. There is also an element (air, fire, earth, and water) that represents each direction, but even different Lakota tribes assign these elements to different directions, so I will not try to specify them here.

So, we collect rocks in the colors of the directions: red, yellow, black, and white and create a circle with these colored stones placed in the directions they represent. At different times of the year, we add various other nature items: red berries for Christmas, yellow flowers for spring, pinecones, driftwood, etc. Our plan is to create a third circle around the first two to represent our trip to Alaska and new beginnings for us as a couple.

The above is the first medicine wheel we created at Briggs Lake back in 2019. We were unable to find rocks in the appropriate colors for this one.

We create medicine wheels and other nature art everywhere we go. We like the idea of honoring nature and leaving a little piece of us each place we visit. For example, Tom balanced five rocks on top of a round floating log in Chapin Bay today. Unfortunately, he didn't have his phone to photograph it, so you will simply have to use your imagination to visualize it.

The two medicine wheels shown in the top photo of the two photos below were created on a boat trip to Watmough Bay last year. As you can see, each color is placed in the direction it represents.

Medicine wheels created outside of Watmough Bay, 2022

Briggs Lake medicine wheel with second ring added in 2021

The photo above shows the original medicine wheel (with a few alterations) that we created at Briggs Lake in 2019, with the additional ring of rocks collected on our trip north into the area of Canada called the Broughton's in the summer of 2021. The rocks we collect from our Alaska trip this year will be added to the outside, making a three-ring medicine wheel. The rocks in the middle represent our loved ones who we keep surrounded in Love and Light.

Havis Amanda anchored in Chapin Bay

After we returned from our kayaking-rock-gathering-paddle, we put away our newly found rocks, prepared and ate a pot of chili, and enjoyed the quiet of this serene little bay before retiring for the night.

Good Night from Chapin Bay - End of Day 77

DAY 78

DESTINATION: PORTAGE BAY

Crossing Frederick Sound on our way to Portage Bay

We were able to sleep in until 7:15 this morning for a 9:00 departure. We left later than usual to avoid fighting a strong current that would have been against us if we had chosen an earlier departure time. Our ride across Fredericks Sound was mostly smooth and uneventful.

As we motored along, Tom and I took turns reading the last 20 or so pages of Mitch Albom's book, *For One More Day*. By the time we finished, we were both in tears. His books have a way of pulling at your heartstrings and making you think about life in ways you may not have considered before. Several are true stories; a few are fiction, but they always have a positive message and are fairly quick reads. We have read six of his books on this trip and will start the seventh one tomorrow.

When we were about three-quarters of the way to Portage Bay, our anchorage for the night, we saw a humpback whale right in front of us. I was able to get a short video of it blowing several times and then diving under. It is the only halfway decent video of a whale we have filmed so far.

Also, good news! Tom figured out the electronic issues he was having and just as he thought, it was an issue with the way the new radio was interfacing with the chart plotter and the Navionics app. It is too technical for me to understand, much less explain, but just know that all is well now. After the corrections Tom made yesterday, the system worked beautifully today. Yea! Another problem solved.

After an easy transit, we arrived in Portage Bay at 2:30 and dropped anchor in a bight right as you come into the bigger bay. So far, it is nice and quiet, and we are the only boat anchored here. We will stay for one night only and then head back to Petersburg early tomorrow.

After a meal of leftover chili, salad, and biscuits, we showered and went to bed early.

Good Night from Portage Bay - End of Day 78

DAY 79

DESTINATION: PETERSBURG

Transiting Frederick Sound on a drizzly morning

Every morning there are clothing decisions to make that are dependent on the weather. If it is raining like it was this morning, the hat gear we choose is different than when it is not raining. For example, on a rainy day, a beanie cap will not do, but instead, a baseball cap will be donned. Why? Because a baseball cap will help to keep the rain off our glasses, whereas a beanie will not. But, then there is the warmth factor that you do get with a beanie cap that you don't get with a baseball cap. The solution I have found is to put the knitted wool half-cap that my friend, Gail, made for me over the baseball cap and pull it down over my ears. It keeps my ears warm and holds my hat on if the wind is blowing. It works like a charm!

And then, depending on how cold it is, we have to determine how many layers to put on under our foul weather gear. I tend to get colder than Tom, so I will usually put on a couple more layers than he does, which makes me look and feel like an astronaut decked out for a moonwalk (or the Pillsbury Dough Girl or the Michelin Gal...take your pick). There is no sense trying to look stylish or in vogue...practicality is the word of the day.

Now, of course, we can drive from the inside helm when the weather is nasty, but if we are dealing with dodging a lot of kelp beds or logs, then piloting the boat from the upper helm is more prudent. This requires more layers of clothes, creates less ease of movement, and necessitates advanced planning for bathroom breaks! Cruising the Inside Passage would never be mistaken for a Caribbean Cruise, that's for sure!

For me, staying warm and dry is key to my physical health and positive mental attitude. As hard as I try not to, I can get quite grumpy when these factors are not in place, so I have become quite proficient at taking care of my physical needs.

So this was a foul-weather gear day. It rained all day, and we bounced back and forth between the upper and lower helms dodging kelp beds and trying to stay warm and dry. Even so, we had fun.

It has become quite comical, really, how many rainy, cold days we have had since we began our journey north. It is the middle of summer, for goodness' sake! What gives?!?

Tom commented that he couldn't remember even one day when we didn't wear one of our pure wool Pollen sweaters that are made in Lund, BC. We both have three of them, and they have become staples of our daily wardrobe. We have honestly gotten so used to wearing foul weather gear with layers of warm clothing underneath that when we do have a dry, sunny day, we feel almost naked without all the layers...a "problem" we would love to experience more often.

So, now, to Petersburg. This was our second stopover in this quaint little town where many businesses all but close up shop on Sundays. We were, however, delighted to find that Inga's Galley was open for business today, so we stopped in for a late lunch of fish and chips and cold draft beer. It was pouring rain, and she only had outdoor seating under umbrellas or a large tent. We opted for the tent. That was a mistake. There was a long table of rowdy men who had chartered a fishing trip and come in afterward for food and beer. They were so loud that we couldn't hear each other talk, so we quickly rectified the situation by moving to an outside table under an umbrella. Way better!

Before our lunch, we did a bit of grocery shopping, but the IGA had very little in the way of fresh vegetables, and the milk was dated back to the third week of June. Ugh! We wondered how they could get away with keeping outdated food on the shelf, but it is Alaska after all, and the remoteness makes timely food delivery difficult at times. We did find Klondike ice cream bars, so that partially made up for the outdated milk. There is simply not much in this world that ice cream doesn't make better.

They do have a great place to buy locally caught fish, so we purchased three nice pieces of ling cod to put in our mini freezer. Petersburg is a fish processing town, so fresh or recently frozen seafood is usually easy to procure.

We came back down to the boat and called T-Mobile's customer service folks to help us with our over usage of data. You see, the issue is that there is no T-Mobile service anywhere in Alaska, so the whole time we have been here, we have been using roaming data. They sent us warning texts that our phone service was going to be shut off if we continued to overuse the cellular data. Yikes! The customer service rep, Robert, was extremely helpful and, with some research, was able to come up with a solution for us: Straight Talk Wireless SIM cards to replace our T-Mobile ones until we get back home. So when we get to Ketchikan, we will go to Wal-Mart to purchase one. The downside is that Tom will need to shut off his cellular roaming data and use my phone for anything other than phone calls or texts unless we are where we can use local Wi-Fi. Cruising in remote places can certainly be challenging from a communication standpoint.

When we got back to the boat, we were still hungry, so Tom made popcorn. He then worked on the timing of us getting back through Wrangle Narrows tomorrow while I worked on today's journal entry. Our transit through the Narrows is very tricky timewise because of the way the current changes in the middle of the channel. Tom is still figuring. Maybe we wait one more day? Decisions, decisions...watch this space.

Oh...by the way... when we were coming into the slip that the harbor master assigned us today, a gentleman about our age walked over to catch a line for us. Come to find out his name was also Tom. He stood out in the drizzling rain for the better part of an hour talking to us about his 29-acre sheep farm on an island in Chili, of all places. And before he was through, he was inviting us to come for a visit and to stay for as long as we wanted...on his sheep farm...on an island...in Chili!!! Seriously!!! And we just might take him up on it one day!

Good Night from Petersburg - End of Day 79

DAY 80

LAYOVER DAY: PETERSBURG

North Harbor Marina, Petersburg

"We must live who we are," said Tom this morning during our Quiet Time. Not who someone else is. Not who someone else wants us to be. Not who society, our family, or even our church expects us to be. No. It is vital to our emotional and physical well-being to simply BE who we are...to be self-realized...self-aware...self-actualized. We must live out our personal truth, our dreams, our destiny...our own Personal Legend as Paulo Coelho teaches us in his book, *The Alchemist.*

This topic of discussion came up this morning from our reading of today's inspirational excerpt from Mark Nepo's *The Book of Awakening.* In it he talks about not being afraid to share our authentic selves, our deepest fears, with trusted loved ones.

He says, *"Somewhere along the way and often with good reason, we learn to fear putting our feelings out in the open, out in the weather of ordinary air, as if our small piece of love will die for exposure to the elements, as if our true feeling will not survive the gaze of others. Yet we all know so very well that without air, nothing can grow."*

Tom and I have committed two things to one another: to be our true authentic self...the self that is messy and quirky and extraordinarily ordinary...and to love and accept one another as we are...without trying to change each other into someone we are not. In order to accomplish these commitments, we have promised to listen and speak from our hearts without judgment. We work on keeping these promises every day.

So that is how our day started...that and a bowl of raisin bran with a cut up banana on top for me and a banana on the side for Tom. Almost immediately after finishing our cereal, I began to experience very strong indigestion pain in my esophagus, stomach and intestines. I took Tums and Pepto Bismol and after about two hours it began to subside a bit. Last night after eating popcorn, I had a bout of acid reflux that also went away with Tums. For some reason, my digestive system is not happy right now. Time will tell, I guess.

Tom checked the oil and all the fluids, and looked over the engine to make sure nothing was loose. As he was working on these maintenance chores, a couple, David and Kathleen, stopped by the boat to introduce themselves. We had been in several anchorages together and had seen one another on AIS. They hail from Seattle and will return home at the end of September. They have had several mechanical issues and were waiting for a replacement part to come in. Nice couple.

We made the decision this morning to wait until tomorrow to leave Petersburg to transit Wrangle Narrows. We both felt good about the decision. We finished up a few more boat chores, then walked up into town to send journal entries 79 and 80. That will be the last journal entries you receive until we return to Ketchikan in three to four days.

We walked back up into town to eat at Inga's Galley for dinner. Tomorrow morning will be a 5:00 leave time, so we will have an "early to bed early to rise" scenario tonight.

Good Night from Petersburg - End of Day 80

DAY 81

DESTINATION: WRANGLE NARROWS/EXCHANGE ISLAND

Looking at the entrance to Exchange Cove from Havis Amanda

Today began as a baseball cap day, but quickly turned into a beanie cap one, when the rainy mist subsided upon entering Wrangle Narrows...at 4:45, mind you. If you remember, way back on Day 47, we transited the Wrangle Narrows from the other direction. I won't replay all the technical information I shared in that journal entry again here, so if you want to refresh your memory, go back and reread the entry for that day.

But let me back up a bit. Tom and I have gotten our morning routine down to a fine art. Each night, Tom decides what time we need to leave the next morning. This is determined by currents, wind, tide changes, and the anchorage situation to which we are traveling. Once that is determined, we usually set the alarm for at least an hour before our departure time. I tend to prefer an hour and a half, just so I can feel relaxed and not rushed, but I can be ready in less than 45 minutes when I need to, like this morning when we got up at 4:00 and left at 4:45. When we have the extra 30-45 minutes, we can do our Quiet Time before we pull up anchor. Otherwise, like this morning, we waited until after we were underway.

Our routine goes something like this: Tom gets out of bed first, gets dressed and does his morning hygiene routine while I am making the bed. It is one of my many quirks, but I hate an unmade bed, so I make the bed first thing. Now, making the bed on our boat is more difficult than in a home where you can walk all the way around the bed. Our bed is enclosed on three sides, so I stay in the bed and make it up around me then crawl out and tuck it in on the one side that is open. Tom says it's kind of an exercise in futility to try to do this task with ease or grace, but he sure likes it when it's done, especially if he doesn't have to do it.

Then, while Tom is making coffee and tea, I do my morning hygiene routine, get dressed and if need be, don my foul weather gear. When I come up the three steps into the pilot house (dubbed the Beer Parlor when it is time for happy hour), the coffee and tea are waiting on the table steeping, a candle has been lit and we are ready to read from *The Book of Awakening* or other inspirational writings, set positive intentions for the day, and talk about anything that comes up for us from the readings. This is also an optimal time to unravel any misunderstandings that might have developed between us, so we give space for that too. As I have said before, we try not to let things fester.

Often during Quiet Time, we discuss the plan for the day's transit and problem solve any issues we think might come up. Like this morning when we were moored in a very narrow slip next to another sailboat. We discussed how best to back out of the slip, and Tom decided that we would both walk the boat back using the lines until we were out of the slip, then climb aboard and take her down the fairway. (We were tied up on our port side to the main dock, which is quite long, so this was possible.) Easy peasy.

The North Harbor Marina, where we were docked, is right inside where the Wrangle Narrows begin. The current rushes right past the entrance, which can make entering or exiting quite a challenge if you hit it at anything other than slack tide. This morning the tide was flooding two and a half knots, so we were interested to see how difficult it might be to get out of the marina. We were surprised to discover that it wasn't hard for us at all.

Transiting the Narrows this time around was quite easy as well. We had to pull over to the side twice to allow very large tugboats to get through some very narrow places, but we handled it just fine. I think we are starting to be old hands at all of this! Do I sound proud? Well, that's because I am!

After we were out of the Narrows, the seas were calm and the winds were light crossing Sumner Strait to then transit down Clarence Strait and into Exchange Cove for the night. We were the only boat in this anchorage at 10:50 this morning, but later in the afternoon two other boats came in and anchored at the entrance to the cove.

This was not a particularly interesting cove to kayak, but we decided we needed some exercise, so we kayaked around for about an hour before coming back to the boat. We were hoping to see bears, but no such luck. We did see two eagles and one sea otter feeding on his back in front of our boat. So cute.

When we got back to the boat, we both fell asleep for about 30 minutes curled up head-to-head on the settee in the pilot house. When we woke, we began dinner preparations.

We had bought three nice big pieces of ling cod in Petersburg, so we marinated and grilled one of the fillets and had stuffing and salad to go with it. I realize stuffing is not what you normally think of with fish, but we were both craving it, so that is what we prepared.

Afterward, Tom washed dishes while I journaled, and then we headed off to bed. We have another early morning and a 40-mile day back to Meyers Chuck tomorrow (which for us is about a six-and-one-hour transit), and we want some good sleep.

Good Night from Exchange Cove - End of Day 81

DAY 82

DESTINATION: MEYERS CHUCK
(and Cassie's Yummy Cinnamon Rolls)

Little islands on our way down Clarence Strait

6:00 Our day started as usual until Tom realized that the electronic gremlins were at work again. This time, it wasn't the radios themselves that were the problem; it was the Vesper system itself. It simply went belly-up.

9:00 Tom had checked everything and found that power was getting to the unit, but the unit itself would not power-up. He tried to call the Vesper folks but didn't have enough cell service to be able to maintain connection with them. Grrrrr...So frustrating!

By losing the Vesper radio system, we not only lose our radio capabilities, but we also lose AIS (Automatic Identification System), which can be pretty crippling when you are cruising. AIS shows you all other boats that have AIS, who they are, how big they are, what type of vessel they are, how far away from us they are, their route relative to ours, and other pertinent information.

Losing our radio means that we have no way to contact the Coast Guard if we need help, no way to get the latest weather forecasts and updates, or hail another vessel. We do still have an older handheld radio, but it does not have AIS.

11:35 Tom was finally able to talk to two different tech help folks and one of them, Amy, suggested he unplug everything and then plug it all back up again. Such a simple solution really, but by George it worked. Such a relief! We decided that Amy was an earthly angel and told her so. Another problem seemingly solved.

We had been traveling for almost six hours and had about an hour and a half to go. If you remember, Meyers Chuck is a teeny, teeny tiny little island that we anchored behind on our way north. It is a sweet place: quaint, friendly and quiet...and then there are those famous cinnamon buns that Cassie makes. We can hardly wait for tomorrow morning to get more!

12:00 Uh-oh...The Vesper system stopped working again! Tom unplugged and replugged again...several times in fact...but no go. Thankfully we had three to four bars of signal on our cell phones at that point, so Tom was able to send an email back to Amy to tell her the bad news.

12:30 The wind picked up to 20 knots about 45 minutes outside of Meyers Chuck, so we were dealing with the tech issues and the weather at the same time. I was at the helm; Tom was on the phone with Vesper and the wind and waves were bashing us...a bit chaotic, to be sure.

1:00 Evidently, Amy forwarded Tom's latest email to Travis, the senior tech that Tom had talked to earlier, and he called Tom to tell him he had found a new unit for us and would work on getting it shipped to us in Ketchikan asap. Yea! He will call or email us later today with the details. So, I guess we had two earthly angels working with us today. Thank you, Travis and Amy! Much appreciated!

1:15 We entered the narrow, curvy entrance to Meyers Chuck and dropped anchor. We really wanted to order Cassie's cinnamon rolls for tomorrow morning, but we didn't write her phone number down the last time we were here, and frankly, we were both too weary and brain-dead to get in the kayaks, go over to the dock to get her posted number, call her to put in an order and then paddle back to our boat-home. It was simply not going to happen. Not on this day, anyway. Sigh...

Tom is making pizza tonight for a light dinner, and then we will pile up in the bed, and as is our modus of operation, fall fast asleep while watching a movie.

Good Night from Meyers Chuck - End of Day 82

DAY 83

DESTINATION: KETCHIKAN

The above photos are of the sleepy community of Meyers Chuck

One thing about the nature of the sea is that it tends to build as the day goes on. It is prudent to leave as early as possible to get to your destination before the seas become too choppy. There is a certain rhythm to the sea that is best to adhere to and not fight against. Mother Nature is going to have her way, so you best get with the program, find her rhythm, and match your rhythm to hers.

I have talked in other entries about how Tom and I have learned to appreciate one another's rhythms, not trying to change each other but acknowledging the grace and beauty in which we each go about moving through our days. Tom is more of a "get-moving-and-get-things-done" kind of person, whereas I am more of a "don't-rush-me-I-need-time-to-think-things-through" kind of person. The good thing is that we are each learning from the other the value of both ways of moving through the world, and so we pull each other to the middle and help balance each other out.

But now the thing about Mother Nature is that she is not going to be pushed or pulled in any direction that she doesn't want to go. She has her own rhythm and is not going to adhere to our wants and needs, so we will just have to adapt to hers. This is never more apparent than when you are out at sea.

So, when we pulled up anchor at 6:30 this morning and slowly motored out of tiny Meyers Chuck, we knew we would be at the mercy of whatever Mother Nature had in store for us. We left 30 minutes earlier than intended, but there was still some chop to contend with. Thankfully, though, the seas did not build in Clarence Strait this morning but instead diminished the closer we got to Ketchikan. A bit unusual, for sure, but definitely welcomed and appreciated. Thank you, Weather Gods!

It was cloudy but not rainy, with winds 20 knots on our nose and wave height two feet or less. An easy, pleasant ride overall, so we drove for much of it from the outside upper helm.

A cruise ship passed us on its way to Ketchikan, as well as other pleasure craft and fishing boats. Ketchikan is a busy place with boats and seaplanes coming and going all day long.

About halfway there, we looked out our port side door and saw a humpback whale cruising right alongside us. We both grabbed our phones and began filming her as she moved smoothly and rhythmically through the water. She stayed beside us for about two minutes and then dove under.

When they dive, they tend to stay down for a while. I asked Google and found out humpback whales can stay down for up to an hour, but most will go down for a dive ranging from four to seven minutes, then come up again for six to eight breaths and repeat the process. Even the whale, which is an intricate part of nature, has to adhere to certain limitations of its own body and adapt to the nature of the sea.

Upon arriving in Ketchikan, we called by cell phone to the harbor master for our slip placement. Once again, as in Petersburg, we were placed in the last slip on that dock next to the main dock, but this time it was a starboard side to tie up. Tom piloted Havis Amanda into the slip without a hitch. I had planned to do so, but I couldn't clearly see the way into the slip, so I turned the helm over to Tom. I have discovered that I don't get nervous if I can see in advance what I am up against, but if I am coming in somewhat blind, I do. I think I am fearful that if I come in at the wrong angle, I won't know how to correct quickly to avoid something bad happening. Tom said I could have docked her easily. I guess I need more help in the confidence department. After I saw how Tom approached the docking, I knew I could have done it. I do try and practice what my son, Rupa, calls, "meditation mind in action," but sometimes I simply fall a bit short. It's ok. I am still a work in progress.

I am not sure I mentioned this before, but Tom had shipped an exhaust elbow to my friend, Gabi, here in

Ketchikan, and we met up with her yesterday to pick it up and go out for dinner. Gabi (Gabriele Beyer) is a very accomplished artist and has her art exhibited in three different local shows this summer here in Ketchikan. She took us to two of them, and they were both delightful.

Afterward, we ate dinner at Cape Fox Lodge. We shared an appetizer of bacon-wrapped scallops and a nice salad topped with grilled halibut then each ordered our own entrée. Gabi ordered the elk burger and an Indian-style curry soup, Tom chose grilled halibut topped with gruyere cheese and dill sauce, asparagus, and roasted potatoes, and I ordered shrimp scampi with the Indian curry soup and roasted potatoes. It was all quite good, but I think Tom's halibut was the best. We, of course, had IPAs on tap, which were decent but not very cold. We opted out of dessert as we were all just too full to stuff one more bite of anything into our bellies. There was live music that was quite pleasant. I was able to use the internet at the lodge to send out one of the journal entries.

Our dear friend, Gabriele Beyer, at one of her art exhibits

Dinner with Gabi at Cape Fox Lodge

Gabi dropped us back off at the marina around 8:00. I talked to Mom, and then we went to bed around 9:00. We will be in Ketchikan until our new radio unit ships to Gabi's address. We are hoping to receive it by Monday. Please cross your fingers for us.

Tomorrow, Tom will install the new exhaust elbow, and we will catch up on boat chores.

Good Night from Ketchikan - End of Day 83

DAYS 84-85

LAYOVER DAYS: KETCHIKAN

Gabi, took this photo of eagle and raven from her home

Owning and living on a Nauticat has its advantages and disadvantages. The advantage is that you meet a lot of very cool Nauticat owners. The disadvantage is that you meet a lot of very cool Nauticat owners. This translates into looking at each other's boats, exchanging Nauticat boat adventure stories, talking about the different systems on each boat, and a gazillion other boating-related topics like where the best anchorages are, the most profitable places to fish for crab, shrimp, and halibut and recommendations for the best local restaurants. (Truth be told, this also happens with owners of other types of boats as well.)

The end result is that a lot of talk happens but very few chores get accomplished. Good thing we're retired and not on too stringent of a time schedule. And, when all is said and done, the chores will still be there tomorrow, so it's all good.

We love to meet and learn from other boaters and, in turn, share our knowledge and experiences with them. It is fun, and it shortens our learning curve tremendously. Honestly, we are grateful for these encounters as they have each enriched our journey in innumerable ways.

Why, just yesterday, as Tom was installing the new exhaust elbow, an elderly gentleman juggling two bags of groceries in his left hand and a set of golf clubs slung over his right shoulder knocked on the side of our boat and said, *"I see you made it in ok."* We realized he had been anchored in Meyers Chuck with us the night before. His name was Al, and we found out he was a recent widower who had lived in Ketchikan all his life. He loved to play golf and drove his boat from Ketchikan to Wrangel (an 89-mile, two-day trip) several times a month just to play on a course there. I mean...who does that? And he is in his 80's, for goodness sake! Simply amazing!

Al gave us some valuable information about the current and wind in Clarence Strait, especially coming around Lemesurier Point. He was a delight! Of course, all boat project work was put on hold for about 30 minutes, but it was worth it to spend time with a local boater sharing invaluable local knowledge.

And then today, a Nauticat owner just a few slips down came by, knocked on our boat, chatted a bit, and invited us down to see his boat. We had just put some left-over pizza slices in the oven that we completely forgot about. In the midst of Laurin and Tom talking Nauticats, I remembered the pizza. I rushed back to Havis Amanda to find the pizza still cooking. I turned the oven off but left the pizza in to keep it warm. Ten minutes went by, but no Tom. Fifteen minutes later, still no Tom. Finally, I trekked back down to Laurin's boat to extract Tom as politely as I could.

Just as we were finishing our pizza, Laurin showed up with his wife, Jackie, to see our boat. They are a very warm and engaging elderly couple about our age or so. They stayed about 45 minutes...more boat talk...no boat work. Sigh...

But the thing is, even though we were "interrupted" two days in a row and taken away from our boat chores to talk boats, we met three really nice people and gained a bunch of knowledge we didn't have before. And hopefully, we were able to share some of the wisdom we have gained from our experiences as well. And you know what? The boat projects were accomplished anyway.

Tom worked all afternoon yesterday replacing the exhaust elbow while I got caught up on journal entries. After we finished our tasks, we walked up into town to eat at Ocean View, a combo Mexican/Italian restaurant we ate at the last time we were here. We ordered pizza and salad to share and enjoyed the atmosphere and good service.

Today, even though we didn't get started until around 3:00, Tom was able to do some route planning while I wrote yesterday's and today's journal entries. I hope to get them emailed to you all while we are at the nearby laundry mat later this evening, which is located near the Safeway grocery store where I will have Wi-Fi. Even in retirement there is so much to do, but we are grateful that we still have the energy and desire to "sailor on" and accomplish whatever needs to be accomplished each day.

Oh, but wait...I forgot to tell you how this morning began. Around 9:00, we received a very loud knock on our boat. The harbor master greeted us with a very gruff, "Well, what are your plans?" Tom explained that we still didn't know when the new radio system would arrive and, therefore, couldn't give him an exact leave date yet. He then told us that the owner of the slip we had been hot berthing in was coming in within the hour, and we would have to move to another slip. We were immediately agreeable, and at this point, his tone softened. He told us which slip to go into, so we quickly changed the fenders and lines over from starboard to port and walked the boat back out of the slip. I drove her down, turned her around, and successfully docked her. What helped me this time was that Tom and I were able to walk down to the other slip and scope it out ahead of time so I could see what was needed for me to successfully dock Havis Amanda. Yea! Mission accomplished!

Well, that is all for today. We are cooking baked sweet potatoes and steamed broccoli for a light dinner as we are both still full of leftover pizza. Later, unless we peter out, we will do laundry and send the latest journal entries. Perhaps we will play cards again tonight. Tom has won four out of the last five games so I have some serious catching up to do.

Good Night from Ketchikan - End of Days 84-85

DAY 86

THIRD LAYOVER DAY: KETCHIKAN

The rain and wind kicked up sometime in the early morning hours, and by early afternoon, as I sat down to write, it appeared to be socked in for the day. As we had not received our new radio unit through the mail yet, we hadn't been able to check the weather conditions out in the strait, but if the weather inside the marina area was any indication of what was going on outside the marina, we were glad to be tied up to a dock all safe and sound, not out battling wind and current on this blustery day. A welcome blessing indeed...all because we had to layover extra days.

Tom and I were talking today about how when things seem to go awry, oftentimes they are a blessing in disguise. Like when the radio unit went belly-up, and we had to order a new one, forcing us to stay in Ketchikan longer than we had planned.

Initially, we said that if we had to do several layover days, we would much rather have been anchored in a beautiful cove somewhere rather than stuck in a marina in Ketchikan. But then, we practiced walking our talk and started looking for the blessings that might come from being here.

The first blessing was the time we spent with my artist friend, Gabi. We visited The Southeast Alaska Discovery Center to view her extensive art exhibit there (as well as another lovely gallery displaying her work), ate a lovely dinner at Cape Fox Lodge and toured a bit more of Ketchikan, all of which gave us a more favorable opinion of the town.

While we were perusing local tourist shops with Gabi, we were given the names of two First Nations jewelry artists to research. Tom and I have been looking for an artist who we could commission to create wedding bands for us that would incorporate carvings of the eagle, raven, sun, and moon. Being given the names of two jewelry artists to check out, was another favorable outcome that resulted from the layover days in Ketchikan.

And then, yesterday, the other Nauticat owners, Laurin and Jackie, gave us the name of a diver to scrub the bottom of our boat and change out the zincs. We wanted to have it done in Friday Harbor, but the port doesn't allow boat owners to do so in the marina for environmental reasons. (Your boat must be hauled out to accomplish this, and we didn't have time to do so before we left to go north.)

So, the young diver, Chevy, and his wife came down today, dove the boat, changed out one bad zinc that was ready to fall off, and scrubbed the bottom. He said that it was very encrusted with barnacles, in fact, the worst boat he had seen in this marina this summer, but that she was now squeaky clean. Tom says Havis Amanda should go much faster now while at the same time using less fuel since there will be less drag on her. Another blessing that occurred because we had extra layover days in Ketchikan.

You know how they say to count your blessings? Well, a couple of other blessings occurred today as well. We took the bus to Walmart to check out buying Straight Talk sim cards to replace our T-Mobile ones until we get back home. If you remember, we have had to greatly curb our data usage. There is not a whit of T-Mobile service anywhere in Alaska, and they have threatened to cut our phone service off completely due to roaming data over-usage. Yikes! Not good!

We were told we could purchase two new sim cards, each with 10GB of data per month, without changing our phone number. That sounded great! Or so we thought.

But, of course, there is more to the story. When we returned to the boat, Tom set out to sign up and activate the new SIM card in his phone. He only got so far before he had to call the Straight Talk people to get help. The customer service rep helped him to get started on the activation process but then told him it would be a full 24 hours before the activation would be complete. This meant he would have no phone usage of any kind until the 24 hours had passed, a detail we were not informed of upfront. Grrr!

Why is it that some angst seems to accompany every blessing? Perhaps it's one way to make sure we humans don't get too cocky and stay humble. We will activate my phone tomorrow, after which we will have to wait another 24 hours, but then, we should both be back in the telephone business.

Later in the afternoon, our friend, Gabi, texted to see if she could stop by. Of course, we said yes! We invited her to have dinner with us...enchiladas and nachos. She accepted and brought gelato and three beers none of us had ever tried before. We had a very pleasant evening eating and telling stories about our lives.

When Gabi departed, Tom finished dishes while I completed today's journal entry. After three days of trying to get the laundry done and the latest journal entries sent, we hope to do so tomorrow...for sure...maybe...

Blessings and challenges alike colored our day, and we learned something valuable from each and every one. Thanks, Universe...I think...

Good Night from Ketchikan - End of Day 86

DAY 87

FOURTH LAYOVER DAY: KETCHIKAN

9:00 OH MY GOODNESS!!! Why is it so incredibly difficult and frustrating to deal with electronics? All we wanted to do was temporarily put Straight Talk sim cards in our phones to use until we got back to Washington and could then go back to T-Mobile. All this because there is no T-Mobile service in all of Alaska, so the whole time we have been here, we have been using roaming data, of which we now have none.

12:00 Tom has spent the last three hours on the phone with T-Mobile and Smart Talk trying to resolve all of this. He was finally able to talk to a customer service rep who was very helpful. Tom is now activated on Straight Talk, but they are still working on getting his data settings finalized. As of now, he has no text, email, or internet. If we ever get this resolved, we will have to go through the whole process again to get my phone activated. AGH! Man! Are we ever being given some lessons in patience! Does it seem like we are learning these lessons yet?

2:10 We are sitting at the local Safeway grocery store because they have the closest Wi-Fi to the marina. We had to come here to download Tom's latest cell phone updates, as the Straight Talk folks think that may be why we are having trouble getting his data going. He downloaded the latest IOS, but unfortunately, this did not solve the problem either. NOPE! We obviously have STILL not mastered the patience lesson!

We are also STILL attempting to find out if the radio unit was shipped out on Friday like the Garmin/Vesper rep said that the CWR people said had happened...but...STILL...no tracking number. That alone was a couple of hours of Tom's day with no resolution in sight. The Garmin/Vesper folks are supposed to call us by 8:00 tomorrow morning with an update. We're crossing our fingers...watch this space...

5:00 Tom is STILL on the phone with Straight Talk reps. Finally, after talking with multiple service reps and going through the same routine with each of them, they said they would connect us to a "higher-up" tech person. The first "higher-up" never called him back. The second two "somehow" got cut off from him and did not call back either.

7:00 I had been holding dinner for quite a long time, so after the last "higher-up" got cut off, Tom decided to bag it for the night and eat dinner. He has been on the phone with Straight Talk, T-Mobile and Garmin/Vesper people a total of 10 non-stop hours just today alone, not counting the three hours yesterday, so before you even ask...

NO, WE OBVIOUSLY HAVE NOT LEARNED OUR PATIENCE LESSON OR WE WOULDN'T STILL BE IN PATIENCE PRACTICING MODE!

And about the laundry that was on our to-do list today? That laundry is STILL in the laundry bags. Maybe tomorrow...or the next day...or...or...

So, what do you think? Do we seem the tiniest bit bitter? If your answer is yes, then you would be correct. We have taken a lot of very deep breaths today to try and stay calm and practice kindness to those who were trying to help us. In fact, we took so many deep breaths that I am surprised we didn't hyperventilate and pass out right there on the floor!

We could sure use some Divine Intervention. If any of you are so inclined to send up a "flash prayer" (as my friend, Marti, calls them) or two, we would be ever so grateful. Hopefully, tomorrow will be less chaotic and more productive. I am hoping that hope really does spring eternal.

Good Night Again from Ketchikan - End of Day 87

DAY 88

FIFTH LAYOVER DAY: KETCHIKAN

Quiet Time this morning

Oh, what a difference a day can make! Thanks to all of you who sent flash prayers, positive thoughts, Light, Love, good juju, and good karma to us and to our phone and radio situations. Whether you sent prayers to God, Jesus, Buddha, Shiva, Great Spirit, Mother Mary, Allah, Yahweh, Source, Creator, Universe, Heavenly Father, Divine Mother, All Our Relations/Ancestors from the North, South, East, and West, or your favorite tree (all of which we have done at one time or another)...IT WORKED!!! What a blessing you are to us. We so appreciate you.

Our day started with an 8:00 wake-up call from Travis, the Garmin/Vesper help desk guy, who had been working on our case for us. He had good news! The CWR Marine company had indeed shipped the radio second day air on Friday, and it was to arrive today. They finally gave Travis the tracking number (which Tom had been begging for since last Thursday), and the radio arrived at my friend Gabi's house in the early afternoon. She lives 40 miles out of town and will bring it in early tomorrow morning. Yea! Finally, some positive news! Our first challenge solved!

After our happy wake-up call, Tom fixed our tea and coffee, and we settled in for Quiet Time. As you know, our Quiet Time consists of an inspirational reading, a discussion of the reading, and setting positive intentions for the day. Well, yesterday, we read from Mark Nepo's *The Book of Awakening*, but we did not take time to discuss it, and more importantly, we did not take time to set positive intentions for our day. Instead, we jumped straight into dealing with the phone and radio issues. So, instead of starting our day on a positive note, we started it from a place of frustration, irritation, and angst. Not good.

I have been taught, and have found from my own experience, that whatever I am endeavoring to do, it is important to start from a place of pure, positive intention.

Unfortunately, that is not what we did yesterday, and so rather than our day unfolding like a river gently flowing downstream, it was as if we were furiously paddling upstream, fighting an out-of-control current raging against us. Again, not good.

So, this morning, we decided we needed to approach the day differently. We set very specific positive intentions; we committed to stay in a mentally happy place; and we asked for wisdom and guidance as to the correct course of action concerning the phone situation.

It is my practice (when I am being my "sane self" and not my "crazed, chaotic-feeling, why-is-the-whole-world-against-me" self) to gather and examine all the information I can about whatever decision I need to make, but then to put aside all that information and just "feel into" the choices that are before me and, as my son, Rupa, says, try to determine which choice "feels lighter." So that is what we did.

After the gathering of info period, we "felt" that we needed to abandon the Straight Talk and T-Mobile carriers and switch to AT&T permanently. Tom said that when he thought about all the options, just thinking about changing to AT&T made him "feel lighter," whereas the idea of dealing with the band-aid we were trying to put on our over usage of roaming data by going with Straight Talk for a month, felt like a very heavy burden. When we looked at how we use our phones in Friday Harbor, as well as when traveling in Canada and Alaska, it made sense to go with a carrier that is widely represented in all three areas...which just happens to be AT&T.

So, we walked ourselves down to the little mall where the AT&T store lives, found out from Juan, the sales guy, what our options were and signed up with them on the spot. We both felt good about the decision. Woohoo! Our second challenge solved.

We then walked back to the boat, ate a quick sandwich, gathered all our laundry together, and headed back up the road to the nearby laundry mat. We were finished in about an hour and a half and walked the clean clothes back to the boat. Finally, after five days of trying to check laundry off our to do list...fait accompli!

We had intended to go out to dinner at the Fish House, a local restaurant that the AT&T guy recommended for their locally caught fresh fish, but we misread the bus schedule and missed the one we needed to take to get us close to that restaurant.

Have you ever tried to read one of those bus schedules? It is like trying to decipher a calculus equation. When we examined the schedule further, we realized we would have to wait a whole hour for the next bus, so we decided to eat in and try again tomorrow night.

We went back down to the boat and fixed a light supper of butter noodles, salad, and cheese bread. Tom worked on designing some boat cards to pass out to new boat friends with our contact info and a lovely photo of Havis Amanda anchored in Kynoch Inlet on them. We printed them out and will use them until we get some glossy card stock, which we feel will enhance the photo.

I talked to my mom, worked on this journal entry, and at midnight, we both crawled into bed, feeling happy and content that our day had been peacefully productive.

We are grateful for everyone and everything in our lives. Thank you all for being a part of our journey.

Good Night Again from Ketchikan - End of Day 88

DAY 89

SIXTH (AND HOPEFULLY) FINAL LAYOVER DAY: KETCHIKAN

Bar Harbor Marina, Ketchikan, Alaska

9:00 Our dear friend, Gabi, arrived this morning with the new Vesper radio unit in hand. Whoopee! She stayed and visited with us for a bit while Tom began installing the radio. After she left to run errands and go on a long hike, Tom contacted Travis at Garmin/Vesper to set up the new radio from his end. Everything appeared to go smoothly...until it didn't.

12:00 Tom is right now trying to input the MMSI number, which identifies us in the AIS system. The radio itself is working, but not that function. Tom attempted to call Travis back, but they would not connect him straight to Travis like they did this morning and insisted Tom leave his name and number for a callback. Go figure. So...again...he waits.

1:00 The call-back from Travis came in, and he stayed on the line to walk Tom through the insertion of the MMSI number into the Cortex radio system. Success!!! Finally!!! Everything electronic seems to be up and running now. Such a relief. No more taking deep breaths...no more hyperventilating...no more passing out on the floor...no more...

2:30 Off to the grocery store for our final provisioning before untying the lines early tomorrow morning and setting off for Foggy Bay. We probably purchased more grocery items than we needed to get us to the next grocery stop in Prince Rupert on Saturday, but...well...you know me. I must have some powerful squirrel energy swirling around in me because I am ALL about being prepared.

3:40 Back on the boat and putting groceries away. We talked to Gabi to see if she would like to join us for dinner at the Fish House, but she was still hiking, so we grabbed the bus schedule and walked up to the bus stop.

4:20 Thankfully, this time we got the time right, hopped on board and were driven to our destination. We both got fresh caught blackened halibut sandwiches and fries that were really good. The people who own the restaurant have their own fishing boat and catch the fish for the restaurant, so it is incredibly fresh and tasty.

6:20 Back on the bus and on our way back to Havis Amanda. Gabi will come down around 8:30 to say goodbye.

8:30-10:00 We had a very nice visit with Gabi. She will be back in Friday Harbor sometime around the first of October, so we will reconnect then. And now, off to bed for a 6:30 leave time in the morning.

Good Night from Ketchikan - End of Day 89

DAY 90

DESTINATION: FOGGY BAY
(Truncated to Bullhead Cove)

Some say that it's a woman's prerogative to change her mind...often, on a whim, and for no good reason, but it has been my experience that men change their minds about as often as women do, on a whim and for no good reason. What happened today was definitely on a whim, but there were good reasons for our change of mind.

We had planned to leave Ketchikan this morning for Foggy Bay to stage for the Dixon Entrance crossing tomorrow. On our way north, we had anchored in Foggy Bay, but our friends, Gabi and Joseph, told us they favored Bullhead Cove. They said the entrance was easier to get into, that there was more swinging room upon anchoring and a decent bottom in which to anchor. They also said it was a prettier spot, with a great view out to Revillagigedo Channel (called Revi Channel by the locals).

We found this all to be true when we <u>both</u> changed our minds, literally in mid-channel, and decided to go into Bullhead Cove instead. We anchored in front of a small islet, jumped into our Fatty Knees dinghy with our crab pot filled with chicken legs and cat food, and headed out to find a good spot to drop our crab pot. We didn't know if this would be a good cove to fish for crab but thought we would give it a try.

We dropped the pot around 11:30, then dinghied over to a beach area to explore. I found several unique rocks and geodes. The geodes looked like quartz crystals to me, but I am not an expert in any way, so I really don't know for sure. I just know they spoke to me and will make a nice addition to our Briggs Lake medicine wheel. We puttered around the beach and made a small medicine wheel and a sculpture out of rocks and an eagle feather (shown in the two photos below) before dinghying back to the boat.

I worked on the journal entry, while Tom scrubbed the hull of Havis Amanda and drove the dinghy around the bay to run the engine. I had put out a nice piece of ling cod to thaw before we left to go exploring, so I marinated it in olive oil, teriyaki sauce, lemon juice and lots of seasonings. I prepared Brussel sprouts to steam, corn on the cob to boil, and sourdough bread to heat in the oven. Mm-um! My mouth is watering at the very thought!

Medicine wheel created on the shore of Bullhead Cove

Rock and eagle feather sculpture created on the shore of Bullhead Cove

We ate our dinner on the back deck and watched the sunset. It was glorious!

We had a wonderful crossing today: warm weather, fair seas, and the joy of being together...it simply doesn't get any better than that. We were glad we had taken our friends' advice to anchor in Bullhead Cove instead of Foggy Bay, as we found it to be a more suitable anchorage all the way around.

This spur-of-the-moment decision to change our plans provided us with the opportunity to venture into unknown territory to discover what magic might just be waiting for us there. Our adventurist spirit had served us well.

Sunset in Bullhead Cove

Good Night from Bullhead Cove - End of Day 90

DAY 91

DESTINATION: PRINCE RUPERT

Sunrise looking back at Bullhead Cove

We arose at 4:00 this morning and untied the lines at 5:00 to get an early start for our nine-hour transit down Revillagigedo Channel, across Dixon Entrance (where we would check into Canada from Alaska), down Chatham Sound, and into Prince Rupert. Crossing Dixon Entrance can be a dicey, lumpy, roly-poly ride, but today, Dixon was on its best behavior, and the seas were relatively calm there, as well as Chatham Sound. Thank you, Weather Gods!

There were several other boats, whose owners we had met at different stages along the way, who were also making the crossing today. It was fun to follow them on our AIS and then to meet up with them when we docked at Cow Bay Marina. As it turned out, Dave and Cathy, a couple we had just met leaving Ketchikan the day before yesterday, ended up right next to us in the marina today.

We hadn't been docked more than about 30 minutes when another boating couple, Marty and Jeri, who keep their boat moored down at Shipyard Cove in Friday Harbor when they are not cruising, showed up at our door to introduce themselves. They had noticed that we, too, hailed from Friday Harbor from the decals on our boat. Needless to say, there was a lot of boat talk amongst us all.

But I am getting ahead of myself. When we called the marina yesterday to get a reservation for tonight, we were told we would be on the outside of the breakwater. But then, when we called to check in right outside the harbor, Max, one of the harbor master's office staff, told us he had put us in a slip instead. That sounded even better...or so we thought. I am going to turn the laptop over to Tom now to describe what happened next.

Tom: *"Three words...TCF. I will let you decipher the acronym. In case you are having trouble, just know...it was not pretty! The only good thing was that Max was standing on the end of the finger to lead us in and give us a hand. Thank you, Max!! This was the furthest slip in, next to the office, boardwalk, storefronts, etc., etc. Get the picture? Lots of onlookers.*

The slip was bow in, port side to, turning to port. Not the best for Havis Amanda (she walks to starboard)...or me...especially at the absolute end of the fairway with boats side tied to the main dock. Did I say tight?

I set up for what I thought would be a fairly straightforward docking. I made my initial turn to port, creeping in under what I thought was good control, only to find out a strong current was pushing me straight toward the boat-filled main dock. S _ _ T!!!

REVERSE...no good...still sliding towards the boats. Forward...get away from the boats! Nowhere to go! I am now sideways in a one-boat slip with my stern literally six inches from crashing into the taxi boat on the main doc and my bow sprit encroaching into the next slip over. Quite a sight! Jandira frantically moved the lines to the starboard side so that we could attempt to turn the boat around, bow out, starboard side to. Max grabbed the lines and pulled Havis Amanda around 180 degrees and got the bow tied. Jandira got the fenders moved over, and we got her tied up. I disappeared into the boat without looking up for fear of the laughter that I was sure was coming from the onlookers above. Pride? None left.

Oh well, as they say, any docking that doesn't hurt the boat, or any boats around you, is a Good One! As I have said before, we sailors have a favorite saying when the anchor goes down: 'Time for an Anchor Down Beer.' I think this calls for Two!"

Yep! It was a fiasco! No doubt about it. But it is these kinds of happenings that make for great stories to tell around the happy hour "campfire." I can't help but wonder if our exit from Cow Marina tomorrow will be anywhere near as entertaining as our entrance. The morning will tell. Watch this Space!

Good Night from Prince Rupert - End of Day 91

DAY 92

DESTINATION: CAPTAIN COVE

*Coming out of dense fog around the Prince Rupert
Harbor area*

You know the expression, "I couldn't see my nose in front of my face"? Well, this morning, for a solid two hours, we could hardly see the bow of the boat in front of us as we left Prince Rupert Harbor. Our transit today was to include going down Arthur Passage into Ogden Channel and finally into Captain Cove, our anchorage for the night. When we left the harbor, there were lots of boats traveling back and forth through the fog and kelp and logs to dodge, but we kept our eyes on the chart plotter and the route Tom had put in for us to follow. When we are in dense fog, we have to totally trust our electronics. And, just like we ask for help from the Debris Dodging Angels when going through a lot of debris, I personally believe it never hurts to enlist the assistance of the Fog Clearing Angels on mornings like this. Which is exactly what we did and look what happened.

The Fog Clearing Angels at work

And...then this. Simply amazing!

When we rounded the corner into Captain Cove, we were pleased to see there was only one other boat anchored in the very back of the cove. Before we dropped anchor, we dropped a crab pot filled with chicken legs at the mouth of a freshwater stream, which is recommended by many as the best place to catch the most crab. Afterward, we anchored in amongst a group of tiny islets, dropped our kayaks, and took off to explore the shoreline. We kayaked around two hours and got some great photos, a couple of which are below.

Captain Cove shoreline

When we got back to the boat, Tom spent the better part of an hour scrubbing the hull. I had intentions of working on the journal entry for today but was so weary that I curled up on the settee and took a 30-minute power nap. I had put two large, sweet potatoes in the oven to bake and spinach in a big pot to steam later before lying down. I woke to the sound of Tom lifting the kayaks back on board, got up, and finished dinner preparations.

Captain Cove shoreline

After dinner, Tom worked on the dishes while I started writing today's journal entry. Usually, when Tom is doing dishes, he puts on music and sings along. Tonight, he played some Nancy Griffith tunes. I found myself with my hands on the keyboard in mid-stroke, pausing to watch and listen to him, and I smiled to myself to see him so happy and free. There is this one Nancy Griffith song, "Tonight at the Five and Dime," that we like to dance to, so when it came on, I went down into the galley and asked if I might have this dance. It was a magical moment.

P.S. There was no current in the Prince Rupert Marina this morning, so exiting was a breeze. Whew!

Good Night from Captain Cove - End of Day 92

DAY 93

DESTINATION: MATH ISLANDS/CLEAR PASSAGE

Leaving Captain Cove this morning

At 7:40 this morning, we had already pulled up anchor and were puttering over to pick up the crab pot we had let soak overnight. We were excited (we caught one large male crab) and disappointed (we caught one large male crab). It was not enough for a meal, but certainly enough for a happy hour appetizer with garlic butter to dip it in. Mmmmm...just like Pavlov's dog, I am already salivating in anticipation at the mere thought. Yum.

As we left the cove, I was at the helm while Tom got out the crab-killing tools and started to work on killing and cleaning the one caught crab. He put the cleaned crab in a ziplock and put it in the refrigerator to keep it cold until we were ready to cook it later this afternoon. I can hardly wait.

We left Captain Cove and headed down Petrel Channel for 23 miles to a part of the Math Islands called Clear Passage. The early morning, patchy fog lifted, and the sun came out, sparkling on the water like diamonds. We had a very peaceful transit down Petrol Channel, enjoying calm seas and warm breezes sprinkled with patches of sun and clouds.

We talked about how very different Northern BC felt in comparison to Alaska, where everything, and I do mean everything, looks and feels bigger than big. Alaska's large expanses of open water and tall, snow-capped mountains are beyond impressive. Now, to be sure, Northern BC also has its share of tall granite mountains (like in Kynoch Inlet and Kwatsi Bay) and large bodies of water (like Queen Charlotte Sound and Dixon Entrance), but there is just an intimate feel to these areas that you simply don't get in Alaska. It is not that we necessarily favor one place over the other. We were just noticing the differences.

We continued on down Petrol Channel and into the Math Islands to our final destination of Clear Passage, making sure to avoid the rocks at the entrance. Tom will take over the explanation from here.

Tom: *"This is a very narrow passage which affords pretty much only a one boat anchorage with very limited swinging room. The wind was being funneled through the head of the inlet, so I decided to tuck into a small nook. This required us to stern tie to shore. We set the anchor, backed down to within 20 feet of shore, and tied to a nice tree. Unfortunately, we now found the wind on our beam, and I didn't like it. I paddled back to shore, untied the line, let the boat swing into the wind, and then tied it to another tree. Problem solved...and you know what that means...Anchor Down Beer Time! Yippee!"*

Stern tie almost complete. Anchor Down Beer Time!!!

We had intended to kayak, but by the time we went through the stern tie process twice, it was about 3:00, so I began to prep everything to make a tuna noodle casserole while Tom got out the large crab cooker to cook our one crab on the bow of the boat. Yes, yes, it was a lot of trouble for one measly crab, but it was only the second one we had caught the whole time we had been gone, and we were determined to enjoy it.

After the water boils, the crab goes in the water for eight-nine minutes, depending on how big it is, of course. Many recipes instruct you to cook them for 15 or more minutes, but I have found from trial and error over the years that that is way too long for my taste. The crab was ready before I could get the casserole in the oven, and freshly cooked crab shouldn't be kept waiting, so we sat out on the stern of the boat and cracked and ate our one beautiful crab. It was finger-licking-good! We have very happy taste buds right now!

The casserole then went into the oven for about an hour while I wrote, and Tom worked on tomorrow's route, which was to be one of the trickiest we have navigated so far. When the casserole was ready, we sat out on the stern again to eat dinner and enjoy the evening.

I came in to write while Tom worked cleaning up the dishes. I kept dozing off with my fingers on the computer keys poised in mid-stroke, so I finally bagged it and got ready to join Tom in bed. I have been especially tired over the last several days. We have been going full tilt from early morning to pretty late at night, and I simply hit a wall.

I crawled into bed thinking I would go straight to sleep, but Tom had a movie queued up that he knew I liked. The movie ended at midnight, and I knew 6:00 would come mighty early. Another night without my preferred eight hours of sleep. Oh well, life is good no matter how much sleep I get.

Good Night from Clear Passage - End of Day 93

DAY 94

DESTINATION: IRE INLET

The skinny entrance into Ire Inlet we had just scooted through

Last evening, Tom spent a considerable amount of time figuring out what time we would have to leave today in order to go through Ala Passage North and the Ala Narrows on our way to Ire Inlet for tonight's anchorage. You see, this passage must be navigated at high water, especially the entrance to Ire Inlet, as it is no more than about 50 feet across and is almost dry at zero tide. Havis Amanda is approximately 45 feet long, so we certainly don't want to get sideways in this narrow entrance.

Tom: *"When we woke this morning at 6:00 to leave our anchorage by 7:00, we were unsure if we wanted to transit the Narrows with the tide ebbing out at 7:00 or flooding back in around 1:00. Back to bed. We needed the sleep anyway.*

We ended up leaving the anchorage at 12:40 and wound our way through Ala Passage, which, if viewed from above, must have looked like we were a couple of drunk sailors. We thought we would be out of the wind, but we were wrong as it was being funneled down through the 50-foot-wide ditch that we had to pass through. It was running like a river through that little cut (exciting, to say the least), but "Captain" Jandira was more than up to the task and brought us through without a scratch!"

There was one other boat already anchored at the head of Ire Inlet when we entered, so we anchored in a spot before and to the right of that boat. Later, another boat came in, stopped to say hello and then went on to anchor at the head of the bay with the first boat. It was around 3:00 already, so no kayaking today.

We prepared a snack of cheese, crackers, grapes, and a sliced ripe peach and sat out on the back of the boat to eat and enjoy the warm, breezy afternoon. Thankfully, I had made enough tuna noodle casserole for three nights, so we didn't have to cook tonight from scratch. Tom made a beautiful salad with all of the basics, as well as fresh strawberries, sliced almonds, feta cheese, and dried cranberries to go with the tuna casserole.

We ate dinner in the pilot house, as it had gotten too blustery and cold after the sun dropped lower in the sky to eat out on the back deck. As per usual, Tom did the dishes while I worked on today's journal entry. It is now 9:15 and still light outside, but the days are definitely growing shorter. Earlier in the summer, it was light from around 2:30 in the morning until 11:00 at night. Simply off-the-chart spectacular to have all that daylight in which to play!

Ok...off to bed now to prepare for a leave time of 6:00 tomorrow morning.

Good Night from Ire Inlet - End of Day 94

DAY 95

DESTINATION: TUWARTZ INLET

Red skies in the morning...sailor take warning

There is a sailor's expression: "Red skies in the morning, sailor take warning...Red skies at night, sailor's delight." **Uh oh.** We have been in an area where we can't get weather reports on the VHS, so we were having to rely on information we got three days ago.

Last evening, when the elderly couple came into Ire Inlet to anchor, they told us the weather was forecasted to be mild for a couple of days. The last weather report we had heard predicted 15-25-knot winds today, so if the gentleman was right, the weather had improved. But...was he right? Or was the red sky this morning warning us to stay put?

Transiting out of Ire Inlet this morning

Well, true adventurers that we are, we decided to "go forth into the unknown" to see for ourselves. We knew there were places along the way that we could tuck into if the "red skies" were right and if the gentleman was right, well, so much the better.

As we pulled up anchor, it began to rain. We had on our lightweight raincoats but not our foul-weather gear because, initially, it was just drizzling. We had to go back through the narrow entrance of Ire Inlet right away, so we had no time to change into our heavier rain gear.

Because Tom wants me to have as much experience in these narrow places as possible, he rarely gets to drive through them, so we decided this morning that fair is fair, and it should be his turn to have all the "fun." As we were transiting through, we discovered that the chart plotter was not entirely correct, so we had to use our eyes and good judgment to carefully navigate through. Tom did a stellar job of getting us safely through to the other side, down Ala Passage, and into Principe Channel...with the help of our On-Call Emergency Navigation Angels, of course! Much appreciated!

We traveled down Principe Channel for about three hours, through Otter Channel, around McCreight Point, and into Tuwartz Inlet for a total of five-plus hours. It looked as though the "red skies in the morning" warning mostly referred to rain, as the seas were calm and the winds were quite light. Yep! We were in good hands today. Thank you, Weather Gods and Sea Goddesses!

Tom describes going through the entrance to Tuwartz Inlet in this way: *"We had a very skinny entrance into Tuwartz Inlet like we did in Ire Inlet, 50 feet or less across, so we had to stay on our toes. The entrance is hard to see until you are right on top of it. As you enter the entrance, the obvious route is also hard to make out as the route is circuitous and blocked by many exposed rocks. Successful entrance and transit require a good, plotted route and prior study so that you have an idea of what's coming. Though the route is not obvious, if you trust the route you have plotted and follow it, it's easily doable. The least depth found on a 3.75-foot low tide was 15 feet at the narrowest part."*

Tom had driven through the early morning narrow sections, so I was to drive through Tuwartz Inlet. I drove through all but the last little section. Even though I had the route plotted in front of me, it just didn't seem possible to go the way the route indicated. I got unnerved at the last minute and turned the helm over to Tom. As usual, after I saw the route in its entirety, I knew I could have accomplished it, so when we leave in the morning and retrace our route back through it, I should be able to handle it just fine. Fingers crossed.

Principe Channel or Otter Channel (Honestly not sure which!)

We motored into the inlet and dropped anchor in a nook in the northeast corner of the inlet. I have been practicing putting on the anchor bridle, which is used to take the shock off of the anchor chain and the windlass. After a bit of hit and miss, I was successful.

We fixed chicken and Swiss cheese sandwiches and chips for lunch with a side of grapes. I worked on the journal entry for today while Tom read about different routes we could take on our way home. Should we basically retrace our steps or find new anchorages to explore? We need to figure this out today, so we will know where to go next. Watch this space.

A decision has been made! Except for a few new anchorages, we have decided on our way south to revisit some of the same anchorages we stayed in on our way north and then revisit several of our favorite spots from our trip up into the Broughton Islands last summer. I will see Ocean Falls, Codville, and Bootleg Cove for the first time, and Tom and I will together experience Pruth Bay, Jones Cove, Nigei Cove, Egmont, and Princesses Louisa for the first time.

We're excited! We have a plan that we feel good about. It gives us a few new anchorages to explore and provides us with the rest and relaxation we both need by going back to some familiar places.

The rain had finally stopped, so after a supper of leftovers and salad, we sat with the doors open and enjoyed the quiet evening. It was now high tide, and the anchorage looked completely different from when we first came in and dropped anchor. These last few anchorages have been in remote, wild places that we have enjoyed immensely. We are so glad we chose to follow the "Outside Inside Passage" on our way back south.

We have become so spoiled with the almost solitary anchorages we have stayed in while in Alaska and in Northern BC, that we are not sure how we will handle being back in the Gulf Islands and San Juan Islands anchored with lots of other boats. It will be quite an adjustment.

Our anchorage at high tide

Good Night from Tuwartz Inlet - End of Day 95

DAY 96

DESTINATION: KHUTZE BAY

Between the mouth of Tuwartz Inlet and Wright Sound

When the alarm rang at 5:00, it was still dark...the first time we had experienced crawling out of bed in darkness since we left in April. Considering that the whole time we were in Alaska, it didn't get dark until around 2:30 in the morning and light again until 4:30ish, that was quite a change for us. It certainly is a sign of fall being just around the corner. So, we gladly put off getting up for 30 more minutes. Yes! More sleep!

Well, not really. We neither one went back to sleep, but instead talked through the upcoming day, and how to better navigate back through Tuwartz Inlet...the narrows that I chickened out on mid-way through yesterday.

It was high tide this morning, unlike yesterday when we transited the narrows at mid tide. The water is deeper at high tide...which obviously has its advantages... but makes it harder to see the underwater rocks. Because of this, it is even more crucial to follow your electronic charts to the letter. *"Stay on your course,"* Tom always says...which I did.

For me, navigating through these tight, rock-ridden routes feels like a combination of nerve-wracking-white-knuckle-hold-your-breath-terror and adrenalin-rush-amusement-park-log-ride-fun. I breathe a huge sigh of relief when I am through and on the other side and somehow manage not to hit a rock or run aground.

For those of you interested in our exact route today, after we came through Tuwartz Inlet, we transited between Farrant and Finn Islands, around the north end of Gil Island, across Wright Sound, down McKay Reach, into Fraser Reach, and finally into Khutze Inlet for the night.

A steady rain intermingled with bouts of fog made up our weather today, so we piloted Havis Amanda from the inside helm station for most of the day. The windows fogged up, so we turned on our fancy "defrost" system of fans and opened doors to keep the airflow going. This helped but made for a cold, breezy, wet ride when the rain blew in the doors. That's one thing you don't deal with when you live in a house on land. Yeah, there are definitely sacrifices we sailors make just to be on the water, but I gotta tell you, it is more than worth it. For example: HUMPBACK WHALES sighted today...three different times along our route!!!

It is very hard to get good snapshots of whales, but Tom was able to catch some of their antics on video. All of the other times we have seen whales, they have primarily been coming up to blow or swimming along going somewhere only they knew the destination of, but today, we sighted this one whale all by itself leaping in the air and flapping its fins. We stopped the boat for a good 10 minutes just to sit and watch it play. It was a sight to see.

When later we rounded the corner to Khutze Bay, our anchorage for the night, we were hailed by the Khutze Watchmen who were doing a study of the bears in that area. The Watchmen are First Nations folks who oversee particular areas. We told them where we planned to anchor, and they okayed our choice. They had a yurt set up from which to do their research and, I would guess, to live on a temporary basis, as Khutze Bay is a ways from any kind of civilization.

We dropped anchor in a steady rain. Low hanging clouds were draped over the tops of the mountains, a wispy mist hovered mid-way above the water. It felt other-worldly and more than a little spooky, as seen in the photo below.

Ghostly clouds draped over the mountain tops in Khutze Inlet

After supper, Tom and I sat in the pilot house with the boat doors open listening to the rain. We were amazed as we watched a group of about 30 seagulls fly around and then land in a couple of trees, lined up eight to ten on each branch.

From a distance, they looked like a string of white Christmas lights strung around the tree. They were too far away to get a decent photo of them, but I think, if you look closely, you can get the idea from the one I posted below.

A string of seagull-Christmas-tree-lights

We have plenty of water caught from the rain-catching system Tom designed a few weeks back, so we will take a nice, hot shower later tonight, then crawl into our toasty-warm and comfy bed. It will feel soooo good after traveling all day in a cold, drizzly rain. I can hardly wait!

We have a 46-mile transit to Kynoch Inlet tomorrow to stay for three days. It is one of our very favorite anchorages, and we are excited to revisit this quiet, serenely beautiful inlet. There is not a whit of cell signal there, so no journal entries will be forthcoming for a few days. Watch this space.

Good Night from Khutze Inlet - End of Day 96

DAY 97

DESTINATION: KYNOCH INLET

Tom spraying off the anchor chain while raising the anchor

Tom and I both woke with a sense of peace this morning, which was, for me, at least, much different than my frame of mind yesterday morning. My mom was to be taken by one of her caregivers and another friend to Anacortes that morning for a nuclear stress test, which consisted of a ferry ride...without me...and a long day of tests...without me...and a ferry ride back...did I mention "without me"...and she's 95 years old! I was experiencing a bit of "bad daughter syndrome" because I couldn't be there with her. I even went so far as to worry what other people would think about me being on a four-month "jaunt" while my elderly mother was dealing with medical issues...again...without me. Even though I had contingency plans put in place for caregivers to take care of any issues she might have before leaving on our trip, I still felt a twinge of guilt at not being there for her. Even though she lives in an assisted living community and is extremely well taken care of, I still felt I was letting her down. And to top it all off...we had no cell service...only the In Reach system...which is cumbersome to use on our end, making communication difficult.

Looking back into Khutze Inlet upon leaving this morning

So, that is how my day started yesterday. But, thanks to our Quiet Time, I was able to talk through those feelings with Tom and come back to my center...my place of inner peace...of accepting "what is." After that, I was mostly able to go through the day knowing I had done all I could to keep her safe in my absence and that the rest was up to Spirit. Thankfully, her caregiver was able to contact us on the In Reach system to tell us that all went well, and the stress test showed no sign of heart problems. Good News! A sense of relief flooded over me that carried me through yesterday and into today.

When we left Khutze Inlet this morning, it had finally quit raining and a few spots of blue sky were peeking through the low hanging wispy clouds. Tom pulled up the anchor and sprayed it and the anchor chain off as it came up from the deep.

Our route today was to come out of Khutze Inlet, turn left, and travel down Frazer Reach into Hiekish Narrows, into Sheep Passage, down Mathieson Channel, and into Kynoch Inlet. Our anchorage at the head of Kynoch Inlet was one of our favorites on the journey north back in May. We plan to stay there for three gloriously peaceful days.

We had a six-and-a-half-hour journey today filled with tall, towering mountains, calm seas, light to no wind, and seagulls gliding along beside us. As we sat out at the upper helm, we talked about how we both felt so peaceful and content...like all was right in the world...well, in our world at least. About how being away from the negative news that is broadcast every day has greatly diminished our overall stress levels. How being surrounded by so much beauty has had such a calming, healing effect on us on so many levels. How we wished our friends and family could experience what we have on this journey. How we will be sad to leave these wild and wonderous places. And how we will most certainly be back!

When we finally turned into Kynoch Inlet, it felt like coming home. We rode along at a brisk seven knots most of the way down the inlet, enthralled by the majesty all around us. We found two "pictures" in the rocks: one of an elephant (top photo below) and another of a face with a droopy right eye and heart-shaped mouth (bottom photo). Can you pick them out of the photos below? We have so much fun looking for faces, animals, and designs that nature has created in the rocks over the years.

As soon as the anchor was down and a crab pot was dropped, a Kynoch First Nations Watchman boat came by and very politely told us we were not allowed to crab in Kynoch Inlet. The First Nations tribe owns the Kynoch land and is trying to ensure it doesn't get over-fished. So, Tom got right back in the dinghy, motored back over, and pulled the pot up to find five crabs had entered the trap in approximately 15 minutes. Sadly, there were five large keepers...if we had been allowed to keep them, that is. Back into the water, they went. I'd say those were some pretty relieved and happy crabs, wouldn't you?

We had tuna sandwiches for lunch and will have leftover enchiladas and salad for dinner. Tom sat on the bow watching a mama bear and her two cubs feeding in the tall grasses over on shore and called for me to come out to watch them with him through the binoculars. So cool!

We are tired but content to be in one of our preferred anchorages for the next few days. We will kayak tomorrow, rest, relax, and just Be.

Good Night from Kynoch Inlet - End of Day 97

DAY 98

FIRST LAYOVER DAY: KYNOCH INLET

Kayaking around the shoreline in Kynoch Inlet

Sleeping in until 8:00 this morning was pure luxury. We had a long, unhurried Quiet Time, leisurely drank our coffee and tea, and read from *The Book of Awakening*. We talked about the journey we are taking together...not just the journey into Canada and Alaska, but the journey we are taking together in life itself and where it might be taking us.

Tom made the comment, *"You and I are born anew every day. We don't just get in a lane and stay there. We take this fork and that fork...we don't let ourselves get stagnant...or complacent. We like to explore and see what's on down the road, and I want us to do that for the rest of our lives together."* Well said. I truly want that, too!

And that is just what we plan to do, so we started this day of exploration by climbing down into our kayaks and heading out. When we were here in May, we kayaked along the north shore but had not explored the opposite shoreline.

We had also not investigated Culpepper Lagoon, which extends two and a half miles southeast of the head of Kynoch Inlet. This Lagoon is entered by means of a shallow 100-yard-long narrows, which is poorly charted and can be intimidating. We kayaked through today about an hour before low water slack but only stayed for a short time as the tide was about to change, and the current would be flooding in against us going back out. We plan to go back in tomorrow during the mid tide ebbing currents so that we can get back through the narrows before the flood begins and enjoy a ride back out.

After our brief exploration of Culpepper Lagoon, we kayaked down the south side of the inlet and got some great photos of the rocks and their unique patterns and colorations. One photo is posted above, and the other is directly below. We kayaked a good ways down that side before crossing the inlet to go back to the waterfall we had visited in May.

When we reached the other side, we pulled our kayaks up on shore and set off to walk up the creek bed to the base of the waterfall. A much smaller stream of water flows down now as the snow from the top of the mountain has mostly melted. There was still enough water, however, to form a nice pool. We plan to come back tomorrow to take our first swim of the trip. It will be icy cold, but we think we are hearty enough to withstand a bit of chill. Afterall, as Tom says, *"Let's explore and see what's on down the road"*...or swimming hole in this case.

Doesn't this swimming hole look inviting? We sure think so!

We picked up several stones there on the beach to bring back on board. We have also been collecting heart-shaped rocks to make a heart medicine wheel as well. Most of the stones here on the beach are sparkly and black...probably granite...and quite unique.

While we were exploring the beach area and listening and watching for bears, Tom found where two big rocks had most likely fallen in a landslide. When they landed they were leaning into each other and formed a cave-like space between them. We crawled in and sat for a bit. We had found our own little hidey-hole. The two photos below give you an idea of what it looks like.

As we were walking back to our kayaks, Tom saw a small field of wildflowers and gathered some to bring back to the boat to make a bouquet for me. (So romantic!) There were two shades of purple, along with white and yellow ones. Quite pretty, really.

When we got back to the boat, we had a happy hour snack of olives and cream cheese spread on crackers...one of Tom's family's recipes and one of our favorites. Tom then worked on the windlass while I started on today's journal entry. Later, we fixed a dinner of sautéed green peppers, onions, mushrooms, and sundried tomatoes over egg noodles with pesto and parmesan cheese. Tom made a crispy-fresh salad and flaky Red Lobster biscuits. Scrumptious!

It is a lovely night, so we may sit out on the back deck...that is if the bugs don't eat us alive...the gnats and deer flies have been a source of some irritation all afternoon.

Ok...enough for now. We will spend one more glorious day in this stunningly beautiful place and then be off to Rescue Bay on Sunday and Shearwater on Monday, where we hope to have cell service and send out the last several journal entries.

Moon over Kynoch Inlet

Good Night from Kynoch – End of Day 98

DAY 99

SECOND LAYOVER DAY: KYNOCH INLET

Dinghying in Culpepper Lagoon

I am going to dispense with the usual and cut straight to the highlights of our day: kayaking in Culpepper Lagoon and swimming in a pool at the base of a waterfall in Kynoch Inlet.

First, Tom got the dinghy ready for us to take a five-mile round-trip ride up into Culpepper Lagoon. We decided against the kayaks because we wanted to go all the way to the head of the lagoon, and we knew the dinghy would be quicker...especially since we planned to swim later and might not have time to do both before the tide changed around 2:00. It is important to time going in and coming out of the lagoon with the tides as there can be fast moving rapids if it is in mid tide, whether it is ebbing or flooding, and we hoped to avoid them both coming and going. This is a neap tide, so we thought it would be doable no matter when we transited through them.

The shoreline in Culpepper Lagoon

When Tom was getting the dinghy ready, the deer flies swarmed all around him, so before we left, we sprayed insect repellant all over us both...Yuck. Thankfully, it did provide us with some relief from those pesky buggers.

Once we got into the lagoon, we puttered around the shoreline, snapping photos of the rocks. As we motored along, we did a lot of ooooo-ing and ahhhhh-ing at the sight of so much beauty on display. Mother Nature sure does have an amazing talent for creating art, doesn't she? Simply amazing!

After our Culpepper Lagoon exploration, we dinghied back to Havis Amanda, gathered together two towels and headed for the waterfall down the way.

When we got to the mouth of the stream, we stopped, pulled the dinghy up on shore, tied her off, scrambled over the creek rocks to the mouth of the waterfall, and began to strip off our clothes.

It is a very protected spot surrounded by rocks, trees, and bushes. If you didn't already know it was there, you would never guess. It was so cool (literally and figuratively) to have our very own private swimming hole.

Refreshed and happy after our swim. Our smiles say it all.

When we first began to test the water, we were both a little hesitant at the thought of putting our whole bodies into such freezing cold water, but in the end, our adventurous spirit won the day. We were not going to deny ourselves this memorable experience over a bit of cold water.

We cautiously dipped our feet in the water, then slowly began to splash it on our arms and legs. We graduated to our bellies and finally splashed water on each other's backs. Brrrrr!!!

There was a lot of squealing and laughing that took place as we worked up the nerve to immerse ourselves in this frigid water, but at some point, we just took the plunge, dropping our whole bodies into the pool.

It was a bit of a shock to our systems (I'm pretty sure our goose bumps had goose bumps!), but it wasn't long before our bodies adjusted to the cold temperature, and we were swimming around giggling and splashing one another like two little kids. When we could no longer stand the cold water, we crawled out and leaned our bodies up against the large, sunbaked rocks that surrounded the pool. After we warmed up a bit, we dried off and redressed, feeling refreshed and happy.

I do believe we will remember this waterfall-swimming-hole experience as one of our fondest memories. We were so glad that we took the "plunge" on this fine sunny day.

Afterward, we dinghied back to the boat and while Tom got busy putting the kayaks and dinghy back on board, I started to work on today's journal entry. When he finished, and while I was still writing, he chopped up red potato chunks to roast and broccoli to steam. I stopped writing long enough to season the potatoes and prepare the lingcod to marinate so it would be ready to grill later. Then, back to writing while the potatoes roasted.

Later, I steamed broccoli while Tom grilled two nice pieces of lingcod. We enjoyed a healthy dinner but came away feeling stuffed (although not too stuffed to partake of several tasty spoonsful of Greek yogurt later in the evening).

We, of course, sat out on the stern of the boat to breathe in the crisp night air and soak up the last remnants of the setting sun on our last evening here. Kynoch Inlet has been our very favorite anchorage so far. Her overall beauty and quietude really can't be adequately described, so I will leave you with a photo of her magnificence.

Good Night from Kynoch Inlet - End of Day 99

DAY 100

DESTINATION: RESCUE BAY

Havis Amanda stern tied in Rescue Bay

We reluctantly pulled up anchor and motored back down Kynoch Inlet into Mathieson Channel at 8:30 this morning. We hated to leave our favorite anchorage of the trip, but grateful to have had three glorious weather days there. We had one of the smoothest seas we have had so far, with little to no wind. It was quite a pleasant morning motoring toward Rescue Bay with no other boats in sight.

We navigated in between several islets to enter the bay at 12:05, and in that we were the first boat in the bay, we got our pick of the anchorages. We dropped anchor in a tiny nook just inside the entrance to get out of what was forecasted to be a northwest wind tonight and tomorrow, and Tom decided to stern tie.

Later that afternoon, the wind came up from a different direction than was predicted, so he pulled up the anchor, and we moved to a better spot, this time without the stern tie. Then, as is typical, the wind laid down. We liked the second anchorage better than the first and decided to stay right where we were.

We embarked on a kayak trip around Susan Island and came upon a massive bed of kelp, as pictured in the two photos below.

Tom paddling through a kelp bed outside of Susan Island

We paddled around for about an hour and a half. We had been noticing for a couple of days that my kayak appeared to be taking on water. On this day, a lot more water was creeping in, so when we got back to the boat, Tom checked it out and found the problem: the seat posts had separated from the hull, which resulted in a crack that allowed water to seep in. In examining his own kayak, he discovered the same issue was starting to occur. He repaired them both using epoxy. Now, we wait to see if it works.

The wind seemed to pick up again while we were kayaking but then died down almost as quickly. We got an updated local weather report from another boater who said the winds had been downgraded. Only time will tell, I guess.

As we were eating dinner, a fellow sailor and his wife, Peter and Ann, motored into the bay. We had met them at the Canadian check-in dock in Van Isle and later ran into them at a few marinas along the way. We hailed them on the radio to say hello. After they had dinner, Peter rowed his dinghy over to our boat to visit and catch up on our respective journeys.

After he left, we had yogurt and fresh mangos, and I finished the journal entry. We leave at 6:00 tomorrow morning for Shearwater to do laundry, provision, and get fuel and water. It would be a five-and-a-half-hour transit, so we crawled into bed early to make sure I could get my required eight hours of sleep. Sleep tight; don't let the bed bugs (or deer flies, in our case) bite!

Good Night from Rescue Bay - End of Day 100!!!

DAY 101

DESTINATION: SHEARWATER MARINA

Sunrise coming down Mathieson Channel

We pulled up anchor at low tide this morning and navigated around rocks that were not visible when we anchored yesterday at high tide. We had a fun passage in very quiet seas, little to no wind, blue skies, and warm temperatures. We steered from the upper helm as we continued motoring on down Mathieson Channel, crossed Perceval Narrows, into Reid Passage (that was a fun ride), down Seaforth Channel, and into Shearwater Marina. This resort/marina was purchased in 2021 by the Heiltsuk Tribal Council, with funds secured through reconciliation agreements. Our plan was to stay for one night to do laundry, provision, get fuel, and water up.

We called into the Shearwater Marina harbormaster to reserve a side tie for the night and were given a spot. We were told our assigned moorage would have no power, but that was not a problem, as we typically run the generator a few hours each day when at anchor anyway.

Upon entering the marina area, we decided to purchase fuel before mooring for the night. The entrance to the marina fuel dock is fairly straightforward, so I had no docking issues, but we certainly did experience some serious sticker shock at how expensive the fuel costs had become. In fact, the price per gallon ($9.00+) was almost double what we paid in Alaska and two dollars more per gallon than when we came through Shearwater two months ago. Unbelievable!

After fueling up, I drove Havis Amanda over to where we were to side tie, and again, the docking was as easy as could be. We immediately gathered together our laundry and our loonies and toonies (Canadian one and two dollar coins) and headed up the dock to the laundry facility at the top of the ramp. We enjoyed the sunshine and played Solitaire on our phones while we waited on our laundry, each winning one game against the other.

After laundry duties, we needed to provision. The small grocery store there was very low on supplies as the barge that brings in food every two weeks was not coming in until Wednesday...two days away. We were fresh-veggie-hungry, but alas...there were none to be had that day. We decided to make do with what they had in stock and the dry and canned goods we still had on board until our next provision stop in Port McNeil.

After all our chores were finished, we started thinking about dinner but decided against eating at the restaurant there above the docks. It wasn't good the last time we were here, and another couple we knew said they had eaten there earlier today, and it was still quite mediocre. We opted for Tom's homemade pizza and bought pumpkin pie for dessert instead. Way better!

There were several folks on the dock that we had met along the way, so it was like old home week. It is always fun to talk boats with fellow cruisers.

Tomorrow, we leave for Ocean Falls for two days. Tom spent a month there in 2019 on his former boat, Evening Star, but I have never been there. It is a very unique place that I am sure I will have much to say about in tomorrow's journal entry.

Shearwater Marina at dusk

Good Night from Shearwater Marina - End of Day 101

DAY 102

DESTINATION: OCEAN FALLS

Looking down Cousins Inlet

After coming out of Shearwater Marina this morning, we took a right into Gunboat Passage (a winding, rock-strewn route that required close navigation), then up Fisher Channel, up Cousin Inlet, and into Ocean Falls. It was a beautiful transit consisting of calm seas and a very light breeze. We have had great weather for cruising for several days running now, including five straight days of sun. It's hard not to have a smile on our faces in weather like this. It's been truly wonderful!

Our destination today was Ocean Falls, a sleepy little town accessible only by boat or plane, where a population of 25 grows to about 100 in the summer. This once-thriving town became almost a ghost town after the Crown Zellerbach Company closed down in the early 1970s. Their factories were in dire need of upgrades and reparations, but the remoteness of the village and the cost of the upgrades made it cost-prohibitive for the company to stay in business. By March 1973, Zellerbach pulled the plug and stopped manufacturing. Ocean Falls was out of business.

This unique community is an inexpensive place to live, but everyday conveniences can be hard to come by. Due to its remoteness, food and other supplies only come in every other week (this after they have been on a supply barge for that long), so fresh produce and basic staples can be difficult to come by.

Most of the houses have long sense been abandoned or are in various states of ruin, but the town still has some of its charm. There is an ice cream shop that also serves a limited breakfast, homemade bread, and various other pastries. Little else can be found in this quaint little town other than a post office, a small public dock, a relatively new state-of-the-art ferry terminal (that is in use only in the summer months), a small craft shop and a pub located in the living room of one of the colorful local residents. Look for the red light on the front porch, signifying the bar is open for business somewhere around five o'clock, that is if he is not working down in town.

As we entered the bay, we dropped a crab pot in front of the old Crown Zellerbach factory before tying up to the small public dock. After we tied up and settled in for the day, Tom and I walked up past the dam that not only powers Ocean Falls but Bella Bella and Shearwater as well. This dam also provides power and water to the controversial hatchery and rearing pen facility for Atlantic salmon smolt for fish farms, as well as for a computer-based cryptocurrency "mining" company that moved into one of the old buildings in 2018.

We continued walking up the gravel road to Link Lake and took a swim. It was cold but very refreshing. I treaded water for a bit of exercise, and Tom sat up on a very long log to get some sun. We swam back and forth from the shore to some lashed-together logs out in the lake that provided an enclosed swimming area.

We were the only swimmers there at first, but later, two other gentlemen came to swim too. One's name was John, a geologist who had retired and moved here over a year ago to live full-time. He said living in Ocean Falls had way more advantages than disadvantages. We didn't get a chance to ask him what they were, but we felt we knew: peace, quiet, a small, close-knit community, a beautiful lake to swim in, and, as John said, nobody telling him what he could and could not do.

We walked back down the hill, stopped at the local ice cream shop, and each ordered a double dip. We sat in the funky outdoor area in front of the shop to enjoy our cool treat. A gentleman across the street was working in his garage building a tree house on land, not up in a tree...but hey...who says a tree house has to be in a tree?

The Ocean Falls folks were friendly yet reserved. We enjoyed our one-day stay but decided not to opt for two. There was not much more to see there, and the swarms of biting gnats almost ate us alive. We chose instead to travel on to Rosco Inlet, which we understand is a lot like Kynoch. We will be up early tomorrow, so it is bedtime for us now.

Nighty-Night from Ocean Falls - End of Day 102

DAY 103

DESTINATION: ROSCO INLET, QUARTCHA BAY

Tom extracting two crabs from the crab pot early this morning

The very first thing we did this morning was to motor over to the head of Cousins Inlet (right off the shore where the hatchery and the cryptocurrency buildings are located) to pull up the crab pot we had dropped to soak all night. Two unfortunate crabs were keepers. Maybe their last meal of salmon heads made up for their early demise this morning. Thank you, tasty crabs, for giving your life for our dinner tonight. Truly.

I drove Havis Amanda back out of Cousins Channel while Tom cleaned the crabs, rinsed off the decks, put away the crab pot, coiled the ropes, and stowed the fenders. We turned from Cousins Channel, into Fisher Channel, and then into Johnson Channel, where tall trees covered the mountains on both sides of the channel. The water was as calm as a mill pond with almost no breeze at all, the sun out in all her glory. Simply magnificent!

Bow-riding crab...he won't be enjoying the view this fine morning

Sun rising over Fisher Channel

Working on today's journal entry

Later, I sat on the stern to work on today's journal entry while Tom piloted the boat up Rosco Inlet about 20 miles and into our anchorage in Quartcha Bay for the night. The transit up this inlet was so enchanting that I simply couldn't bring myself to stay inside. As we motored along, I couldn't help but ponder the whole of our journey north up to this point...knowing full well it would be coming to an end much quicker than we would like.

A dear friend of ours wrote a comment to one of our recent journals that mirrors what Tom and I have often talked about: *"What is evident more than anything else, is how much this really is a journey, yours and Tom's journey. Not just a cruise in a boat to a single destination, but an experience and passage of growing, exploring,* and *loving."* So very true.

Which then brought to mind the following excerpt from *The Book of Awakening,* by Mark Nepo, that Tom and I read each morning: *"The simple rose, at each moment of its slow blossoming, is as open as it can be. The same is true for our lives. In each stage of our unfolding, we are as stretched as possible...It helps to see ourselves as flowers. If a flower were to push itself to open faster, which it can't, it would tear. Yet we humans can and often do push ourselves. Often we tear in places no one can see. When we push ourselves to unfold faster or more deeply than is natural, we thwart ourselves. For nature takes time, and most of our problems of will, stem from impatience...Perhaps one of the hardest remedies to accept for our pain of becoming is that wherever we are in our path...no matter how flawed or incomplete...is a blossoming unto itself."*

This has been a hard lesson for me to learn throughout my lifetime. I tend to be a perfectionist, who probably never perfected anything, honestly, but that certainly never stopped me from trying. Truth be told, I still have these tendencies, but I am trying to learn to accept that wherever I am on "the path" is perfectly ok.

As Tom put it, *"Don't be like a rubber band that is stretched too tight or past its limitations, or you will break. But, if, on the other hand, you behave like a rubber band that has become brittle from being too stagnant and not growing, you can break as well."* Wise words from a very wise man.

As a couple, our intention for this four-month journey on the water, as well as our life journey together in general, has been to learn and grow and evolve...to become the very best versions of ourselves as individuals and as a couple that we can possibly be.

In reference to this, Tom recently said, *"You and I are like two peas in the same pod, nourished by the same roots, growing together as one."* How beautiful is that?

So, as each day brings new anchorages, new acquaintances who develop into new friends, and new adventures to experience, we are growing, being careful not to grow too far too fast. And, along the way, we are becoming more accepting and supportive of where each of us is on our individual journey to wholeness.

OK...enough philosophizing for one day.

As we entered Quartcha Bay, we dropped a crab pot from the bow of the boat to be picked up tomorrow morning before going to the head of Rosco Inlet. We maneuvered slowly, searching methodically to find a suitable place to anchor, as our electronic charts did not match the actual ground. The charts showed us on the ground when we were actually in deep water. Hmmmm...that's unsettling. Go figure.

We dropped the anchor, weren't satisfied, pulled it up, and reset it in deeper water. When we were finally happy with the anchorage, I worked on the journal entry for the day while Tom plotted tomorrow's route and routes for the next couple of days.

The wind picked up considerably, creating white caps in the bay where we were anchored, so we opted not to kayak. It is typical in these long, winding fiords for the wind to funnel down through the channel in the afternoons. It was very breezy, which helped to keep the deer flies at bay, and thankfully, no biting gnats seemed to be in the area. We have bites all over us from those pesky little critters in Ocean Falls yesterday.

A bit later, Tom cooked the two crabs we caught this morning, and I prepared boiled red potatoes and carrots. We had eaten nachos for happy hour and were not very hungry, so a lighter dinner was in order.

It has been a glorious day, and we are grateful to be alone in this spectacular anchorage for the evening.

Anchored in Quartcha Bay

Good Night from Quartcha Bay - End of Day 103

DAY 104

DESTINATION: CODVILLE LAGOON

Motoring south down Rosco Inlet

I awoke to Tom consulting the Navionics app on his phone. He was determining if it would be more prudent to leave for Codville Lagoon this morning rather than stay in Rosco Inlet one more day. It would give us two days in Pruth Bay, where we could obtain up-to-date weather info, before going to Jones Cove to stage for coming around Cape Caution. By leaving today, we would also have one extra day in case we needed to wait out the weather before going around the Cape, which can be quite intimidating if not transited with weather, wind, and current carefully considered.

So, that is what we did. It was already 8:00 (we had planned on this being a sleep-in morning...boohoo), so we had to hop to it, as Rosco Inlet to Codville Lagoon takes around five and a half hours, providing us with an ETA of approximately 1:00. These anchorages can fill up fast, so we didn't feel that we had any time to waste.

After we pulled up anchor, we had to scoot over and pick up the crab pot we soaked overnight. It was very low tide, and we were a little worried that the pot might be in water too shallow to pull Havis Amanda alongside to grab and haul it in without running aground. Thankfully, that wasn't the case, so we raised the pot and took off.

Tom cracking and picking crab meat from the shells

Yea! Four keepers today! Tom killed, cleaned and refrigerated the crabs. He then sprayed off the decks and the crab-killing tools while I piloted the boat. We transited back down Rosco Inlet, into Johnson Channel, to Fisher Channel, turning left into Codville Lagoon for the night. The plan is (although that certainly could change on a whim) to transit to Pruth Bay tomorrow for one or two days, depending on the weather forecasts for coming around the Cape on Sunday or Monday, whichever day looks better. Time will tell. Watch this space.

It was an overcast day, with calm, glass-like seas, little wind, and cooler temperatures today than yesterday. When we arrived at Codville Lagoon, we surprisingly had cell signal, so I called my mom to check in, and then we both checked our email. I sent yesterday's journal entry and began to write today's, while Tom began cracking open the shells and picking out the crab meat. We will have some for tonight and save some for another meal. The gnats were a bit pesky, but we put out our super-duper Thermacell bug-repellant dispenser, and that helped a lot.

Tom teases me that he has lost me to my writing, and I think he is only partly kidding, so I will wrap up for the night. We will spend a nice evening eating fresh crab and other goodies before retiring to watch a movie. Unless, Tom is up for losing another Flip 8 card game before going to bed that is. Ha Ha!

Good Night from Codville Lagoon - End of Day 104

DAY 105

DESTINATION: PRUTH BAY

Turn your head sideways...how many faces can you make out?

The photo above is one of the best examples of Water Totems we have ever taken. These totems completely surrounded the shoreline of Codville Lagoon this morning, so we got some amazing photos and videos on our way out.

Dense fog enveloped us as we motored for four hours in Fitz Hugh Sound on our way to Pruth Bay for the night. It was like motoring through a bowl of creamy clam chowder. On top of the fog, much of the transit was littered with logs, kelp beds, and "aircraft carriers" (floating logs carrying a line of seagulls) that had to be dodged and maneuvered around all morning. Even so, we were grateful for calm seas and very light winds all day. I can't imagine going through this much fog and debris if the seas had been choppy and the wind howling. All I can say is thank goodness for GPS, radar, and AIS, without which we would be getting out our paper charts, dividers, and protractors.

Motoring through the soup down Fitz Hugh Sound...Spooky

It was a tiring day as we were constantly looking down at the electronic chart plotter and back up at the "road" ahead of us to watch for debris, boats that didn't have AIS, and whales. Yes, whales. I was at the helm when I saw a "big log" over on my starboard. Then it moved.

That's when I told Tom, *"That's a whale!"*

To which Tom replied, *"Nah, that's a log."*

To which I said excitedly, *"NO, THAT'S A WHALE!!!"*

And sure enough, it was a humpback whale resting on the surface of the water. I think we surprised it as much as it surprised us, but it quietly slipped under the water and was gone. Earlier today, Tom saw a humpback right beside the boat just before it went under, and before that I saw one swimming in the opposite direction we were headed. Each time, they were alone. Often, you see them in groups called pods, but today, they were playing a game of solitaire.

We were almost to Pruth Bay when the fog finally lifted. It was a welcome relief to be able to see clearly in all directions. At that point, we were only five miles from our destination at the end of Pruth Bay. When we arrived there, we dropped anchor in 55 feet of water in front of a shoreline of exquisite rocks, shown in the photo directly below.

I prepared a large pot of homemade chicken noodle soup and a small salad and Tom made biscuits. I made enough for tomorrow evening as well, in that we will have a nine-hour transit day around Cape Caution.

We had planned to go around the Cape on Monday, but in looking more closely at all the factors that needed to be considered, we decided we would go on Saturday instead. The wind, wave height, and current will be more in our favor on Saturday, so we will do it all in one day instead of breaking it up into two. Our morning wakeup call will be at 5:00 so...early to bed, early to rise, will make Tom and Jandira rested and wise.

Good Night from Pruth Bay - End of Day 105

DAY 106

LAYOVER DAY: PRUTH BAY, CALVERT ISLAND

West side of Calvert Island

The VHF radio woke us this morning at 4:00 with gale force warnings in the Central Coast area where we are presently anchored, as well as the area we would have been traveling through today rounding Cape Caution. Tom crawled out of bed to go in and listen to the whole weather report so he could get a more complete picture of the upcoming storm. This gale was not predicted yesterday but began developing offshore early this morning and is now forecast to continue into Sunday. So...once again...our plans changed, and we decided to stay in Pruth Bay until Monday. This is a perfect example of why we always in-corporate a few extra days in our schedule in case we have to hold over somewhere to wait out bad weather. It's ok though...now we will have time to explore this beautiful island.

Calvert Island is home to the Hakai Beach Institute. According to the Douglass resource book we use, *"In 2010, the fly-fishing resort at the head of Pruth Bay was sold to the Tula Foundation and became the Hakai Beach Institute...It is a private research and conference center, but visitors are welcome."* We were told by a gentleman that we met on staff that they work closely with the UW Marine Labs in Friday Harbor, where we live. Small world. The grounds are beautifully kept, with well-maintained trails that are mostly boardwalks. The trails lead through the woods and out to several white, sandy beaches with incredibly unique rock formations.

We kayaked over around noon and hiked the trail out to the west side of Calvert Island. We puttered around the beach and walked up to a lookout high above the beaches. We had a wonderful afternoon in nature and were so glad the gale force winds kept us from going around the Cape today, or we would have missed seeing some really beautiful parts of nature here on Calvert Island, as can be seen in the photos below.

We were honestly speechless at the sight of the stunning rock sculpture pictured below. Can you see the praying women and child in the middle of the rocks? They have their backs to us and appear to have head coverings similar to those worn in the time of Jesus. They are right below the large white vertical rock in the center. This rock sculpture felt holy to us, like we had walked into a nature-made chapel of sorts. We created our own offering to nature on the side of it to show our gratitude for such sacred beauty.

Our very own nature altar

We had an incredibly lovely day doing all the things we love: kayaking, hiking, being in nature...and most of all...being with one another.

Good Night from Pruth Bay - End of Day 106

DAY 107

SECOND LAYOVER WEATHER DAY: PRUTH BAY

West side of Calvert Island. Almost looks tropical, doesn't it?

We went to bed with rain, woke up with rain, and enjoyed the almost constant rain all day today. It was heavenly! Yes, the rain foiled our planned kayak back to the beach, but what it did give us was a peaceful sleep-in day with the rain as a backdrop, time to take a nice hot shower, time for a longer Quiet Time, time to thoroughly listen to the weather report for tomorrow for our planned Cape Caution rounding, time for me to bake banana-nut muffins, oatmeal cookies and prepare enchiladas for dinner as well as time for Tom to plan and put in routes all the way to Bootleg Cove, our first stop in the Broughton Islands after we leave Port McNeill.

It also gave him time to work on the saltwater pump that began acting up yesterday, which, as you can see from the photo above, he is doing as I write. The saltwater pump is the washdown for the anchor and anchor chain, but it is now also designed (by Tom) to rinse and wash the dishes in saltwater before a final rinse in hot potable water. This helps us to conserve potable water in between fill-ups when we are out at anchor for several days in a row. It looks like it is probably an issue with the pump itself, of which we do not have a spare until we get to a marine supply place. "Ahhh, well...it's a boat,"...as sailors frequently bemoan when things go awry. She's still a work in progress, that's for sure...much like we humans are...but that's ok. As Mark Nepo says in *The Book of Awakening*, *"I am growing...I am carried toward the Light...I lack nothing."* Well said.

After Tom finished working on the saltwater pump (it turns out it was the pressure switch that he was able to get working well enough to get us home), we prepped for a dinner of enchiladas that would be enough for tomorrow evening as well. We have a nine-hour transit tomorrow, so it will be nice to have leftovers to heat up and not have to start from scratch after such a long day.

Since we didn't get off the boat today, due to the ever-constant rain, we didn't get any new photos, so I have included a few more from yesterday below. We will most certainly return to Pruth Bay on our next trip north. The natural beauty of this island fed our souls in ways it is hard to explain. It simply must be experienced in person.

Good Night, again, from Pruth Bay - End of Day 107

DAY 108

AROUND CAPE CAUTION
DESTINATION: WALKER GROUP
COVE

Transiting Fitz Hugh Sound

Our route today took us from Pruth Bay back down Kwakshua Channel, down Fitz Hugh Sound, into Queen Charlotte Sound, around Cape Caution, down Queen Charlotte Strait, and finally into a group of islands called the Walker Group. We anchored in Walker Group Cove, a tiny cove located off Staples Cut, for the night.

Having two "forced" layover days in Pruth Bay for weather was a Godsend, as the sea conditions today were much more favorable than had we left to come around Cape Caution on Saturday as we had originally planned. We had a low westerly swell with rippled seas, which is just about as good as it gets. We motored through some light fog during the first half of the day, with a mixture of sun and clouds the last half. We had lots of logs and kelp beds to dodge, so we were both on point most of the day. (Thankfully, so were the ever-watchful Debris Dodging Angels!)

In fact, the sea conditions were so favorable that we commented at least a dozen times how easy a "cape-rounding day" it had been. Whoever orchestrates the weather up there...thank you, thank you, thank you!!!

Motoring through light fog in Fitz Hugh Sound

Our anchorage for the night, Walker Group Cove, is almost completely landlocked. Its shores are covered with old-growth cedar and spruce trees, and nightly entertainment is provided courtesy of resident sea otters and loons. Kelp and small logs dotted the water as we entered, making for a limited choice of anchorages. Plus, there is only room for two boats due to the cove shallowing not far past the entrance and a rock awash at 12 feet. We dropped anchor twice as the first time the anchor didn't hold. The second attempt was a success, with the anchor catching and holding solidly.

Walker Group is a beautiful set of islands and is a kayaker's paradise, but we got in too late in the day and were too tired after our nine-hour transit to do so. Maybe next time.

We fixed a small snack of cheese and crackers and sat out on the back deck to rest before heating up leftover enchiladas. One other boat was already in the cove when we got there, and while we were having our snack, a smaller sailboat came in, looked around, and decided it was too crowded and too shallow and anchored across the cut just outside another small cove. They had five folks on board a 32-foot sailboat. I just can't imagine where they all sleep! It makes me even more grateful to have Havis Amanda as our boat home.

After our happy hour snack, I began working on today's jour-nal entry while Tom checked routes for tomorrow and did some boat maintenance chores. He then heated up the leftovers, we ate, he did the dishes while I wrote and then off to bed for us both.

We have a short travel day tomorrow of only four hours to get to Port McNeill, where we will probably stay for two days to fuel up, water up, provision, do laundry, and eat out at the local pub called The Devils Bath that we enjoyed so much on our way north.

My day is over now, and Tom is calling me to bed.

Good Night from Walker Group Cove - End of Day 108

DAY 109

DESTINATION: PORT MCNEILL, NORTH ISLAND MARINA

The teeny tiny cut Tom drove through this morning. Holy Moly!

We left our anchorage in Walker Group Cove this morning at 7:25. Tom drove through the narrow cut shown above to get back out into Queen Charlotte Strait. The rain had stopped, and there were low hanging clouds, but they were very wispy and easy to see through. The seas were calm and the winds light. It is truly incredible just how good the seas and winds have treated us of late...a blessing we don't take for granted.

We motored down Queen Charlotte Strait for five hours, one hour longer than we thought it would take. The extra hour of travel time was due to a two-knot current pushing against us for most of the way. It was such a pleasant ride that we didn't mind the extra hour of cruising. The skies were simply enchanting, as you can see from the photo below.

Motoring down Queen Charlotte Strait in unusually calm seas

We arrived at the North Island Marina around 12:30 and were given a starboard side to spot on B Dock. Two marina staff came down and caught a line for us...a very easy docking all the way around.

We went down to pay for our planned two-night stay only to find out that when you reserve a spot on their website, there is a glitch in the system. If you want one night, you click on the date you want, but if you want two nights, you have to click on the dates for three nights. Wait. What? There is no indication on their website that alerts you to this glitch, so how would you know?

The dock staffer was very nice about it, but he had "no room in the inn" for tomorrow night. That meant we had to do laundry, fuel up, water up, provision for the next couple of weeks, and shower all in one day. We had hoped to stretch it out over two days as we were quite weary from the Cape Caution rounding yesterday, but that was not in the cards, so we hustled up and were able to get all our chores accomplished before dinner time.

North Island Marina and Port McNeill Boat Harbor

Thankfully, we finished in time to go to the Devil's Bath Brew Pub for salad and pizza for dinner. It was delicious and very relaxing. It has been one of our favorite places to eat out, and honestly, there haven't been many.

When we returned from dinner, I worked on today's journal while Tom worked on the generator, as it was still leaking oil. It is now 9:10, and he is still at it. Hopefully, he can wrap it up soon, as we are both exhausted and longing to slip our freshly showered bodies in between freshly laundered sheets. On that note, I will say:

Good Night from Port McNeill - End of Day 109

DAYS 110-111

DESTINATION: BOOTLEG COVE

End of Queen Charlotte Strait

I woke yesterday with symptoms of a UTI (urinary tract infection) that got worse as the day went on. I had brought symptom-relieving, over-the-counter meds with me but no antibiotics. I very rarely get UTIs, so I didn't really think it would be an issue. I was taking the meds for symptom relief, which helped, but as anyone who has ever had a UTI knows, nothing but an antibiotic will likely cure the infection. Even though I knew I couldn't get an antibiotic without a prescription, I very foolishly thought maybe I would be ok without one. Now, my father, the pharmacist, would have chided me for this foolish notion, and honestly, I knew better as well, but I didn't think I would be able to get a doctor's appointment on such short notice, especially since we couldn't stay in the marina but one day.

My symptoms got worse overnight, so today began with a mildly frantic email to a doctor friend of ours in Friday Harbor to see if he could call in a prescription for an antibiotic to the local pharmacy here in Port McNeill. Though quite sympathetic, he said he could not prescribe meds in a foreign country (I did not know this) and recommended finding an urgent care center. We had to be out of the marina by 11:00, so we thought this might be difficult to do, but we started looking online and found a medical clinic, and miracle of miracles, they had just had a cancellation for 10:40 this morning.

I walked up to the harbormaster's office to plead my plight, and they said as long as we were out of the marina by 1:00 it would be ok, so we got directions and took off walking...one mile each way. This normally wouldn't have been an issue, but we were on a time schedule, and I wasn't feeling up to par, so it was a bit of a struggle for me.

We made it to the clinic on time, and I explained our time issue with the marina. They kindly expedited my appointment, and I was in and out of there in about 30 minutes (although $100 poorer) prescription in hand. We walked straight to the pharmacy, explained our time issue to them, and they, too, worked fast to fill my prescriptions and get us on our way.

We got back to the marina at 12:30, untied the lines, and pulled away from the dock, this after a bit of trouble untangling ourselves from between two boats that had been tied up too close to us the day before. Thankfully, Tom was able to inch forward and back enough times to finally get us out of there without damage to anybody's boat, including ours. Whew! That was too "close" for comfort!

Our transit across the southern end of Queen Charlotte Strait and into the Broughton Islands was full of fog, boats, and debris, but we made it through safely. August is typically quite foggy and true to form, we have had a lot of fog the last several days. Sailors long ago nicknamed August Fogust because of this.

All along the way, we could hear boaters hailing other boaters on their VHF, determining how to pass one another. In limited visibility, clear communication is needed to determine an agreed upon passage...red to red or green to green as we say...or in other words...port to port or starboard to starboard. The area around Port McNeill is very busy with the BC ferry, fishing boats, and pleasure crafts coming and going, and navigating through fog complicates things a bit...very doable, of course, but staying focused and attentive is required for safe passage.

The landscape was beautiful on our route today which included Spring Passage and Retreat Passage to finally anchor in Bootleg Cove, aptly named as it had been the perfect place for bootleggers to hide from authorities during the days of prohibition. The entrance to the cove cannot be seen from Retreat Passage as it looks like a dead-end bay. It is very sheltered, protected, and quiet...a nice layover anchorage to rest and heal from my UTI infection.

Looking across Spring Channel to mountain ranges in BC

We had planned to stay only one night in Bootleg Cove, but after dinner, I started to feel very flu-like...you know...that all-over achy, headachy feeling, most likely due to the urinary tract infection raging through my body. I went to bed feeling quite ill and woke up that way this morning. I pretty much stayed in bed all day drinking lots of liquids and taking antibiotics and Tylenol. Tom puttered around while I slept, watching a black bear feeding on the shore, working again on the generator to try and find the leak, and reading up on boat stuff.

I got up around 3:00 and began working on yesterday's and today's journal entries. I still felt poorly, but better overall than yesterday. We will head to Viner Sound tomorrow, which, thankfully, is only about an hour and a half away. I will rest more there and hope to be on the mend soon.

One thing we have learned on this trip, is how to deal with and adapt to the many different situations (including illnesses) that present themselves to us daily. We are grateful for each experience, even the difficult ones, though not necessarily in the moment that their happening. It is usually after we have had a chance to process the event and can see it from a higher perspective, that we can began to recognize the blessing and feel gratitude for it. You know...hindsight. Ok...I am fading fast, so:

Good Night from Bootleg Cove - End of Days 110-111

DAY 112

DESTINATION: VINER SOUND

Rocks along the way in Cramer Passage

When we left Bootleg Cove, I was still feeling punky, although better than yesterday. It was a mostly clear day with drooping clouds, but not troublesome in any way from a seeing-our-way-forward perspective. In fact, as you can see from the photo below, the cloud-shrouded mountains were incredibly beautiful. Again, the seas and winds were calm. Our passage only took us an hour and a half, a far cry from being in Alaska, where the transit to our destination for the night could sometime take all day. As I have mentioned before, EVERYTHING is simply BIGGER in Alaska.

As we motored down Viner Sound, we had hopes one of our favorite anchorages from last year would be empty of other boats, but to our disappointment, there was one boat already anchored there. Viner Sound only has room for two boats, and we didn't want to be that close to another boat, so we opted to go across the way and anchor in another little cove called Viner Sound South. We were glad to be settled in for the day.

Hornet Passage just before turning into Viner Sound

This islet in Viner Sound South graced our "backyard"

Tom got both kayaks down, as I had decided it might do me good to get out in the fresh air and get some mild exercise. We were rewarded with two bear sightings. They were both meandering around shore, turning over rocks looking for grubs, small mussels and shells. Every now and again they looked up from scrounging around for their lunch to check us out, but neither one offered to come close to us and only moved away when they thought we were getting too close to them. We were thrilled to share this space with them for about an hour, after which I paddled back to the boat to rest while Tom paddled further down the shoreline. Later, we prepared a light supper and crawled into bed early.

Sunset in Viner Sound South

Good Night from Viner Sound South - End of Day 112

DAY 113

DESTINATION: SIMOOM SOUND

Kayaking in Simoom Sound

We slept in this morning as we only had an hour and a half transit over to Simoom Sound. It was very nice to have a slower-start morning. We pulled up anchor around 9:30 and headed out. When we reached the end of Viner Sound, we hit a very dense fog bank, as thick as any we'd been in up to this point. Now, it is one thing to pilot the boat through dense fog when you are out in a wide-open channel or strait...there you have debris and boats to worry about hitting but a lot more space to maneuver around them. I must tell you, however, that it felt quite different to me today navigating in very tight quarters around islets, islands, and rocks AND worrying about dodging boats and debris. Thankfully, we had very little debris and met no on-coming boats, but most of all, we were thankful for our GPS, chart plotter, and radar systems that saw us safely into Simoom Sound. (And our Debris Dodging/Fog Lifting Angels were spot on as well.)

When we rounded the corner into McIntosh Bay, we were pleasantly surprised to find the fog had lifted there, and the sun was shining brightly. It is a beautiful area with lots of small islets to kayak around, so, literally, the minute we dropped anchor, Tom was getting the kayaks in the water and telling me, "Hurry, *Honey, this day's gonna go by fast!*" Tom was so anxious to be out on the water kayaking I could literally feel him vibrating from the top of his head to the bottoms of his feet in anticipation.

I wasn't quite ready yet...I still had to get into my rubber boots, retrieve my water bottle, don my baseball cap, grab a plastic bag (to gather shore rocks, carry an extra jacket, and my phone for photos), and, of course, pee...when I realized Tom had been standing impatiently in the doorway with the kayak line in one hand and the boat pole in the other, waiting to help me into my kayak. (Tom holds the bow line from my kayak and uses the boat pole to hold the stern of the kayak in place so it holds steady as I am getting in. Works like a charm.)

You see, I am a methodical-be-prepared-for-any-scenario kind of person, which I am sure drives Tom to distraction at times, as it takes me longer to get prepared for all of my perceived scenarios than it does him. To his credit, though, he has learned just to give me more time...to tell me in advance what time he would like me to be ready to leave...so I can then judge what I have time to get done and what I have to leave for later. But today, his excitement to be in the kayaks was just too much for him. In fact, I thought he might just vibrate right out of his skin.

We started paddling around the shoreline when we heard a "CLOP" sound over on the rocky beach. We knew right away it was a bear. We paddled over to get a closer look and watched this shiny black bear turning over rocks foraging for his lunch. Two days in a row, we had been graced by the presence of black bears peacefully walking the shore looking for food, paying us no mind except to occasionally look up to make sure we weren't going to steal their supper.

We then paddled over to this small rocky beach to get on to shore to walk around a bit. This shore was connected to the shore where we had previously sighted the bear. Tom climbed up on this big egg-shaped rock, and I got the photo below. After he climbed down, we saw the bear again...on shore...the very same shore we were on. Yikes! Tom was not the least bit bothered, but I certainly was. I hurriedly scrambled to get back to the kayaks, but thank-fully, the bear was not at all interested in us and just kept right on eating.

Each time we have encountered bears, I have learned something new about them. I have learned to be respectful and quiet, not act in any way threatening, not to get too close, and most importantly, that they are far more interested in scrounging for their food than bothering us. And, of course, we ALWAYS carry bear spray, even though, thankfully, we have never had to use it.

After that, we paddled around several other islets and down a couple of narrow inlets. Tom stayed close to shore, but I paddled a little way out, being bear-aware, as they say in all the guide-books. We both got hungry at the same time and decided to go back to the boat for an early happy hour of nachos and crab dipped in garlic butter. I have been feeling much better from my UTI but have had quite a lot of indigestion discomfort for the last several days, so I didn't eat anything else for dinner except yogurt. Tom had a turkey and Swiss cheese wrap, I wrote and he did dishes, and then we sat out on the back of the boat to enjoy the sunset. Tom said it was a mackerel and mare's-tail sky, which can signify rain in a few days. It had been a lovely day in our little piece of paradise. We went to bed happy and content.

Tom resting on top of a large egg-shaped rock

Good Night from Simoom Sound - End of Day 113

DAY 114

DESTINATION: KWATSI BAY

Water Totems in McIntosh Bay, Simoom Sound

The Water Totems we observed in McIntosh Bay this morning were quite different from the ones we have encountered throughout our journey. In the McIntosh Bay totems, we couldn't distinguish any faces, but there were still many unique patterns and colorations...albeit more grays, tans, and golds than in other places. Intriguing.

The fog was high enough this morning that we could see clearly to pilot Havis Amanda out of McIntosh Bay and into Tribune Channel. The seas were calm, with almost no wind to speak of and literally one small log to dodge coming down the channel. There were towering rocks on our port for most of the way, and the patterns and colors were so exquisite that we chose to drive very close to shore so we could see them better, rather than in the middle of the channel like we often do. It was plenty deep enough, and with no rocks to avoid, it was a safe and pleasant ride. We commented that we were doing it "Colin's way." Our English friend, Colin Banks, loved to putter along the shoreline no matter how long it took him to get to an anchorage. After today, we can definitely understand the value of doing so.

Towering rock wall in Tribune Channel

When we arrived in Kwatsi Bay, there was a boat in the exact spot we wanted to anchor in, but thankfully, they were pulling up anchor and leaving, so we were able to drop anchor in approximately the same spot we anchored in last year. Tom lowered the kayaks into the water, then remembered he needed to work on the saltwater pump, which had quit again earlier today. He spent about 20 minutes on it, and it appears to be good to go. We shall see.

We climbed into our kayaks and paddled for the shoreline. The rocks in this bay are truly stunning. When we were here last August, we took photos of what we called Zebra Rocks. These rocks were the inspiration for the first mandalas I had ever created straight from nature. My earlier mandalas were primarily abstracts. The Zebra Rock mandalas have an abstract quality but are clearly representative of nature. I did a series of these nature mandalas last year and plan to do more this winter from the new photos we took this year. Below is a photo of these same rocks taken just today.

Zebra Rocks in Kwatsi Bay...Incredible!

When we returned to the boat, I worked on the journal entry for the day while Tom put up the kayaks and then started preparing three batches of cream cheese and olive spread. We will be in Lagoon Cove Marina tomorrow afternoon, and they host a daily Happy Hour. Everyone brings an appetizer, and Dan and Kelly, the owners of the marina, provide spot prawns that are freshly caught each day.

Last year, we brought the cream cheese and olive spread as our contribution to happy hour, and they loved it so much that Tom made another batch just for them. When we called for reservations this year, they said they would save us a spot on the dock as long as we promised to bring the cream cheese and olive spread. HA HA! So, Tom made three batches: one for happy hour, one for Dan and Kelly, and one for us. Triple Yum!

I am still having some very painful indigestion issues, so we opted to cook a mild dinner of boiled potatoes and carrots...again. I am beginning to think that either the antibiotic for the UTI or the new bladder meds might be causing the indigestion. Tomorrow is the last day for the antibiotics so I should know then if that is the culprit.

We are now one of three boats in this bay, anchored side by side. It is a beautiful evening here in Kwatsi Bay with towering mountains on all sides, floating logs acting as aircraft carriers for tiny seagull-type birds, Tom singing along to Cat Stevens as he makes cream cheese and olive spread, and the boat gently swinging back and forth on the anchor. I really don't think I could ask for a more perfect ending to a very perfect day.

Good Night All from Kwatsi Bay - End of Day 114

DAY 115

DESTINATION: LAGOON COVE MARINA

Kwatsi Bay has been one of our favorite Canadian anchorages for a couple of years now, so we had a bit of a lump in our throat as we left this morning on our three-and-a-half-hour journey to Lagoon Cove Marina, which, it just so happens, is one of our favorite places to dock. We usually ask for the Honeymoon Dock as it is located a little bit away from the main dock and provides us with more privacy.

As I mentioned in yesterday's journal entry, Lagoon Cove has a tradition of hosting a daily happy hour where all boaters who want to participate bring an appetizer, and the owners, Dan and Kelly, serve fresh prawns caught daily with homemade cocktail sauce. The happy hour today was well attended and lots of tasty treats were offered by boaters from Canada and the US alike.

We met a couple from Kirkland, WA, Pat and Dennis, who own an American Tug and invited us to come aboard to see it. They were a lovely couple a tad older than us and had lots of stories to share. Pat was a former teacher, is very open-minded about different spiritualities, and loves many of the same authors and artists I do, so we had much in common to talk about. She also talked about her recent experiences with bone cancer, a brain tumor, and being treated with proton therapy. Of course, Tom and Dennis talked boats, boats and more boats for almost two hours. It made for a nice evening for us both.

Tom and I have spent so many wonderful hours and days alone together, not conversing with another living soul, that it was a bit over-stimulating to be around a group of folks all talking at once. Tom says we almost have to reteach ourselves how to be sociable when we have been alone for long stretches of time. It is truly lovely to meet new folks and swap boating adventures, but honestly, we cherish our alone time with one another far more than being in a crowd of people. I guess it is about finding a balance between the two.

That was pretty much the jest of our day. We will be on our way to Forward Harbor tomorrow, another one of our favorite anchorages from last year and the place of Tom's proposal, so it is quite special to us.

Lagoon Cove Marina at sunset

Good Night from Lagoon Cove - End of Day 115

DAY 116

DESTINATION: FORWARD HARBOR

Coming out of Havannah Channel into Johnston Strait

We left Lagoon Cove this morning at 7:00, navigated through a tricky section called The Blow Hole, down Chatham Channel (where multiple range markers must be lined up and followed to avoid shallow areas, kelp beds, and rocks), and into Havannah Channel, which empties into the infamous Johnstone Strait.

When we rounded the corner to come out into Johnstone Strait, we had a bit of wind, so Tom put the mizen and jib sails up to take advantage of this light breeze. Which...of course...promptly died. Sigh. This is very typical of the Pacific Northwest...you have wind...you don't have wind...you have wind...you don't have wind. But it's all good! We love it all!

We had mixed weather reports for Johnstone Strait today. The VHF predicted gale force winds later this evening, and other sources, like Predict Wind and Windy, showed only 5-10 knots of wind this morning and 10-15 the rest of the day.

It is very hard to know which source to trust, so we usually try to strike a balance between them all. We opted to go for it.

Mizen and jib up in Johnstone Strait...Tom at the helm

There was some light fog and the seas had about a one-foot chop...way calmer than Johnstone Strait can sometimes be. We were grateful for the Weather Gods and Sea Goddesses smiling on us again today.

We came out of Johnstone Strait into Sunderland Channel and then into Wellbore Channel, which led us into beautiful Forward Harbor. We were the third boat to anchor here, but by suppertime, there were ten boats all swinging in the breeze. One of the last boats that came in had a springer spaniel on board. Now, don't get me wrong, I love dogs. In fact, at one time in my life, I had six dogs and three cats, but I think you have to be on the other side of nuts to cruise for long spans of time with an animal on board that you have to dinghy to shore multiple times a day to do its business. Thank goodness Tom and I are on the same page about this...NO ANIMALS ON BOARD!!! EVER!!! Ok...I am coming down off my very opinionated soap box now. I am so glad to get that off my chest and on to the rest of today's happenings.

When we dropped anchor, Tom put the kayaks down. We paddled to shore to hike a short trail through the woods to a rock-filled beach in another bay. We putzed around the beach looking for rocks for the medicine wheel we will add to down at Briggs Lake when we get back home. This whole summer, we have collected stones in red, yellow, black, and white to represent the four directions in the Lakota First Nations tradition. We are short of black ones, so we mostly gathered those. We came across this ancient tree that had fallen over with its intricate root system exposed for all to see. Fascinating. We created a small nature sculpture on top of it and others all along the shoreline.

Root system of the ancient tree on the beach in Forward Harbor

When we got back to the trailhead, we stepped into our kayaks and paddled around shore for a while. The water is crystal clear here, and you can see multi-colored rocks shining up from the ocean floor. Stunning! The wind picked up, and we didn't want to have to paddle hard against it to get back to the boat, so we headed back.

Sun-kissed path through the woods in Forward Harbor

We fixed and ate too much food for dinner and were completely stuffed. When we get home, we are going to return to our intermittent fasting regimen. We both feel better, healthier and have more energy when we are doing so. Not long after dinner, dishes, and writing, we retired for the evening.

Good Night from Forward Harbor - End of Day 116

DAY 117

DESTINATION: SHOAL BAY, PHILLIPS ARM

Good morning from Forward Harbor

We left Forward Harbor at 7:00, the sunrise reflecting off our stern as we motored out of the bay. It was a beautiful morning to go through Whirlpool and Greenpoint Rapids, the first at slack and the second at around two knots going with us...both as easy as falling off a log. We had a three-hour transit with mill pond seas and soft, gentle winds.

We motored most of this gorgeous day from the upper helm. Tom spent most of his time trying to get me to go back inside to rest...I didn't. I haven't felt well for several days now. I seem to be over the UTI, but somewhere in the middle of dealing with that, I started having what I thought was severe indigestion. I take meds for that and acid reflux, so it made sense with my symptoms, except none of the meds were easing my pain.

After a few days of discomfort and me developing a hacking cough that grew worse when trying to talk, we figured out it was more likely bronchitis. I have been treating symptoms now for a couple of days and am some better, but it was a welcome relief when we got to Shoal Bay today to go in and sleep for three hours while Tom kayaked for a while by himself.

Motoring down Chancellor Channel

When he came back, he did some research on various alternative anchorages for us to try out next trip, checked all the engine systems, topped off the engine fluids, and took a brief nap himself out in the pilot house on the setee, not wanting to wake me by crawling in bed beside me.

When we got up, we played Flip 8 and then began working on dinner. Tom chopped peppers and onions while I sauteed fresh mushrooms and heated water for noodles. Our dinner consisted of egg noodles topped with pesto, seasonings, sauteed peppers, onions, sundried tomatoes, and mushrooms. I made a small semi-Greek salad with grape tomatoes, cucumbers, and feta cheese tossed with a French vinaigrette. It all blended together nicely.

After dinner, we sat out on the back of the boat soaking up the late afternoon sun, just talking about this and that and enjoying being together in such a beautiful place. From our anchorage we can look straight up into Phillips Arm...such stunning beauty on display for our evening pleasure.

Phillips Arm towering behind Havis Amanda

Good Night from Shoal Bay/Phillips Arm - End of Day 117

DAY 118

DESTINATION: LUND HARBOR MARINA

Cordero Channel

We left Shoal Bay at 7:30 this morning to light wind, some clouds, rippled seas, and breakthrough sunshine. Today was a day of timing three different rapids: Dent, Gillard, and Yuculta...one right after the other. Timing is crucial if you want to go through all three at slack, which most boaters choose to do. When we talk about rapids and show photos or videos of us going through rapids at slack tide, it doesn't look tricky at all, and for the most part, it's not, but we still have to stay vigilant, for even at slack the current can pull the boat into rocks or the shore. It is an exciting ride, though, to transit them when they are all squirrely...it sorta feels like we're skirting across the top of a pot of boiling water...being pushed and pulled around willy-nilly. Woohoo! Here we gooooo!!!

For those of you who like to follow our route, it was as follows: Shoal Bay to Cordero Channel, through Dent,

Gillard, and Yuculta Rapids, into Calm Channel, down Lewis Channel, past Desolation Sound, into Thulin Passage, and finally into the small town of Lund. This transit was super easy, even with lots of boats and logs to dodge around.

If you remember, when we came into Lund on our way north, we had high winds coming into the marina blowing us off the breakwater, and I had trouble getting the boat tied up. (The breakwater in Lund is a floating concrete dock that protects the marina from tides, currents, waves, and storm surges and has room for several boats to side tie to.)

Today, the winds were lighter, so the docking went well. Tom stepped off first and then I did, and we walked the boat back to the end of the breakwater, as I had docked the boat further in than Tom had wanted. We tied her up, and Tom set about getting the dinghy down so we could dinghy over later to pay for our two-night moorage fee and to eat at the Boardwalk Restaurant.

When we were here last, the restaurant was having trouble getting and keeping staff, and we just barely were able to get a table. Today, they were closed all day for the very same reason. We were very disappointed as they have really good food and a great atmosphere. We are hoping to have better luck tomorrow.

Instead, we ate at the motel restaurant, which is typically mediocre, but tonight was decent. We enjoyed sitting under an umbrella at an outside table watching boats come in and go out of the marina as we dined on halibut fish and chips and a couple of IPAs. It was very nice not to have to cook, and I am quite sure Tom was delighted not to have to do dishes while I wrote.

After we returned to Havis Amanda, it was so hot that I laid down for about 20 minutes under our aft cabin fan to cool off. It has been very hot today, and I don't do well in the heat, so I was feeling pretty wrung out.

Later, we watched from the breakwater as the sun gradually dropped lower and lower in the sky. This marina is very congested with boats of all types and sizes, including water taxis from Savary Island, going back and forth from early morning until after dark. It is quite entertaining to watch. No dull moments in this thriving little town.

We were getting eaten up by mosquitoes, so we came in and lathered Benadryl Gel all over our bites. I finished the journal entry, called my mom and joined Tom in bed to...you guessed it...start watching a movie only to fall asleep mid-movie. Yep...that is what happens when you get old!

Sunset over Lund Harbor Marina

Good Night from Lund Harbor Marina - End of Day 118

DAY 119

LAYOVER DAY: LUND HARBOR MARINA

Lund Harbor Marina

We slept in until 7:30 (Tom) and 8:30 (me). It was a layover-provision-laundry day, and we could move at a bit slower pace. When I crawled out of bed, Tom was already calculating the weather, wind, tides, and currents for the next few days. We had planned throughout the whole trip to finally experience Princess Louisa this time around, but in looking at weather windows to cross Georgia Strait, we either needed to cross this Monday or wait until the following Monday. When we took everything into consideration, we decided it would be most prudent to cross this Monday, which meant forgoing Princess Louisa, at least for this trip. We both felt good about the decision. We will arrive back in our home port of Friday Harbor either Friday the 2nd or Saturday the 3rd of September...as long as "God's willing and the creek don't rise."

The above expression is one I have heard all my life. I always thought it meant that we would "get there" (wherever "there" was) as long as God was willing and the creek water didn't rise so high we couldn't get across it to the other side. Imagine my surprise when our friend, Joseph Bettis, informed us it was his understanding that the word "creek" did not refer to a small stream, but instead to the First Nations tribe, the Creek.

That piqued my curiosity, so I went online to do a bit of research. I found that some historians attribute Benjamin Hawkins as having been the first person to ever say these words and that he did so in a letter to then President of the United States, George Washington, when he was General Superintendent for Indian Affairs and had responsibility for the Native American tribes south of the Ohio River, one of which was the Creek Indians. In a letter to the Commander in Chief, Hawkins stated that he would return to the nation's capital, *"God willing and the Creek don't rise."*

Hawkins was said to be a college-educated and well-written man who would not likely have made a grammatical error, so the capitalization of Creek most likely would be a reference not to a small body of water but to the Creek Indian Nation. If the Creek 'rose,' Hawkins would have to be present to quell the rebellion.

On other sites, I read theories that discounted the above explanation entirely, believing it to simply relate to a small, meandering body of water commonly called a creek. So, it seems we may never know the true origin and meaning of this expression, and maybe, in the great scheme of things, it doesn't really matter anyway.

But now, back to the day at hand. After the decision was made to forgo a stopover in Princess Louisa this year, we got started on our day of chores. At this marina, we usually tie up on the breakwater. It is cheaper as there is no power, and if you tie up in the main part of the marina, they require you to raft up with other boats if need be, and we don't like doing that. So, to get to the grocery store, laundry, restaurants, etc., we kayak or dinghy over to shore to take advantage of these amenities. When we have a lot to carry back and forth, the dinghy is the best choice.

We did our grocery shopping first, as they tend to run out of fresh produce pretty quickly. Today, I was able to purchase lettuce, spinach, onions, green peppers, cucumbers, and cherry tomatoes, which was good, but no fruit except for some raspberries and no other green vegetables.

Provisioning when you're cruising can be a challenge in certain locations, especially when it comes to finding fresh fruits and green veggies. This is a source of frustration for me but a good test of my willingness to release my expectations, accept what is, and go with the flow. After all, unless I can magically create these fresh food items from water, sand, shells, or rocks, I better learn to live with and be grateful for what is available to me at any given moment, realize that things are not always going to go my way and find new, inventive ways to use the foods I do have on hand.

While I was grocery shopping, Tom rowed the dinghy back to the boat, loaded up the laundry, brought it back to shore, hauled it up the hill, and put it all in to wash. When you live in a house and have access to your washing machine 24 hours a day, don't have to haul it back and forth to a laundry mat...sometimes by dinghy and sometimes by dragging it in a cart...and don't have to pay for each load you wash and each load you dry, you forget how challenging it can be just to have clean clothes. I must say, however, it's worth every bit of inconvenience to be able to experience being in wild and wonderous places away from traffic, noise, politics, and news. I would gladly haul laundry, groceries, and other items to be able to have the experiences we have had the past four months.

After I finished grocery shopping, Tom hauled the groceries back down to Havis Amanda while I changed out the laundry and waited for it to dry. When he came back to wait with me, we played a few rounds of Solitaire on our phones. Tom, of course, beat me every time. He says he has to beat me at something as I usually beat him at cards. We have fun no matter who wins.

As we were rowing back with the laundry, we passed our friends, Jim and Suzanne, side tied on the main docks. We knew they might be coming into Lund for the night, so it was great to see they had made it. We made plans to join each other for supper at the same restaurant we ate at last night.

It was a delightful evening of boating stories including docking fiascos, engines blowing up, anchors dragging, whale and bear sightings, great anchorages, terrible anchorages, best places to hike and swim...well, you get the picture. After three and a half hours, we said good night and rowed back to the boat, stopping on our way back to pick up a jug of homemade kombucha from Jim and Suzanne. We made short work of that jug of deliciousness in less than 24 hours! Um-um good!

When we got back to the boat, we had brownies with raspberry yogurt on top; I wrote, Tom did the breakfast dishes, and then off to bed for us both. I am ever so grateful for the productive day we had today and look forward to the restful sleep we will receive tonight.

Good Night from Lund Harbor Marina - End of Day 119

DAY 120

DESTINATION: BALLET BAY

Motoring into Ballet Bay

Being out on the breakwater in Lund Harbor Marina can be a roly-poly place to be, especially when you are getting wind coming in from the northwest. Because the swells build up right there at the breakwater when there is a wind, it can beat the daylights out of any boat that is tied up there, especially if the boat is on the outside of the breakwater.

Which is exactly where a 45-foot sailboat had to tie up last night when there was no room anywhere else on the docks. A 20- knot wind was blowing them roughly onto the dock and was not scheduled to lighten up till much later that evening. The boat was really taking a beating, and the two sailors were frantically trying to position more fenders to keep the boat from crashing into the dock over and over through the next few hours. Tom suggested they come inside the breakwater and raft up with us for the night. They declined saying their vessel was a steel boat, and they were going to put out more fenders and try to weather the weather until things calmed down, which they did. Within a few

396

hours, the wind and the waves laid down for a long summer's nap. All's well that ends well!

Ok...now to today's happenings. We untied the lines and motored away from the breakwater at 7:30 in a 10-knot wind. As the day progressed, the waves built, varying between one-three feet following seas, and the wind howled at a consistent 17 knots. It was roly-poly but not too terribly uncomfortable, and we had a beautiful sunny day of motor sailing. We kept the mizzen sail up to steady the boat but were only able to keep the jib up for a short time as the wind was smack-dab behind us. We weren't really trying to sail for the pure joy of sailing, as much as we were trying to get a little push from the sails for speed.

We arrived in Ballet Bay at 11:30 after a four-hour transit down Malaspina Strait. The entrance into the bay is narrow and rock-strewn, so we took our time and remained watchful.

When we got further into the bay, we saw that there were several other boats already anchored there to get out of the wind. We first thought we might have to go over to Fox Cove instead, but once deeper inside the bay realized there was plenty of room for us to anchor. In fact, after we anchored, several more boats came in, and all found suitable spots to drop their anchors. All total, there were 11 boats anchored here for the night, including our friends, Jim and Suzanne, who came in late this afternoon.

We ate a grilled turkey and Swiss sandwich for lunch. I wrote for a while, and Tom napped in the sun on the back of the boat. Later, I put sweet potatoes in the oven to bake and spinach in a pot to steam while Tom made a beautiful salad with lots of goodies in it.

Afterward, we took in the beauty of our surroundings and watched as even more boats came into the bay for the evening. It was a warm, sunny evening with a soft breeze and a few gusts of wind here and there.

Jim paddled over on his paddle board to say hi and to deliver a tiny little glass bottle filled with beach sand, sea glass, and small stones that Suzanne had made to hang up in our boat. So sweet! We found the perfect spot!

I came back in to finish the writing, and Tom did some research on how to tie various decorative knots. We ate a small bowl of yogurt with fresh raspberries and a squirt of chocolate syrup on top for dessert around 8:30.

Ok...time to stop writing. Tomorrow, we layover here in Ballet Bay. We will sleep in, kayak and just lay low and relax!

Sun setting over the entrance to Ballet Bay

Nighty-Night from Ballet Bay - End of Day 120

DAY 121

LAYOVER DAY: BALLET BAY

Rock groupings in Ballet Bay

We woke to mostly blue skies, a very light breeze, and wispy mare's tail clouds stretched across the horizon. It was warm, so we sat out with our tea and coffee to have our Quiet Time. It was serene, even with ten boats still in the bay. On this lazy Sunday morning, we could hear some folks doing exactly what we were doing, some pulling up anchor to continue on to their next destination, and others still tucked inside their boats, sleepily beginning their day. It was lovely.

Our friends, Jim and Suzanne, were leaving this morning to travel to Egmont Public Dock to stage for transiting Jervis Inlet tomorrow into Princess Louisa for a few days. They stopped by on their way out of the bay to say goodbye, and we wished them fair winds and following seas.

We then ate a bowl of Raisin Bran (plain for Tom and raspberries and Agave on top for me), got the kayaks down, and took off to explore the bay and the many islets and rock groupings dotting the landscape. The rocks are nothing special as far as colorations or patterns, but they are interesting in their own right. This is a quiet anchorage with some houses perched along the shoreline and some tucked back in amongst the trees, some quite fancy and others in various stages of dilapidation.

As we were kayaking past this one home, the owner was sitting out on his golf cart watching the world go by, so we said hello and stopped for a chat. It turns out that his family had lived on Savary Island for many years but spent time in Ballet Bay as well. In 2000, he bought 20+ acres here and built a beautiful 4,000-square-foot home. He told us his power bill was $3,000 a month. Can you imagine? He is looking to sell the house and the land, as he said the upkeep had just become too much for him and his wife. Any takers out there?

We kayaked further, circumnavigated a small islet, and came back into the bay through the north entrance. We returned to the boat, and I sat down to write. Tom stayed in his kayak and puttered around the hull of the boat, scraping growth off at the waterline and cleaning off some exhaust soot.

When Tom finished his chores, we sat on the stern watching boats coming in to anchor and enjoyed a happy hour beer. It was so pleasant, we found it hard to tear ourselves away to go in to prepare dinner.

Tom cut up little red potatoes to roast and prepared a beautiful salad while I made homemade chicken salad for wraps. What a great galley team we make!

I finished writing for the day, then talked to my mom while Tom washed dishes. Later, we curled up in bed to watch a movie. We have an early day tomorrow as we cross Georgia Strait, so no late-night viewing this night. We will go to bed with the chickens and get up when the rooster crows us awake.

Evening skies in Ballet Bay

Good Night from Ballet Bay - End of Day 121

DAY 122

ACROSS GEORGIA STRAIT
DESTINATION: NANAIMO

Leaving Ballet Bay...But wait a minute!!! Who's at the helm?!?

Leaving Ballet Bay at 6:50 this morning gave us an early start for our transit down Malaspina Strait on our way to make the crossing of Georgia Strait. We checked the wind apps again this morning to find that nothing had changed: 5-15-knot winds diminishing to light winds later in the day.

When we entered Malaspina Strait, the wind was on our nose, but we had current with us, so only about one foot of chop. The sky was overcast, with a few rays of sun peeking through. Whisky Golf, a restricted military munitions test area in Georgia Strait, was open for transit, so we were good to go.

After we passed the southern end of Texada Island, and entered Georgia Strait, the seas built to three-four-foot chop (with wind still against us and current still with us). The ride was choppy, but there was a rhythm to it. Tom remarked that instead of constantly bracing against the chop, that finding the rhythm of the chop and moving with it, was more enjoyable and a lot less tiring and stressful.

I thought about how that is true of my life. When I am constantly bracing myself for what might happen...worrying about what terrible thing might occur...then I am fearfully living my life from a place of what if. On the other hand, if I can live in the present moment, be in the flow of things, and not argue against what is, then I can operate from a place of grounded peace.

I truly believe that what I resist persists, so I am trying to take life as it comes and just roll with it. One of my biggest challenges, for sure. Yep...I am STILL a work in progress, even after 71 years of living, and I most certainly will be for the remaining years of my life.

But back to the task at hand. After a six-hour crossing of Georgia Strait, we turned into Newcastle Island Passage to get fuel and water: $8.50 a gallon Canadian! Geez Louise! Seriously?!? It's a good thing we are almost home!

It was important to follow the markers and stay aware of our surroundings as we motored down this skinny, shallow channel. There were lots of boats and float planes transiting on all sides of us, and honestly, some of them didn't appear to know the "rules of the road." Yep...a boat-plane-traffic-jam at its best!

We pulled into a jam-packed Mark Bay but found an anchorage in front of the Dinghy Dock Pub. We took a much-needed shower and headed over to the pub in our kayaks for an early dinner.

They were out of the cod fish and chips but had red snapper, which I hadn't had since my days of deep-sea fishing in Fort Myers Beach, Florida, so I decided to give it a try. Tom ordered a hamburger with mushrooms, cheddar cheese, and fried onions (which they weren't), and yam fries. My red snapper and chips were better than his hamburger and yam fries...but let's just leave it at that.

When we got back to the boat, Tom was still hungry and fixed us a cookie sheet full of nachos. I wasn't the least bit hungry, but I sure did eat my fair share. I finished up today's journal entry while Tom did the few dishes left from coffee and tea this morning.

As the sun dipped down behind the skyline of Nanaimo, we sat out back and watched pleasure boats and water taxis travel to and fro between the pub on Protection Island and Nanaimo proper. Never a dull moment as they say. Tomorrow: sleep in, kayak, hike Newcastle Island, and do boat maintenance.

Eating at the Dinghy Dock Pub

Good Night from Nanaimo - End of Day 122

DAY 123

LAYOVER DAY: NANAIMO

Mark Bay in the foreground...the city of Nanaimo in the background

Quite a few boats had already left this morning when we woke at 7:30 to sunny blue skies, warm temperatures, and planes, pleasure boats, and water taxis already creating a very busy atmosphere here in the bay. We were having a leisurely Quiet Time with coffee and tea when Tom got a call from his youngest son, Nathan, who works for the family business, to help him prob-lem solve a technical issue.

Afterward, I set about fixing cheese toast, and Tom began working on trying to figure out where the leak in the generator was coming from. This has been an ongoing problem for a while now.

He had taken out one of the hatches to the engine bay and turned around to look at something on his phone. He forgot the engine compartment was open, stepped backward, and fell into the bay, hitting his lower back on the frame of the engine bay hatch and pulling his groin muscle. Thankfully, nothing appeared to be broken, but I am quite sure he will have some bruising and soreness.

Can you guess what his first statement to me was, even before we determined he was ok?

Tom: *"Don't let the cheese toast burn."*

Don't let the cheese toast burn?!? Seriously?!? Here I am, worried that he might have seriously injured himself, and he is worried about the cheese toast?!? Well, I guess that is typical Tom...he does love bread above all other foods in the universe!

I know exactly how falling into the engine bay must have felt to him, as two years ago, a similar thing happened to me. Unbeknownst to me, Tom had opened the engine bay door/hatch and had propped it open part-way. We had been sitting out on the back of the boat when he told me the "hatch" was open, which I took to mean the sunroof hatch. I went down into the boat from the upper helm for something and, as I always do, came down the steps into the boat backward. This meant I didn't notice that the engine bay door was open, didn't cue in that the "hatch" Tom was referring to was the engine room hatch, not the sunroof hatch, and without looking, stepped backward into nothingness, falling straight back into the bay and hitting a plastic milk crate full of stuff. When I fell, I hit the pole holding the engine bay door open, and it fell in on me, adding insult to injury for sure.

The door was so heavy I couldn't hold it open. I yelled for Tom, who finally heard my muffled cries for help through the closed engine bay door and came running to help me. I was pretty sure I had broken a rib or two as several years ago, I fell into the engine bay of another boat and broke a rib, so I knew what it felt like...OUCH! We were anchored out in Echo Bay, Sucia Island, and there didn't seem much reason to go home at that point. I mean, after all, there is really very little you can do for broken ribs but endure the pain of the healing process for about six weeks. When we got back to Friday Harbor, I had my ribs x-rayed and, sure enough, two broken ribs on the lower left side. DOUBLE OUCH!!!

Now, of course, one can get hurt no matter what their living situation, but after living aboard four different boats over a 16-year span of time, I have found there just seems to be a lot more things to "trip" you up when you are living aboard a boat. I have broken ribs on two separate occasions, sprained my right arm, pulled my hamstring, cut and scraped my hands, and stubbed my toes more times than I care to remember.

But you know what? I wouldn't trade the experiences of living aboard a boat for all the gold in Fort Knox, as it has made me a more mindful person. I have learned to move with intention and care, to pay attention to my surroundings, and to hold on moving around on the boat, especially in choppy seas.

Tom in the engine bay looking for the generator leak

I have also learned what essentials I truly need and have become a minimalist where "stuff" is concerned. I mean, really, how many pairs of shoes do I really need? Truth be told, I have never been the shoe hog in my family...that honor goes to my mom. I was a jewelry nut, though, until the last couple of years. In fact, right before we left on this four-month journey, I consigned over half of my jewelry. It felt so good to know someone else would enjoy the jewelry I had stuck away in my closet and not worn for years.

While I was writing, Tom finally figured out the generator problem. He thinks he can temporarily fix the issue until we get home and can order the part, an oil pressure switch. Yea! One more hurdle tackled and hopefully solved.

Remember a few entries back when I wrote about how important flexibility is to boating life? (If I didn't write about it, I definitely thought about it and filed it away somewhere in the deep recesses of my mind to write about later...later being now.) Well, our plans to kayak over to Newcastle Island to hike will just have to wait until the next time we are in this area, as there are just times that boat maintenance must take precedence over fun. This was one of those times.

Update on the generator: Unfortunately, Tom wasn't able to fix the oil pressure switch, so he ordered one that should arrive in about a week. Until then, he will watch the generator closely and keep it full of oil.

After Tom finished up his engine bay work, and while I was preparing dinner, he washed the salt water off Havis Amanda that had splashed all over her on our choppy ride across Georgia Strait yesterday.

After dinner, dishes, and journal writing, we sat out on the back deck to watch the stars come out and listen to the saxophonist serenading us from across the bay. We leave at 6:15 tomorrow morning to go through Dodd Narrows at 7:15 at high water slack. Should be a piece of cake.

Alright, time to close for the evening.

Nanaimo at nightfall

Good Night from Nanaimo - End of Day 123

DAY 124

DESTINATION: PORT BROWNING MARINA, HAMILTON COVE

Tom pulled up anchor shortly after sunrise this morning to time our transit through Dodd Narrows by 7:15...high water slack. Lots of boats followed our lead (or maybe we followed theirs) to stage to go through the Narrows when the current was least squirrely. As we reached the entrance to the Narrows, we saw a large tug carrying a fuel truck and crane traveling through quite slowly. As it is best to go through one at a time, all boats behind it had to slow down and wait for it to transit first. Everyone we saw go through handled the current with relative ease.

Tom at the helm transiting Dodd Narrows at high water slack

We motored down Trincomali Channel, into Plumper Sound and finally entered Hamilton Cove to drop anchor in front of Port Browning Marina. All total, we were moving for about six hours. It was a peaceful ride with quiet seas, some sunshine, and a few boats here and there.

I took an hour rest around 10:00 as I had been up most of the night with food poisoning (from what I don't know) and had only slept for about four hours total. For those of you who have never had food poisoning, you don't want a detailed description...and for those who have...you *really* don't need a reminder of what it was like. Right? Right!

I was queasy most of the morning but by early afternoon began to feel better, so we kayaked up to Port Browning Pub for a late lunch. I had a Tai noodle dish and Tom ordered pizza. Both dishes were quite satisfying. We treated ourselves to a double dip of strawberry cheesecake ice cream in a waffle cone. Double Yum! We had leftovers from our pub lunch for dinner, played cards (I won!) and went to bed to watch a movie.

Crescent moon over Hamilton Cove

Good Night from Hamilton Cove - End of Day 124

DAY 125

LAYOVER DAY: HAMILTON COVE

We slept in until 8:30 this morning, and it felt so so good. We had a very long Quite Time, looking back over our four-month journey and discussing plans for future adventures yet to come. It was delightful! As this was the next to last day of our trip before heading back to Friday Harbor, we planned to clean up the boat, take inventory of our remaining supplies, clean out the fridge, and take a shower. Tom also worked for a while on fixing something or another that had to do with the aft head (which is definitely over my "head"...ha ha). It seems he came up with a solution of some kind.

I gathered together all of the many bags of rocks we had collected from beaches, trails, and shoreline kayaking. (There were a lot of rocks!!!) I then set about to organize them and put them into smaller ziplock bags to make it easier to carry them to Briggs Lake, where we will add another ring of black, white, red, and yellow rocks to our already existing two-ring medicine wheel.

We are very much looking forward to getting back in physical shape in order to resume our hiking regimen. Unfortunately, being on a boat for four months is not conducive to staying physically fit. There were very few trails in BC and even fewer in Alaska that were accessible by boat. We will have some serious training to do to get back in shape to walk long distances again, but we are determined to do so and to return to our intermittent fasting lifestyle of eating.

Later, we fixed a light supper of boiled potatoes, carrots, and onions (once again), a cool, crisp, tossed salad, and, of course, bread. We had had a late lunch and weren't very hungry. I made some banana bread, which we will have for breakfast in the morning, but in full disclosure...I broke down and had a nice, healthy square of it before climbing into bed with Tom.

Tomorrow will be my last journal entry. One hundred and twenty-six days of consistently writing every day has brought me back to my writer-self, and I am ever so grateful for that. This winter, I plan to edit all 126 journal entries for spelling and grammatical errors but will most likely change very little of the content of the entries. I wanted the daily musings to be just that: our thoughts, insights, worries, fears, joys, and challenges. I wanted the entries to be what we were thinking, feeling, and experiencing every day. I wanted to write like I talk...in my own voice...not write a collection of polished essays. I hope I have succeeded. I certainly have enjoyed trying.

Good Night from Hamilton Cove - End of Day 125

DAY 126

FINAL DESTINATION: PORT OF FRIDAY HARBOR

Leaving Hamilton Cove on our way home to Friday Harbor

Beginnings and Endings.

We began this journey 126 days ago, and today marks the last day...the end of our four month long magical journey. We have had ups and downs, highs and lows, health and illness, rain, sun, clouds, fog, cold temps, hot temps, wind, no wind, choppy seas, calm seas, current with us, and current against us...Yep, we have pretty much had it all, and it has all been good.

We learned a lot more about sailing...in Northern BC as well as Southeast Alaska...and we are better sailors because of it. Our commitment and love for one another deepened daily, and we are the better couple for it. I mean, we figure if we can live in a "hallway" of approximately 350 square feet with one another for four months, 24 hours a day, and not only not kill each other but actually revel in one another, we can together face and handle anything that comes our way going forward.

But now to the day at hand. When we left Hamilton Cove for Friday Harbor this morning, the sun was low in the sky, creating a look of shimmering crystals on the water. It was enchanting. Our trip home was uneventful but pleasant.

As we piloted the boat from the upper helm, we reminisced about all of the many wonders we had seen and the many challenges we had faced. We attempted to put it all in perspective, to accept that the end of the trip, with our mixed feelings of sadness at our beautiful journey coming to an end, mixed with the joy of reconnecting with our friends and family, was just as important to experience and accept as the beginning was when we were so full of excitement and anticipation of what grand and glorious adventures awaited us.

When we pulled into Friday Harbor, we were met by our dear dock friends: Rand, Mark, and Jeff. We threw them a line and then jumped off to help tie up the boat. We stood around and talked for a bit before "putting the boat to bed."

Approaching Friday Harbor Marina

We watered up the boat before going to eat at Downriggers Restaurant and then on to visit Mom for a while. She was very excited to see us, as we were her. I knew I had come back to reality when the first thing she said to me when I walked in the door was, "Since you're here, you can take Little Buddy out to the bathroom for me." Some things never change. Yep! Definitely back to reality!

We returned home, relaxed out on the back deck and watched the sun go down before coming in to get ready for bed. It felt surreal to be back in our home port, tied up to a dock, surrounded by people, but comforting as well. **Endings.**

Beginnings.

And now a new chapter of our lives begins, and we are excited, looking forward in delicious anticipation to discover what is to come. Watch this space!

Good Night from Friday Harbor - End of Day 126

And...

End of Our Four-Month Long Journey up the Inside Passage into Southeast Alaska.

Oh, but wait... there's more to the story...

Below, you will find three photos: one of our wedding day four months later, one of the medicine wheel we created at Briggs Lake, and one of the heart under the Great-Grandmother Tree. The medicine wheel and the heart were created with rocks brought back from Northern British Columbia and Southeast Alaska to commemorate our journey.

THE NEXT CHAPTER...

January 3, 2023...Tom and Jandira's Wedding Day

It was a cold, blustery day, but the love emanating between us warmed our hearts. It was our wedding day...a day filled with excitement, joy...and, of course...profound LOVE and deep COMMITMENT to one another. We are extremely grateful for all the angels (earthly and heavenly) who had a hand in bringing the two of us together and to Spirit who orchestrated it all from somewhere above. To have found each other at this time in our lives truly is a bit of a miracle. We feel so very blessed!

AND, FINALLY...TO
MY READERS...

I wish you strength and courage
to meet whatever comes your way,
And the wisdom to accept the "issness"
of each moment of your day.
I wish you dreams to follow and goals to achieve,
Exploration and adventure to search for and
seize.
And when all your yarns have been spun,
The peace to know your journey is done.

In Light, Jandira

www.ingramcontent.com/pod-product-compliance
Lightning Source LLC
Chambersburg PA
CBHW051129120626
46547CB00012B/733